Tiling

STANLEY®

Tiling

Joseph Truini

The Taunton Press

To Marla, Kate, and Chris, for their unwavering devotion, support, and love

The Taunton Press
Inspiration for hands-on living®

The Taunton Press, Inc.
63 South Main Street
PO Box 5506
Newtown, CT 06470-5506

Email: tp@taunton.com

Editor: Peter Chapman
Copy Editor: Diane Sinitsky
Indexer: Jim Curtis
Jacket/Cover design: Stacy Wakefield Forte
Interior design: Stacy Wakefield Forte
Layout: Jennifer Willman
Photographer: Joseph Truini (except where noted)

The following names/manufacturers appearing in *Tiling* are trademarks: Alpha Professional Tools®; American Olean® Belmar™ and Graphic Effects™; Corian®; Daltile® Imagica™, Porada™, Season Wood™, Tiger Eye™, and Uptown Glass™; DensShield®, Durock®; Hardiebacker®; Kevlar®; Laticrete® 255 MultiMax™ and PermaColor®; Mapelastic™; Quick-Pitch®; Schluter®; Speed® Square; WonderBoard®

Library of Congress Cataloging-in-Publication Data

Truini, Joseph, author.
  Stanley tiling : a homeowner's guide / Joseph Truini.
     pages cm
  Includes index.
  ISBN 978-1-62710-941-3
  1. Tile laying--Amateurs' manuals. I. Title.
  TH8531.T78 2015
  698'.9--dc23
                          2015032237

Printed in the United States of America
10 9 8 7 6 5 4 3 2 1

About Your Safety: Construction is inherently dangerous. Using hand or power tools improperly or ignoring safety practices can lead to permanent injury or even death. For safety, use caution, care, and good judgment when following the procedures described in this book. The publisher and Stanley cannot assume responsibility for any damage to property or injury to persons as a result of misuse of the information provided. Always follow all manufacturers' safety, installation, and operation warnings and instructions provided with the products and materials. Don't try to perform operations you learn about here (or elsewhere) unless you're certain they are safe for you. The projects in this book vary as to level of skill required, so some may not be appropriate for all do-it-yourselfers. If something about an operation doesn't feel right, don't do it, and instead, seek professional help. Remember to consult your local building department for information on building codes, permits, and other laws that may apply to your project.

STANLEY® and the STANLEY logo are trademarks of Stanley Black & Decker, Inc. or an affiliate thereof and are used under license.

FIRST AND FOREMOST, I'D LIKE TO THANK ALL the talented and hardworking people at The Taunton Press. Thank you in particular to Executive Editor Peter Chapman, who displayed immeasurable patience and good humor throughout this endeavor. This book, and the process of writing it, was made much better by Peter's gentle guidance, skillful touch, and steady hand.

And my appreciation to the book layout and production team—including Lynne Phillips, Rosalind Loeb Wanke, Stacy Wakefield Forte, and Jennifer Willman—who managed to mold my tangled mess of images and words into a precise, concise, readable design.

This book wouldn't have been even remotely possible without the extraordinary support and generosity of Jimmy Tiganella and his son, James, of Classic Tile in Oakville, Connecticut. Jimmy served as my tile-setting guru, technical advisor, photo model, muse, and friend. He kindly invited me to his job sites and shared his skillful manner and professional approach to tiling. And Jimmy always showed great patience in answering my relentless barrage of questions, which I delivered at all hours of the day and night. For this and much more, I am eternally grateful.

I'd like to express my sincere thanks to the following people who went out of their way to provide me with information, photographs, technical data, and products: Rich Citro and Terry Baskin (Schluter Systems), Sarah Findle (Daltile), Brent Luecke (Marazzi Tile), Carmen Rionda (Mexican Decorative Accessories), MaryAnn Nuzzo (Tile America), Nora DePalma (American Standard), and Sarah Windham (Stanley Black & Decker).

CONTENTS

STANLEY

CHAPTER ONE

CHOOSING TILE

Tile shown: Marazzi Oxford

IF YOU LIKE SHOPPING FOR building products—and who doesn't—then you're going to love shopping for tile. For every tiling job, there are literally dozens of choices, so you're sure to find a tile color, pattern, size, and style to satisfy your personal taste and design criteria.

Of course, having so many options can sometimes be overwhelming, even paralyzing. To simplify the selection process, it's important to first become familiar with the different types of tiles available and then learn some basic tiling terminology. Once you've gained that knowledge, you'll know what to look for at the home center or tile store, and you'll be able to quickly narrow down the number of options to find the perfect tile for your project.

In this chapter, I'll present a detailed overview of the commonly available tile options, focusing on the four most popular types: ceramic, porcelain, stone, and glass. Here, you'll also find recommendations on where to install each type of tile.

And one last bit of advice: Be sure to start tile shopping as early as possible. In many cases, tile must be ordered and shipped from the manufacturer or local distributor, and that could take anywhere from one week to a month, depending on the specific tile chosen and the quantity needed.

Walk around any tile store and you'll see hundreds of tile samples on display, but nearly all of those tiles fall into just four basic types: glazed ceramic, porcelain, natural stone, and glass. Now within each tile type there are several variations, including color, shape, size, and texture, but knowing the benefits and features of each type can help lead you to the correct tile for your project.

Glazed Ceramic Tile

When most people think of tile, it's glazed ceramic that they're imagining. It's the ubiquitous 4-in. x 4-in. glossy white tile installed in thousands of bathrooms across the country. It's the colorful square tile used on countless kitchen countertops and backsplashes.

A These glazed ceramic tiles reflect the rustic look and texture of natural stone. The 12-in. x 12-in. floor tiles are complemented by matching 3-in. x 6-in. tiles on the backsplash wall. Tile shown: American Olean® Belmar™ Tortoise.

This display board of glazed ceramic tile shows the various tile colors but also available sizes, shapes, and mosaic-sheet layout.

The old-world beauty of handcrafted terra-cotta pavers is perfectly captured in this low-maintenance glazed ceramic tile.

TIP When shopping for tile, bring along a sketch of the room, including all pertinent dimensions. Also, bring snapshots of the area that'll be tiled. And lastly, show the salesperson photos from books and magazines as examples of the tile design you'd like to replicate.

B

C

TIP Ceramic tile is often referred to as a white-bodied tile because its clay core or body is white. (Although some ceramics have a dark pink core.)

Ceramic tile became popular—and remains so today—for three valid reasons: It's easy to install, highly stain resistant, and affordable. In fact, it's the most affordable type of tile. Glazed ceramic also comes in many more colors than most other tile types.

Glazed ceramic tile is made from an earthy mixture of mined clays and other natural minerals. The putty-like mixture is extruded, stamped, or otherwise shaped into tiles, topped with a glaze, and fired in an extremely hot kiln. The resulting tile has a glossy, easy-to-clean surface that's impervious to staining.

Ceramic tile is relatively thin and soft, which makes it very easy to cut and install. However, those characteristics also make it weaker and less durable than some other tile options. That's why glazed ceramic is usually reserved for walls, countertops, backsplashes, vanity tops, and tub and shower surrounds. It's not that you can't install glazed ceramic tiles on floors. It's just that there are better options, including porcelain or natural stone.

The other disadvantage is that if you drop a hard or sharp object onto a glazed ceramic tile, you could chip the glazing, which would reveal its white core.

B A new manufacturing technique known as visual imaging adds texture, contrast, and brightness to this contemporary-style tile. Tile shown: American Olean Graphic Effects™.

C The delicate, feathery veining of travertine is available in low-maintenance glazed ceramic tile. Tile shown: Marazzi Province Quebec.

Porcelain Tile

Porcelain tiles now represent the fastest-growing segment of all tiling products. They're made from ultrafine porcelain clays that are fired at much higher temperatures than ceramic tiles. As a result, porcelain tiles are much harder, denser, more durable, and less porous than ceramic or natural stone tiles. Porcelain tiles are also less likely to crack and they have superior resistance to moisture and staining. And, unlike ceramic and most stone tiles, porcelain can be installed indoors or outdoors.

Porcelain tiles are produced to exacting standards in controlled manufacturing plants, which ensure quality, consistency, and uniform sizing, while virtually eliminating defects. And they're available glazed and unglazed. Unglazed porcelain is commonly called color-body or full-body tile, meaning that the surface color is uniform throughout the thickness of the tile. If you accidentally chip the surface of a color-body tile, it's much less noticeable because there's no glazing.

The intrinsic properties of porcelain—hardness, denseness, and extreme resistance to moisture and staining—make it an ideal floor tile. In fact, most tile contractors are trending away from ceramic and only installing porcelain tiles on floors. Plus, porcelain tiles are often available in bigger sizes than ceramic or stone, making them perfect for tiling floors in large, expansive rooms.

The two minor drawbacks to porcelain tiles are that they're typically more expensive than ceramic tiles and a bit more difficult to cut. Now, most porcelain tiles can be cut with a manual score-and-snap tile cutter, but there are some porcelain tiles that are so hard, you must cut them with a motorized wet saw.

Porcelain tiles come in virtually every imaginable color, pattern, and texture, including many that resemble natural stone, especially marble. In fact, you're likely to find more

A The popularity of large-format tiles is showcased in this high-style bath. The 20-in. x 20-in. glazed porcelain tiles capture the bold grain pattern and rich texture of natural slate. Tile shown: Daltile® Porada™ Deep Grey. B Capture the look of stained concrete with color-body porcelain tiles. This floor combines 4-in. x 48-in. tile planks with 8-in.x 48-in. planks set in a staggered brickwork pattern. Tile shown: Daltile Imagica™ Midnight.

TIP Order all ceramic and porcelain tile needed for a room at the same time. That'll increase the odds of getting all the tiles from the same lot number. Tiles manufactured from different lots are often slightly darker or lighter in color.

TIP Glazed tile is a good choice for allergy sufferers because it doesn't support allergens and it can easily be scrubbed clean.

porcelain tiles that look like stone than you are to find different types of real stone tile. Again, that's because as a manufactured product, a tile company can simply engineer a new tile to whatever shade, pattern, or texture it desires—even if it doesn't actually exist in nature.

And while stone-look porcelain tiles may not look exactly like real stone, they come pretty close. More importantly, however, porcelain doesn't have any of the imperfections or weak spots inherent in natural stone. The result is a floor that resembles stone but is much more durable and easier to maintain.

C The look of natural-stone slabs and hardwood planks comes together in this color-body porcelain tile floor. Tile shown: Marazzi Fontanella Milan. D This shower floor features an attractive glazed porcelain tile done in a pinwheel pattern with center dot. The tile has the chiseled edges and rough texture of natural travertine. Tile shown: Marazzi Archaeology Troy.

This wood-plank floor is actually a color-body porcelain tile floor. The 8-in. x 48-in. and 12-in. x 48-in. tiles are near-perfect reproductions of weathered wood planks, right down to the rough texture, rich wood grain, and knots. Tile shown: Daltile Season Wood™.

Wood-Plank Porcelain Tile

The latest porcelain products are porcelain-tile planks that mimic wooden floorboards, right down to the realistic-looking wood-grain texture (see pp. 82–95). Some of the planks resemble weathered barn boards, while others look like richly stained hardwood. Porcelain-tile planks typically measure about 6 in. wide x 36 in. long, but longer and wider planks are starting to be introduced.

Testing Tile Toughness

When shopping for porcelain tile, check its surface hardness rating to ensure it'll stand up to foot traffic in your home. A test developed by the Porcelain Enamel Institute (PEI) rates tiles from 0 to 5. The higher the number, the more abrasion-resistant the tile is. And be aware that PEI hardness ratings only reflect a tile's hardness and durability, not price or quality.

PEI GROUP 0:

Not recommended for floors. Typically installed on walls only.

PEI GROUP 1:

Light foot traffic. Install in rooms where shoes are seldom worn, such as bathrooms. Can be used on walls.

PEI GROUP 2:

Medium foot traffic in homes but not recommended for kitchens, entryways, or steps.

PEI GROUP 3:

Medium-heavy foot traffic. Suitable for all residential and light commercial flooring applications.

PEI GROUP 4:

Heavy foot traffic in homes, medium commercial, and light industrial installations.

PEI GROUP 5:

Extra-heavy foot traffic. Suitable for all residential, commercial, and industrial applications, including floors exposed to extremely high foot traffic, abrasive dirt, and excessive moisture.

Note that some tiles are rated for hardness according to the MOHS Test, which is based on a scale from 1 to 10, with 10 having the hardness of diamond. For residential floors, a rating of at least 5 will ensure excellent wear resistance.

Natural Stone Tile

When it comes to authentic, natural, enduring building materials, few products can compete with real stone tiles. Sliced from great slabs of granite, slate, marble, travertine, and limestone, natural stone tiles bring old-world charm to the modern home. And while there are porcelain tiles that resemble stone and even cost less than stone, for the discriminating homeowner, nothing compares to the natural beauty, texture, and color that only Mother Nature can create.

Stone tile is most often installed on floors, but it can be used to cover virtually any surface. However, since stone is fairly expensive, it's best used where it'll have the greatest impact, such as in a foyer, kitchen backsplash, or master bathroom. And most natural stone tile lines also include complementary accent pieces, such as bull-nose edging, chair rail, medallions, and rope moldings, which are carved from stone.

Stone tiles come with one of three surface finishes: polished (glossy), honed (matte), or tumbled (roughened)—although not all types of stone are available in all three finishes. For example, tumbled marble is commonly available; tumbled slate is not.

Working with stone tile is similar to other types of tile, except that you can't cut stone with a manual score-and-snap tile cutter. You must use a motorized wet saw for all cuts. And certain stone tiles must be set in a very specific type of mortar. For example, white and light-colored marble tiles must be set in white mortar because standard gray mortar will telegraph through and darken the surface. Green marble tiles should never be set with mortar that contains high amounts of lime because it can cause the marble to cup and warp.

When considering stone tile, keep in mind that stone is relatively soft and porous. So, it must be sealed and then resealed on a regular basis to prevent staining. And stone, being a totally natural product, often contains tiny fissures, holes, and chips. These "defects" add character and beauty, but they also create weak spots in the tile and crevices that collect dirt.

Here are two examples of tumbled marble tiles. One is a manufactured glazed porcelain tile; the other is cut from natural stone. Can you tell the difference? The porcelain tile (near left), while realistic looking, can't match the totally random pattern, shading, and texture of real stone (far left).

Travertine, a type of limestone, is highly prized for its warm, rich color and rustic charm. This display board shows the travertine components available for tiling a wall.

Glass Tile

Glass tile is the hottest trend in tiling today, and it's easy to see why: It's colorful, shiny, contemporary, iridescent, and stylish. And glass tile is a relatively "green" product: It takes half as much energy to produce glass tiles as it does most other tiles, and many manufacturers are now using recycled glass.

Glass tile is most often installed on kitchen backsplashes and in bathrooms, especially around tubs, showers, and sinks. It's also installed on bars, vanity tops, and occasionally on kitchen counters.

As its name implies, this trendy tile is made from glass formed into squares and rectangles. There's no clay body or glazing, just pure glass. And it's available in an amazing array of eye-catching colors, from subtle pastel shades and bright, bold colors to highly reflective surfaces, opaque hues, and sparkling crystal-clear glass.

There are two methods of producing colored glass tiles: Ordinarily the tile itself is simply made from colored glass. Other times, the color is applied to the back of a clear glass tile, adding depth and dimension to the tiled surface.

Besides being made of glass, not clay, glass tile differs from traditional tile in another important way: It's available in much smaller sizes and is most often sold in mosaic-tile sheets. The glass tiles used in mosaic sheets range in size from about ½ in. sq. to 2 in. sq. However, the latest design in glass-tile mosaics feature narrow rectangular tiles that are usually $9/16$ in. wide and 2 in. to 12 in. long.

Mosaic-tile sheets are typically about 12 in. sq., which makes installation go much easier and faster. The individual glass tiles are assembled into sheets by either fiberglass webbing adhered across the backs of the tiles or by a piece of paper glued to the top of the tiles. The paper is removed after installation and prior to grouting.

A Glass-mosaic tiles are extremely popular for tiling kitchen backsplashes. Here, the mosaic sheets are composed of both glass and stone tiles. Note that the stone tiles match the granite counter. B Tiling backsplash walls with small-diameter tiles makes the space appear larger. The wall shown here is covered with 12-in. x 12-in. mosaic sheets made up of ⅝-in.-sq. glass tiles. Tile shown: Marazzi Crystal Stone II Pearl.

TIP Before installing glass tiles, wipe the back of the tile with a lint-free cloth to remove any dust or dirt. Otherwise, the debris might show through the tile.

Glass-tile mosaic sheets come in two basic styles: all-glass mosaics, which comprise only glass tiles, and glass-and-stone mosaics that combine glass tiles with natural stone tiles in the same sheet.

Glass tiles are also available as individual field tiles but, again, in much smaller sizes than traditional tiles. (Field tiles refer to the full-size tiles set in the main area or "field" of an installation.) Most field-glass tiles range in size from about 2 in. sq. to 8 in. sq., and that includes the popular 3-in. x 6-in. subway-style glass tile.

Care must be taken when installing glass tile to prevent the mortar from showing through the tiled surface. Start by using white thinset mortar, not traditional gray thinset. And after applying the mortar with a notched trowel, use a smooth trowel to level and flatten the ridges in the mortar. If you don't, the ridges will be visible through the glass tile.

Despite being wildly popular, glass tile does have two distinct drawbacks. First, it typically costs more than any other type of tile, except for some extremely rare and exotic natural stone tile. And second, it's not very well suited for floors. By its very nature, glass is relatively soft and susceptible to cracking and scratching. And, more importantly, glass is slippery when wet.

Now, that doesn't mean you can't install glass tile on a floor. You can, as long as you accept its limitations and obey this extremely important rule: Be sure the glass tile chosen is specifically engineered for floor installations. Confirm with the tile manufacturer that the glass tile has passed the stringent standards of the American Society for Testing and Materials (ASTM) and has been approved as a flooring material.

C This eye-popping tub surround is covered with 12-in. x 12-in. mosaic-tile sheets that feature clear and translucent glass tiles interspersed with tiles cut from natural marble and slate. Tile shown: Marazzi Crystal Stone II Pewter. **D** This contemporary and urban-inspired bath is tiled with 1-in.-sq. mosaic-glass tiles. Unlike typical mosaics, however, this one features tiles in a range of colors, iridescent tones, exotic prints, and geometric patterns. Tile shown: Daltile Uptown Glass™ Exotic Black. **E** Stone, glass, and gleaming stainless steel all come together in this mesmerizingly modern wall treatment. The random-block mosaic comes in mesh-backed sheets measuring approximately 12 in. sq. Tile shown: Daltile Tiger Eye™ Indo Stainless.

Terra-Cotta Pavers

The four types of tiles previously mentioned—glazed ceramic, porcelain, stone, and glass—represent a vast majority of the tiles sold today. But there's an additional tile that's worth mentioning: terra-cotta pavers.

Terra-cotta is a thick unglazed ceramic tile made from natural unrefined clay. The clay is baked at very low temperatures until hard. In some regions, the tiles are still sun-baked outdoors. (Terra-cotta, translated from Italian, means, baked earth.) These rich, russet-brown pavers are also known as Saltillo tiles, after the Mexican state of Saltillo where terra-cotta pavers are still made by hand.

Terra-cotta pavers are typically installed on floors but can also be used on bars, tabletops, counters, and vanity tops. And in warmer regions that aren't subjected to below-freezing temperatures, pavers are commonly installed on outdoor patios, walkways, steps, and walls.

> **TIP** Apply a sealer to terra-cotta pavers prior to installation and grout will clean off easily and not stain the surface.

The pavers are extremely popular in Southwestern- and Spanish Colonial-style homes. And although prices vary widely depending on country of origin, terra-cotta pavers are pretty affordable, costing about the same as mid-priced glazed ceramic tiles.

Unlike other types of tiles, terra-cotta pavers are usually a bit irregular, meaning that they're not all exactly the same size or perfectly flat or square. And while those irregularities add charm and character, they also affect the installation: Terra-cotta pavers must be set in a thicker mortar bed with wider grout joints.

Pavers are also much thicker than the average tile, sometimes as thick as ¾ in., and are relatively soft and very porous. It's important to apply a sealer immediately after installation to prevent staining. Or, pay a little extra and buy factory-sealed pavers.

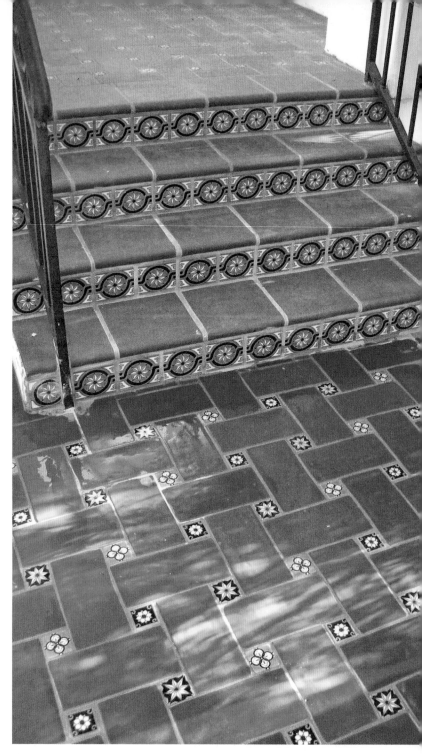

This outdoor staircase features authentic terra-cotta pavers that are adorned with deco tiles on the stair risers and floral-pattern dots on the landings. Tile from: Malibu Ceramic Works Terra Cotta.

> **TIP** Terra-cotta pavers are best cut on a wet saw, but small notches and short cuts can be made with a jigsaw fitted with a carbide-grit blade.

The rustic warmth of handcrafted terra-cotta pavers is reflected in this glazed ceramic floor. The floor pattern is composed of three sizes of tiles: 6 in. x 6 in., 12 in. x 12 in., and 18 in. x 18 in. Tile shown: Marazzi Super Saltillo Saguaro.

TIP Standard terra-cotta pavers have relatively sharp, square edges and corners. For a slightly "softer" look, consider installing Super Saltillo pavers, which have rounded edges and corners.

And be aware that the color of the pavers is dependent on where the clay comes from. For example, pavers from Italy or Portugal are often darker than those from Mexico. Shading differs even from one Mexican state to the next. So, when buying terra-cotta pavers, be sure to order all that you need from the same manufacturer.

Lastly, if you can't find terra-cotta pavers in a color that you like, you can simply stain them to the desired shading.

CHAPTER TWO

TOOLS AND MATERIALS

IF YOU'RE AN ACTIVE DO-IT-YOURSELFER, you probably already own many of the tools needed to install tile, including a tape measure, utility knife, framing square, chalk reel, level, and cord-less drill. However, there are several specialty tools that you'll also need, such as a tile cutter, grout float, carbide-grit hole saw, mixing paddle, tile nippers, and various types of trowels.

Fortunately, most tiling tools are relatively affordable, and the ones that aren't, such as a motorized wet saw, you can rent by the day. In this chapter, I'll take a detailed look at all the tools required to set tile, including personal safety equipment. I'll also cover many of the tile-setting materials you'll need, ranging from thinset mortar and tile grout to cement backerboard and crack-isolation membranes. Selecting the proper materials (and installing them correctly) is the single most impor-tant factor in producing a professional-quality, long-lasting tile job.

You'll be able to find most tile-setting tools and materials at any well-stocked home center, but some specialty items will be available only at a tile store or tile distributor. And don't forget that tool-rental dealers and most home centers carry a wide variety of tile-setting and demolition tools, which you can rent.

Safety Equipment

Tile work, especially tile demolition, can be hazardous and dangerous. However, for a small investment you can easily protect yourself from flying shards, nasty cuts, choking clouds of dust, and ear-splitting noise. Here, I'll take a quick look at the safety gear needed to protect your eyes, lungs, hearing, even your hands and knees.

Safety goggles

There are two basic ways to protect your eyes: with safety glasses and with eye goggles. Safety glasses are similar to normal eyeglasses but fit more snugly to your face and provide better side protection and better protection against high impact. Eye goggles are held in place with an adjustable elastic head strap, which fits tightly to your face to completely seal out dust and debris.

When properly worn, safety glasses and eye goggles will provide adequate protection. Safety glasses are more comfortable to wear and easier to put on and take off, but eye goggles offer better protection from flying bits of debris. The smart choice: Buy both types and wear the one that best suits the job at hand.

> **TIP** When shopping for eye protection, confirm that the glasses or goggles are equipped with impact-resistant lenses. Make sure eye protection complies with ANSI Z87.1.

Respiratory protection

Breathing in airborne dust and dirt can irritate your nasal passages and esophagus and eventually damage your lungs. Unfortunately, tile work, especially tile demolition,

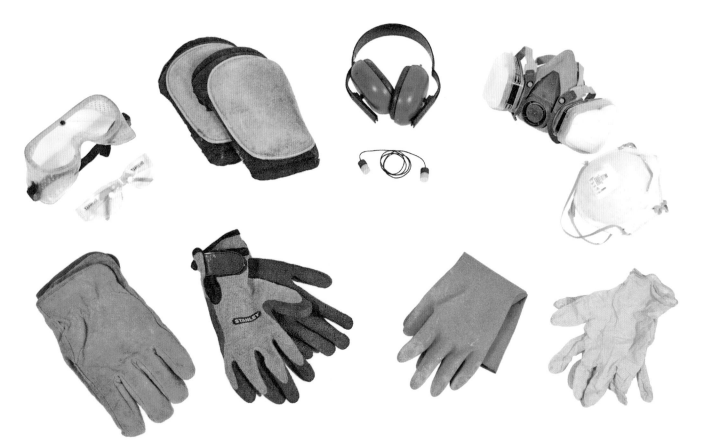

Protect yourself with the following safety gear (top row): eye goggles and safety glasses, kneepads, earmuff hearing protection and earplugs, respirator and dust mask; (bottom row): leather work gloves, all-purpose utility gloves, rubber gloves, and disposable latex gloves.

is sometimes a dusty, dirty endeavor. But you can easily protect your lungs with a two-prong attack: Wear a disposable dust mask for general dust protection and a half-mask dual-cartridge respirator as protection from particularly thick, irritating dust or noxious fumes.

Wear a dust mask when mixing thinset mortar or tile grout, which contain silica dust. It can also offer protection when drilling or cutting cement backerboard. A dual-cartridge respirator fits very tightly to your face and can be worn any time, but is particularly effective at filtering out superfine dust, dirt, smoke, and fumes. It contains two replaceable prefilters and two replaceable cartridge filters. Check to be sure that the filters are rated for the type of environment in which you'll be working, and replace the filters as recommended by the manufacturer.

Older homes may be constructed with materials containing asbestos or other hazardous substances. Before doing demolition work on an older home, have a professional check for the presence of these materials. Never attempt to do demolition work yourself if hazardous materials are found; hire a licensed remediation specialist.

TIP If your safety glasses fog up when wearing a dust mask, switch to a respirator. A tight-fitting respirator will often prevent fogging.

Hearing protection

The two most effective ways to protect your hearing are with in-ear plugs and over-ear muffs. Soft in-ear plugs are affordable, comfortable, and fit tightly in the ear canal to block out sound; just be careful not to press them in too far. They're available as two individual plugs, or as two plugs tethered together by a flexible plastic cord.

Earmuff-style hearing protection clamps tightly over the ears and is held in place by an adjustable head strap. This type of protection is a bit bulkier than in-ear plugs, but ear muffs are a lot easier to put on and take off.

Be sure to safeguard your hearing when operating a wet saw, impact driver, reciprocating saw, right-angle grinder, electric chipping hammer, or other power tool. Also wear hearing protection during noisy phases of demolition work, such as when pounding tiles loose with a hammer.

TIP Before inserting an earplug, cup it in a closed fist and exhale warm air onto it for several seconds. Next, gently compress the warm plug by rolling it between your thumb and forefinger. Then quickly press the plug into your ear and hold it in place with your fingertip until it expands and wedges itself into the ear canal. Repeat to install the second earplug.

Work gloves

You'll need three different kinds of gloves to protect your hands and fingers from cuts, splinters, punctures, bruises, and irritations.

Wear leather work gloves when handling sharp shards of broken tile or sheets of plywood and cement backerboard.

For general, all-purpose protection during all phases of construction, wear utility work gloves. Choose a pair that's composed of resilient Kevlar® fibers and features a non-slip, sure-grip coating on the fingers and palms.

Tiling requires working with a lot of water and mixing wet materials, including mortar, grout, and sealers. So, it's important to protect your hands with rubber gloves. Wear thin disposable latex or nitrile gloves when applying grout sealers and other light-duty jobs. But when mixing and handling mortar and grout, don a pair of heavyweight PVC (polyvinyl chloride) gloves. Look for a pair that extends up to the elbow for maximum protection and has a jersey-cotton lining for comfort.

Kneepads

Tiling, especially floor tiling, requires you to spend a majority of the time on your knees. A good pair of kneepads can offer protection from cuts and bruises and reduce fatigue and joint pain. There are a wide variety of kneepads available, and they all work pretty well. However, the kind with a hard outer shell and thick, soft interior pad provides the best combination of cut protection and all-day comfort.

TIP Kneepads with wide elastic straps and hook-and-loop closures are more comfortable to wear and easier to put on and take off than the kind with buckles or latches.

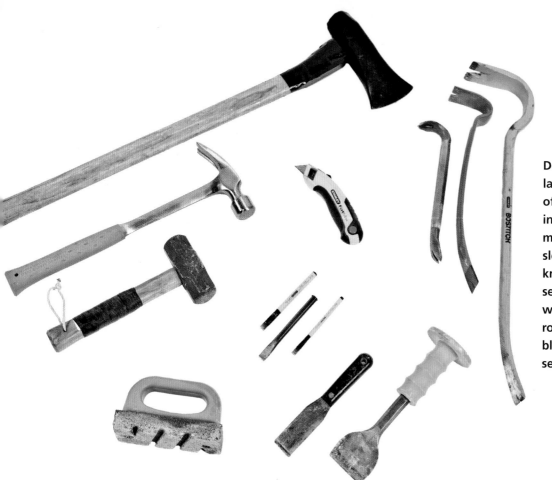

Demolishing old tile installations requires an arsenal
of rough and rugged tools,
including (from left): an 8-lb.
maul, framing hammer, 3-lb.
sledge, retractable utility
knife, three-piece cold chisel
set, cat's paw, flat pry bar,
wrecking bar, and (bottom
row) rubbing stone, stiff-
blade putty knife, and brick-
set chisel.

Demolition Tools

Most DIY tiling projects are renovations of existing tiled
spaces. Therefore, the first step is usually tearing up and
removing the old tiled walls and floors. And for that, you
need demolition tools. Here, I separate the tools into two
distinct groups: pounding tools and prying tools. I also
include a few miscellaneous tools that can help with the
demolition process. Again, be sure to wear all the necessary safety gear during demolition.

Pounding tools

Heavy-headed tools that are used to pound tiles loose
and break apart substrates include a 3-lb. sledgehammer,
long-handled framing hammer, and maul.

The 3-lb. sledge might be the smallest of all sledgeham-
mers, but it provides plenty of power for pounding tiles
loose and cracking the hardest, most stubborn tiles into
small pieces.

An 8-lb. maul is ideal for heavy-duty demolition jobs,
such as busting out old cast-iron bathtubs.

Drive a stiff-blade putty knife or thin pry bar behind an
old tile to pop it loose.

A framing hammer is preferred over a curved-claw nail hammer because it has a long handle for better leverage and a straight ripping claw that's superior for prying and chopping. A 22-oz. or heavier framing hammer is well suited for demolition work.

A maul is a firewood-splitting tool that's a cross between a sledgehammer and an ax. It's ideal for busting up large-format tiles, knocking down tiled walls, even shattering cast-iron bathtubs. An 8-lb. maul is sufficiently heavy and will provide plenty of tile-busting power.

Prying tools

This category includes a variety of different prying tools, including a wrecking bar, flat pry bar, cat's paw, stiff-blade putty knife, cold chisel, and brick-set chisel. Each of these tools can be driven beneath the tile or behind the substrate by a framing hammer or small sledge. Then, the tile or substrate can be pried loose and discarded.

A cat's paw is indispensable for pulling nails and other fasteners, and the stiff-blade putty knife can be used for scraping, prying, and popping tiles loose. Cold chisels are designed for cutting metal but are also useful for chopping through tile, mortar, grout, and cement backerboard. The brick-set is commonly used to cut brick, stone, and concrete block, but it, too, is ideally suited for demolishing tile.

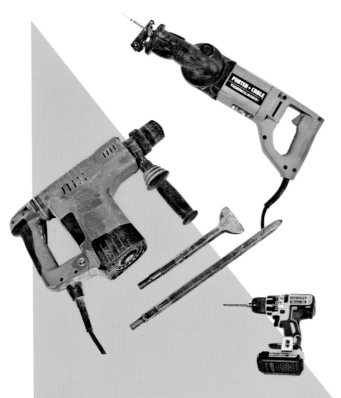

When a tile-demolition job calls for a little extra muscle, reach for an electric chipping hammer, cordless drill/driver, and reciprocating saw.

Miscellaneous Demo Tools

Here are a few extra tools that often prove helpful during the demolition phase:

A cordless drill/driver provides a quick and easy way to remove screws when disassembling walls and floors. It's also useful for screwing down the subfloor to the joists below.

A reciprocating saw can be used to cut through nail-embedded wood framing, plywood subfloors, and drywall.

When removing tile from a large floor, rent an electric chipping hammer. It can be fitted with a wide chisel blade or pointed bit to quickly pulverize tile into tiny pieces.

A retractable utility knife is useful for a wide variety of cutting and slicing jobs. Keep plenty of extra blades on hand, and consider upgrading to carbide-tipped utility-knife blades. They cost a bit more than standard blades but stay sharper much longer.

An abrasive rubbing stone can be used to grind off the last remnants of mortar or grout from the subfloor. This Flintstonian hand tool is simply a handle fitted onto a chunk of supercoarse stone. Rubbing the stone back and forth will smooth the roughest surface in a matter of minutes.

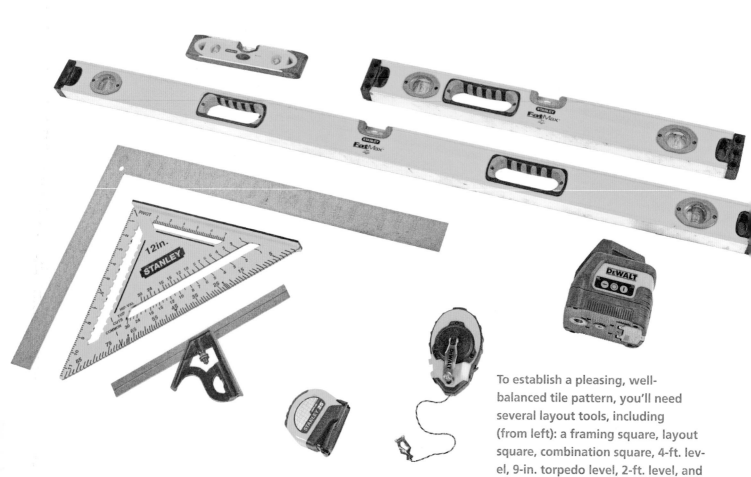

To establish a pleasing, well-balanced tile pattern, you'll need several layout tools, including (from left): a framing square, layout square, combination square, 4-ft. level, 9-in. torpedo level, 2-ft. level, and (bottom row) 25-ft. tape measure, chalk reel, and laser level.

Layout Tools

You'll need a small number of layout tools to measure the space and establish the desired tile pattern. These are ordinary carpentry tools, so you may already own them; any that you don't have are commonly available and relatively affordable.

Here, I divided the layout tools into two groups: alignment tools and measuring and marking tools. Depending on the size of the job and complexity of the tile pattern, you may not need all of these implements.

Alignment tools

Alignment tools help ensure a precise and true layout, especially when it comes to marking level (horizontal) and plumb (vertical) lines. This tool group includes various sizes and types of levels, including a 2-ft. and 4-ft. level, and a 9-in. torpedo level. When tiling large, expansive spaces, consider using a 72-in. or even 78-in. level.

To accurately mark layout lines across the substrate, use a chalk reel. Start by filling the reel with powdered chalk; blue chalk shows up well on most surfaces. Next, pull out as much string as necessary, stretch it tight, and then snap the string onto the surface to mark a perfectly straight layout line. Chalk reels are available in a few different sizes, but a 100-ft. model is adequate for most tiling jobs.

Accurate layout lines can also be established with an electronic laser level. Once considered a pro-only tool, laser levels are now available in a wide range of prices and features. A laser level provides a quick and accurate way to project layout lines across floors, up walls, around corners, and onto ceilings—all at the same time, if desired. Look for a self-leveling model, which automatically adjusts itself, even if set on an uneven, sloping surface. Laser levels are also available at most tool-rental dealers.

Now, while a laser level certainly makes tile layout faster, easier, and in some cases, more accurate, it's not absolutely necessary. Long before the advent of laser levels, tile setters were getting excellent results using a level, framing square, and chalk reel.

Measuring and marking tools

It's possible to lay out virtually any tile job with just three measuring and marking tools: a 25-ft. or longer tape measure, framing square, and combination square.

A tape measure is indispensable throughout the entire tiling project, but is particularly useful for confirming that layout lines are properly spaced, parallel, and precisely positioned to create the desired tile pattern.

The carpenter's framing square provides not only a quick and reliable way to lay out and mark lines but also to check the squareness of layout lines. In other words, it can be used to confirm that a line is square, or precisely 90°, to a wall or other surface. It's also helpful for determining if two crisscrossing lines are square to each other and form a perfect 90° angle. The importance of establishing square layout lines can't be overstated. It would be nearly impossible to install tiles if the layout lines are out of square.

A combination square has an adjustable 12-in.-long steel rule that can be used to mark and check square lines and 45° layout lines, which is useful when setting tiles diagonally. And when you're setting tiles, the combination square is handy for marking cut lines onto tiles prior to trimming them to fit.

A layout square is also invaluable for marking and checking square and angled layout lines. Often called a rafter square or Speed® Square, this triangular-shaped tool can also be used as a guide fence on the wet saw.

Cement Backerboard Tools

Cement backerboard is an ideal substrate for setting tile. It's hard, flat, and moisture-resistant, and mortar bonds tenaciously to its surface. Unfortunately, it's not the easiest material in the world to cut. Here's a quick look at a few of the tools you'll need when working with backerboard.

Cutting tools

The simplest, safest way to cut backerboard is with a carbide-tipped scoring tool. Simply score the surface of the backerboard with the tool's sharpened carbide tooth. Rake the tool along the cut line two or three times to form a

deep groove. Then, bend the sheet until it snaps along the groove. Be sure to wear a dust mask or respirator; backerboard contains silica dust, which is hazardous and can damage lungs and nasal passages.

There are specialty portable circular saws designed for cutting cement/masonry materials that have proper dust shrouding and blade guarding. Use one of these saws with a carbide-tipped or diamond-grit blade specifically designed to cut these materials.

Use a 4-ft. or longer level to check for plumb and to ensure that several tiles are all in the same plane.

Cut large holes and notches into backerboard with a jigsaw fitted with a metal-cutting blade. The small, hardened teeth cut slowly but leave behind a very smooth, clean edge. A carbide-grit jigsaw blade also cuts backerboard but is sometimes difficult to find in stores. The best way to cut small holes into backerboard is with a drill and carbide-grit or diamond-impregnated hole saw.

A pair of electric shears provides a fast, easy, and relatively clean way to cut most backerboard. And this versatile tool can make all cuts: straight, curved, notches, and holes. Electric shears are rather expensive to buy, but they're typically available for rent at any well-stocked tool-rental dealer.

Electric shears slice through most types of cement backerboard with a minimum amount of effort, noise, or dust.

Miscellaneous backerboard tools

Two additional tools that can make working with cement backerboard much easier are a T-square and a cordless impact driver.

A 48-in.-long T-square provides a quick and accurate way to mark square, straight cut lines onto backerboard sheets.

A cordless impact driver is the best tool for setting the screws used to secure backerboard. It's important to drive the screws just slightly below the surface of the backerboard, not too deep, nor too shallow. While you can use a standard cordless drill to set the screws, the impact driver

gives you much better control to consistently drive screws to the correct depth.

Tile-Cutting Tools

Here are the five most common tile-cutting tools. You may not need all of them for every tiling project, but with these tools in your arsenal, you'll be able to execute all of the necessary cuts in any type of tile.

Manual tile cutter

Consisting of little more than a tiny scoring wheel and lever handle, a manual score-and-snap tile cutter is a marvel of engineering. Here's how it works: Set the tile on the cutting table and place the cut line directly below the scor-

> **TIP** To eliminate any chance of an electrical shock when using a wet saw, always plug the saw into a GFCI-protected electrical outlet.

To work cement backerboard, you'll need (from left): a 4-ft. T-square, circular saw, cordless impact driver, carbide-tipped scoring tool, jigsaw, and electric shears.

STANLEY

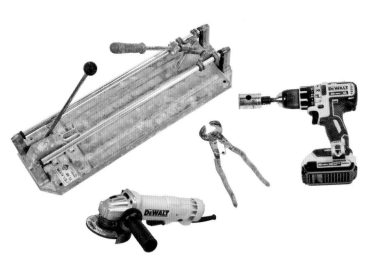

A manual score-and-snap tile cutter is quick, quiet, and easy to use. It can cut all types of tile, except natural stone. The model shown here has two lever handles: one for scoring, and one for snapping.

Popular portable tile-cutting tools include (clockwise from left): manual score-and-snap tile cutter, tile nippers, cordless drill with carbide-grit hole saw, and right-angle grinder.

> **TIP** Manual tile cutters can be used to cut ceramic, porcelain, and glass tile but not natural stone tiles. You must use a motorized wet saw or right-angle grinder to cut stone tiles.

ing wheel. Lower the handle until the scoring wheel contacts the tile. Firmly press down and then push the handle forward to score a line across the surface of the tile. Now press down on the handle to snap the tile in two. (Note that some manual cutters have two handles, one for scoring the surface and another for snapping the tile.)

When shopping for a manual tile cutter, keep in mind that price is a good indicator of quality. Avoid bargain-priced cutters, which will cut roughly and inaccurately. An alternative to buying a tile cutter is to rent one from a home center or tool-rental dealer.

Wet saw

A motorized wet saw is perhaps the most valuable of all tiling tools. It can be used to make any cut—straight, angled, notched, square cutout, even circular holes—in any type of tile, including natural stone and the densest, hardest porcelain. Its high-speed motor drives a diamond-impregnated, toothless blade that easily slices through tile.

The saw is equipped with a water pump that continuously showers the spinning blade with water, reducing friction (which cools the blade) and flushing away the soggy slurry of tile dust. The spinning blade sprays a fine mist of water out the back of the saw, so set up outdoors or in a garage. Wet saws are sold at home centers, but unless you're planning several more tiling projects, it's probably smarter to rent the saw than to buy it.

A motorized wet saw provides a quick, precise way to execute any type of cut in any type of tile. The saw sits above a water tub that holds an electric pump, which continuously circulates cooling water over the spinning blade.

A motorized wet saw has a toothless abrasive blade that cleanly slices through the thickest tiles with little effort. Hold the tile down flat on the sliding table, then push the table forward to cut the tile.

Bore holes through all types of tile with a cordless drill and abrasive hole saw. Use a wet sponge to cool down the hole saw during the drilling process.

A portable right-angle grinder is useful for making the tough cuts, including plunge cuts to create square or round holes. The grinder's spinning wheel shoots out a thick stream of dust, so always work outdoors and wear the appropriate safety gear.

TIP When using a hole saw to bore pipe-penetration holes in tile, always select a hole saw that's slightly larger in diameter than the pipe. That way, the pipe will comfortably fit through the tile even if the hole is slightly off center.

Right-angle grinder

When fitted with a carbide-grit or diamond-impregnated cutting wheel (blade), a portable right-angle grinder will easily slice through any type of tile, including natural stone. This powerful, handheld tool is particularly useful for cutting irregular shapes, notches, and circular and square holes. It can also be used to cut cement backerboard.

TIP Before operating a right-angle grinder, inspect the cutting wheel for cracks, fissures, or chips. If you see any flaws, replace the blade. Never cut with a damaged wheel; it could fly apart, causing serious injury.

Abrasive hole saw

The quickest, cleanest way to cut holes in tile is with a carbide-grit or diamond-impregnated hole saw. Unlike a standard woodcutting hole saw, an abrasive hole saw doesn't have teeth or a pilot bit. Instead, the rim of the saw is encrusted with supersharp tungsten-carbide or diamond grits that grind through the hardest, thickest, most resilient tile in a matter of seconds. Abrasive tile-cutting hole saws are sold individually or in multipiece sets. They range in size from about ¾ in. to 3¼ in. dia.

Tile nippers

Tile nippers might be the most basic of all tile-cutting tools, but they're indispensable just the same. Tile nippers are essentially pliers that are armed with durable carbide-tipped jaws, which can chomp through virtually any tile. Now, you'd never use nippers to slice a tile in half, but they're invaluable when you need to remove a small bit of tile, snip off a corner, or make a semicircular cut to fit around a pipe or other obstacle.

The trick to using nippers is to nibble away at the tile a little at a time. Take too big a bite, and you're likely to crack the tile. When done, the cut edge will be a little ragged, but you can smooth it with a diamond-impregnated file, if desired.

When shopping for tile nippers, choose a pair that has long handles and comfortable, non-slip grips. Some models feature a compound-action mechanism that greatly increases cutting leverage while reducing hand fatigue.

TIP Prior to using tile nippers, score the cut line on the tile with a utility knife or carbide-tipped scoring tool. That creates a relief point, which can help prevent the tile from cracking beyond the cut line.

Tile nippers are invaluable when you need to notch a tile around an outlet or other obstacle.

TIP Always wear safety glasses when using tile nippers as protection from flying bits of glazing and tile.

Tile-Setting Tools

It's surprising how few tools are required to set tile. In most cases, all you need are a few trowels, a putty knife or two, and a drill equipped with a mixing paddle to blend the mortar.

However, the exact style and number of tools required often depends on the size and type of tile. For example, large-notch trowels are typically used when setting large-format tiles. And the opposite is true when installing smaller tiles. Setting glass tile requires both a notched trowel and wide-blade putty knife. Here's a quick look at some of the most commonly used tile-setting tools.

Trowels

There are literally dozens of different types of trowels available, but they're all used for the same purpose: to spread mortar. Tiling trowels can be divided into two basic categories: notched and smooth.

A notched trowel has notches cut along the edge and end of its steel blade. The notches are typically square-cut, but V-shaped and U-shaped notches are also common. The purpose of the notches is to create ridges in the mortar, which helps the tile bond more securely.

The edges of smooth trowels aren't notched. These tools are used to apply a thin skim coat of mortar and to smooth and flatten mortar applied with a notched trowel. A trowel will often have one notched edge and one smooth (unnotched) edge. Or, it might have one size notch along one edge and a different size notch along the opposite edge, effectively doubling the tool's usefulness.

Spreading mortar with a notched trowel creates well-defined ridges in the mortar. These ridges are crucial to the tile installation: When a tile is pressed down, the ridges compress, creating a vacuum-like pressure that locks the tile in place.

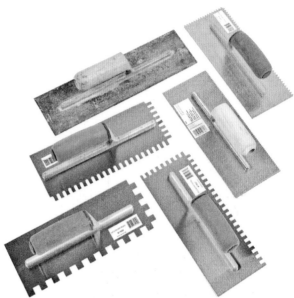

These six trowels represent just a small sampling of the many sizes and types of trowels available for spreading mortar. Note that most of them are notched trowels. Large-notch trowels are typically used for setting large tiles; small-notch trowels are recommended when working with smaller tiles. And note that the smooth trowel (upper left) has no notches.

Besides trowels, you'll also need the following tile-setting tools (from left): ½-in. drill with mortar-mixing paddle, rubber mallet, assorted putty knives, retractable utility knife, and suction cup.

Putty knives

Putty knives are general-purpose tools used for a variety of tasks, such as applying and smoothing mortar, scraping trowels clean, picking debris out of the mortar bucket, and scraping rough spots off walls and subfloors.

Putty knives come in a wide range of sizes, which are indicated by the width of the blade. They also come with either a flexible blade or stiff blade. Flexible blades are best for smoothing and applying mortar, while stiff blades are meant for scraping and chiseling. For most tile jobs, you can get by with four putty knives: a 1½-in.-wide stiff-blade knife and 1½-in., 3-in., and 5-in. or 6-in. flexible-blade knives.

Drill and mixing paddle

The quickest, most efficient way to mix thinset mortar is with a ½-in. electric drill and metal mixing paddle. Don't try using a smaller drill or you might burn out the motor.

Shopping for Trowels

Determining which trowel to use for each tile job might seem a bit daunting, but it's actually very easy. First, the tile manufacturer will often indicate what type and size of trowel to use right on the box of tile. This information is also typically printed on the back of the mortar bag. And if all else fails, visit the website of the tile or mortar manufacturer. There, you'll find detailed installation instructions, including which tools to use.

When shopping for trowels, resist the temptation to buy bargain-bin models. Cheap trowels typically have thin metal blades that can easily bend out of shape and hard, uncomfortable handles. Spend a few bucks more for mid-priced trowels that are made of thick, resilient steel and have cushioned rubber handgrips.

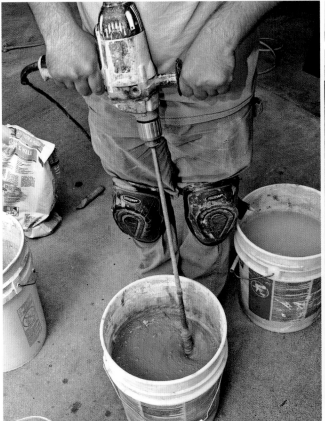

Mix thinset mortar in a 5-gal. bucket. Add the water first, then the mortar, and mix well for at least five minutes using a drill and metal mixing paddle.

Tap tiles into the mortar with a rubber mallet and thick wooden tapping block. Slide the beveled end of the block across the floor to check for any misaligned tiles.

Add water to the bucket first, then sprinkle in the mortar. Run the drill at high speed and continuously raise and lower the paddle throughout the mixing process to thoroughly blend the mortar. Mix well for at least five minutes, then let the mortar slake, or rest, for 5 to 10 minutes. The brief respite allows all the ingredients to coalesce.

Immediately after mixing the mortar, lower the paddle into a bucket of clean water. Then run the drill at high speed to rinse any mortar off of the mixing blades.

Mallet and tapping block

Tiles, especially large-format tiles, are often embedded into the mortar by tapping them with a rubber mallet and wooden tapping block. A 1½-lb. mallet is sufficient for most tile installations, though a slightly lighter dead-blow hammer would work just as well.

The tapping block, which is also known as a beating block, is usually 1½ to 2 in. thick, 6 in. wide, and 10 to 12 in. long. You can buy tile-tapping blocks, or make one easily enough from a fir 2x6 or 2x8.

The end of the block is beveled at a sharp angle, which serves a very important function: After tapping the tiles into place, slide the block across the surface. If any tile is sitting too high or too low, the beveled end of the block will catch on the tile. This height discrepancy is known as lippage. A certain amount of lippage is acceptable, and in some installations, even unavoidable, but it shouldn't be so great as to feel uncomfortable underfoot or create a tripping hazard.

Suction cup

Sometimes you need to pull up a freshly set tile (either because there's too much mortar underneath or not enough). If you need to pull a tile, use a large suction cup. Simply stick the cup to the tile and lift. If the tile won't budge, slip a stiff-blade putty knife beneath the tile and gently pry up as you pull on the suction-cup handle. Suction cups are sold at home centers, tile stores, and through online retailers.

> **TIP** Suction cups won't stick to dusty surfaces, so be sure to wipe clean the surface of the tile and the underside of the suction cup. And lift straight up on the handle; if you pull to the side, the suction cup will slide off.

Flooring roller

You won't need a flooring roller for every tiling project, but it's an absolute necessity when installing uncoupling membranes (see p. 31), radiant-heat mats (see p. 70), and other sheet goods that must be pressed down into mortar.

A simple J-roller works fine, but a triple-wide roller with a front handle provides much more leverage and delivers greater downward pressure. Flooring rollers are sold at home centers and tile stores but are also typically available at tool-rental dealers.

A flooring roller is required when installing sheet goods, such as the uncoupling membrane shown here. The pressure from the roller ensures a good bond with the thinset mortar.

Grouting Tools

There are only a few simple hand tools needed to apply grout to the joints between the tiles, but each tool is important.

Margin trowel

A margin trowel is typically used by concrete contractors but is also ideally suited for mixing tile grout. It has a narrow but stiff blade that cuts through the thickest grout without bending. And its square nose scrapes the bottom of the bucket to thoroughly mix all the grout. It's also perfect for scooping grout out of the mixing bucket.

Rubber grout float

A rubber float is easily the most important of all grouting tools. It's used to smear grout across the tiled surface and force it deep into the joints. However, to properly apply grout, you must use a high-quality rubber float that has a thick, dense pad. Inexpensive floats have thin, soft rubber pads that compress too easily, making it impossible to force in the grout deep into the joints.

Grout sponge

After the grout is applied with the rubber float, a grout sponge is used to clean the excess grout from the surface of the tiles. Unlike a typical square-edged scrubbing sponge, a grout sponge has rounded edges and corners, which glide over the fresh grout without disturbing it. When using a grout sponge, be sure to rinse it clean and wring out the excess water after each swipe across the floor.

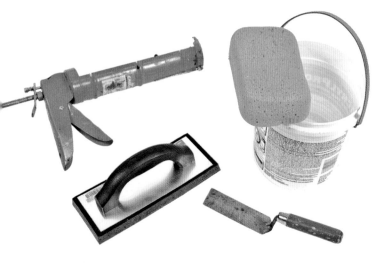

When it comes time to grout the tile joints, you'll need the following tools (from left): a caulking gun to seal around the tiled surface, a rubber float to apply the grout, a grout sponge and bucket to clean off excess grout, and a margin trowel to mix the grout.

Tile-setting substrates include (back row): cement backer board and extruded polystyrene panel. Other commonly used setting materials include (front row, from left): grout, modified LFT thinset mortar, unmodified thinset mortar, and liquid waterproofing membrane.

Cement backerboard is screwed in place, and then the joints are covered with self-adhesive mesh tape and thinset mortar.

Caulking gun

After grouting, it's often necessary to apply caulk around the tiled surface, especially where it abuts a dissimilar material, such as a wood cabinet, window trim, plastic-laminate countertop, or aluminum threshold. That's because tile and other materials expand and contract at different rates. If you fill these gaps with grout, the grout will eventually crack and crumble as the two surfaces move apart.

To solve this problem, use a caulking gun to fill all perimeter joints with a silicone or "siliconized" sealant. These types of sealants are often labeled as Tub and Tile Caulk. And if you can't find a caulk color to match the tile, use clear sealant. It'll fill the joint and be less conspicuous than a contrasting color.

Tile-Setting Materials

It wasn't so long ago that tile was typically applied to either moisture-resistant drywall or plywood. While these two materials are still occasionally used for tiling, there are much better substrates available for setting tile, especially in wet areas and rooms regularly exposed to high humidity. Here's a look at the most popular tile substrates and other tile-setting materials.

Cement backerboard

The most popular tile substrate by far is cement backerboard. It's produced from several different manufacturers and is essentially a sheet of cement—commonly ¼ in. or ½ in. thick—that's reinforced by fiberglass mesh. It's

Use a rubber grout float to force grout down deep into the spaces between the tiles. Tip the float on edge and smear the grout diagonally across the joints.

After applying the grout, use a damp grout sponge to clean off the excess grout from the tiled surface. Wipe diagonally across the tiles to avoid pulling out any grout.

installed much like drywall: screwed in place and then taped over the joints. Only instead of using paper tape and joint compound, backerboard seams are covered with self-adhesive mesh tape and thinset mortar.

Cement backerboard is readily available at home centers and lumberyards in 3-ft.-wide x 5-ft.-long sheets. When installing backerboard, be sure to follow the manufacturer's instructions implicitly, and don't take any shortcuts. For example, when installing backerboard to a subfloor, always set it into a bed of mortar. And be sure to follow the fastener size and pattern, as recommended by the manufacturer. Using the wrong screws, spacing the screws too far apart, or driving the screws too close to an edge or corner will weaken the substrate and adversely affect the tiled surface.

Extruded-polystyrene substrate

The newest tile substrate, known by the trade name Kerdi-Board, is totally different than any other type of backerboard. First, it contains no cement but instead is made of extruded polystyrene (think, Styrofoam). That makes the panel extremely lightweight, remarkably easy to cut, and, most importantly, 100% waterproof.

Extruded-polystyrene substrate panels (aka Kerdi-Board) are lightweight, easy to cut and install, and ideal for wet areas like a shower or tub surround.

Waterproofing Membranes

When tiling showers stalls, tub surrounds, and other wet environments, it's highly recommended that you apply a waterproofing membrane to the cement backerboard. (Waterproofing isn't required for Kerdi-Board.)

There are two basic ways to waterproof walls, shower pans, and floors: using moisture-blocking fabric or liquid membrane. The woven fabric comes in sheets and is adhered to the backerboard with thinset mortar. All seams and corners are sealed with strips of fabric, which are also set in mortar.

Liquid waterproofing membrane is applied to the backerboard with a paint roller. You must apply two coats, but once the rubber-like liquid cures, it'll form a barrier to seal out water. (We used AquaDefense liquid waterproofing in the shower stall project on p. 96.) And as an added benefit, the moisture-blocking fabric and liquid membrane both also help prevent cracks in the backerboard from transferring through to the tile.

Liquid waterproofing membranes apply as easily as paint. Simply roll it on, allow it to dry, then roll on a second coat. The entire process typically takes less than an hour.

TIP It's important to leave ⅛-in. expansion space between the backerboard sheets and to stagger the joints so that the corners of four sheets never come together at one intersection.

It's also available in many more sizes and thicknesses than cement backerboard. Sheets are available in eight thicknesses, ranging from ³⁄₁₆ in. to 2 in., and five sizes from 32 in. x 48 in. to 48 in. x 120 in., although not all thicknesses are available in every size. (For the tub surround project on p. 132, we used 4-ft. x 8-ft. sheets of ½-in.-thick Kerdi-Board.)

There's a cement-free reinforcement layer laminated to each side of the polystyrene panel. The reinforcement layer, in turn, is topped with anchoring fleece webbing that creates a suitable surface for installing tile. Kerdi-Board can be used in place of cement backerboard for all typical tiling applications, including floors, walls, ceilings, countertops, tub decks, and more.

Uncoupling membranes

Uncoupling membranes represent the greatest advancement in tile-setting technology since the advent of thinset mortars. That's quite a claim for a product that's little more than a thin sheet of polyethylene plastic.

When properly installed, an uncoupling membrane adds rigidity to the subfloor, provides superior support for the tile without dramatically raising the floor height, creates a continuous waterproof barrier below the tiles, and prevents cracks and movement in the subfloor from passing through to the tile or grout joints.

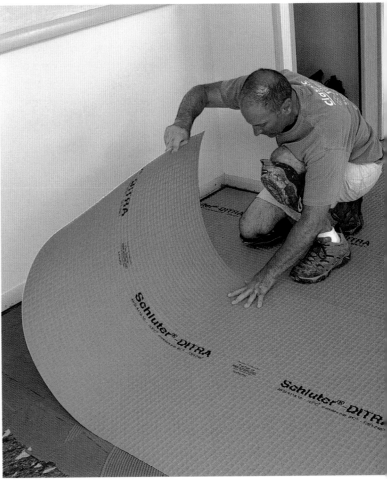

The standard uncoupling membrane (left) has a surface that's punctuated with small, square dimples. The opposite membrane (right) has octagonal dimples, which accept radiant-heat electrical cable. The back surface of each membrane is covered with crack-isolation fabric.

Uncoupling membranes are set in a bed of thinset mortar, pressed down with a flooring roller to ensure proper adhesion, and then topped with mortar.

Ditra-Heat is a new underlayment product that doubles as an uncoupling membrane and platform for installing electric radiant-floor heat. The electrical cable is simply snapped down between the octagonal dimples.

Stamped into the surface of the membrane is a grid of small, square dimples. Each dimple angles back to form a dovetail shape, which provides an anchoring point for the mortar. The underside of the membrane is covered with crack-isolation fabric that isolates any cracking in the subfloor.

Uncoupling membranes are typically adhered to the subfloor with latex-modified thinset. The membrane is then pressed down with a flooring roller to ensure proper adhesion. Once the mortar hardens, the dimples in the top surface are filled with unmodified thinset. You can set the tiles immediately, or wait for the mortar topcoat to cure, and then apply fresh mortar and set the tiles.

There's a new type of uncoupling membrane that also serves as a platform for installing electric radiant-floor heat. Made by Schluter®, it's called Ditra-Heat and its surface is stamped with octagonal-shaped dimples. Once the membrane is mortared to the floor, electrical heating cable

is pressed down between the dimples. The nice thing about this system is that you can run the cable in any direction and into any section of the membrane, allowing you to provide heat precisely where you need it.

Thinset mortar

Thinset mortar is the material of choice for bonding all types of tiles to virtually any surface. And although there are several different types of mortar, they can be divided into two basic groups: modified and unmodified.

Modified thinset contains chemical polymers, such as acrylics and latex. When mixed with water, the polymers dissolve and make the mortar more flexible, much stronger, and more resistant to freeze/thaw cycles. Most tile jobs are set in modified thinset mortar.

Unmodified thinset, as you may have surmised, contains no polymers. It's simply a mix of Portland cement, fine-grain sand, and a water-retention compound that helps the cement properly hydrate. You can mix unmodified thinset with water or a liquid polymer additive, which essentially creates modified thinset.

Now within each group, there are many different formulations of thinset. For example, LFT (large format tile) modified mortar is a non-sag thinset specifically made for setting large, heavy tiles. There are fast-setting mortars and mortars recommended for outdoor installations.

Choosing the Right Mortar

Identifying the appropriate mortar for your installation is easy. Check with the tile manufacturer or read the instructions on the bag of mortar. There, you'll find all pertinent information, including recommended substrates, appropriate tile types, size of notched trowel to use, detailed mixing directions, and square-footage coverage rates per bag.

Most tiles are set in standard gray mortar (either modified or unmodified) but glass tile and light-colored marble must be set in white thinset. And certain natural stone tiles, such as green and black marble, must be installed with a special thinset, such as an epoxy-bonding mortar, to prevent the tiles from warping or cupping.

Have three 5-gal. buckets on hand when mixing mortar. Use one as a mixing bucket for blending the mortar, another as a water bucket for adding water to the mixing bucket, and the third one as a rinse bucket. Fill it with water for rinsing the mixing paddle clean of mortar.

Mix the mortar in a 5-gal. bucket, using a ½-in. electric drill and paddle mixer. To fully hydrate one 50-lb. bag of mortar, you'll need to add about 1½ gal. of water. However, it's best to mix only about half of the bag at a time. Working in smaller batches requires mixing more often, but it allows you to work at a more leisurely pace.

Add about 3 qt. of water to the bucket, then pour in some dry thinset mortar. Mix well, then add a little more mortar and mix again. Continue until you've added about half of the bag, and the mortar is the consistency of yogurt: thick, lump-free, and smooth enough to spread easily. If the mortar is too thick, add a bit more water. If it's too runny, mix in more mortar. Then allow the mortar to slake, or rest, for 5 to 10 minutes.

And keep in mind that the amount of mortar you'll need will depend not only on the size of the project but also on the size of the notches in the trowel. Obviously, trowels with large notches will apply more mortar than small-notch trowels. And it doesn't take much of a change in notch size to dramatically influence coverage. For example, using a ¼-in. x ¼-in. square-notch trowel, the coverage rate for one 50-lb. bag of mortar is 75 to 90 sq. ft. If you use a slightly larger ¼-in. x ⅜-in. square-notch trowel, the coverage rate drops to 55 to 65 sq. ft.

Mix grout in a 1- or 2-gal. bucket using a margin trowel. And be aware that a little grout goes a long way, so only mix a little at a time.

TIP To determine which type of grout to use for your specific tile installation, contact the grout manufacturer or visit its website. You can also find all relevant information on the back of the grout bag.

Tools for Grout Repair

When it's time to regrout an existing tiled surface, you'll need a few specialty tools to do the job correctly. To start, you'll need a grout saw to scratch out the old grout from between the tiles. This simple hand tool has a carbide-grit-encrusted blade that quickly grinds through the hardest grout. Both long-handled and compact grout saws are available for just a few dollars each. And the pointed end of a can opener is useful for removing grout, especially from hard-to-reach spots.

If you need to remove a lot of grout from a large area, save yourself some time and trouble by using an oscillating multi-tool. Install a carbide-grit grout blade and grind out the grout in a matter of seconds.

After removing the grout from between the tiles, use a grout brush to clean out any dust and debris. The brush's narrow, contoured head and stiff bristles fit perfectly into tile joints.

For small- to medium-size grout repairs, fill the joints with premixed grout. Force the grout into the joints with a rubber float. Use a 3-in.-wide plastic putty knife to apply grout into corners, crevices, and other tight spots that you can't reach with the float.

Lastly, use a thick grout sponge to wipe the excess grout off the tiled surface. Be sure the sponge is damp—not dripping wet—and rinse it clean after each swipe across the tiled surface.

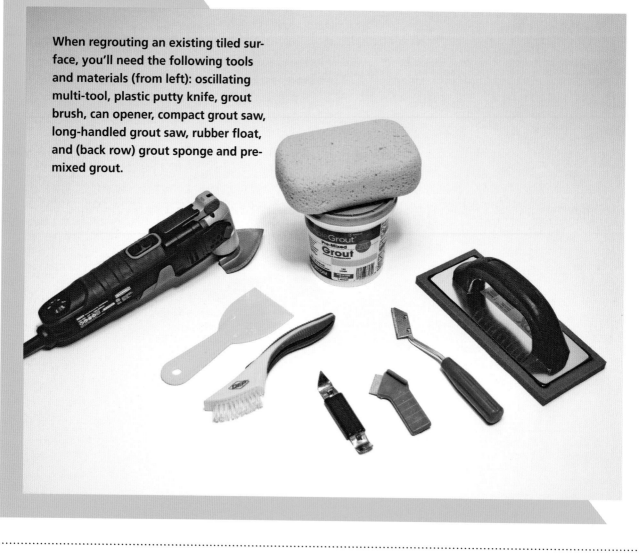

When regrouting an existing tiled surface, you'll need the following tools and materials (from left): oscillating multi-tool, plastic putty knife, grout brush, can opener, compact grout saw, long-handled grout saw, rubber float, and (back row) grout sponge and premixed grout.

Tile grout

Cement-based masonry grout is used to fill the joints between the tiles. You can buy ready-to-use premixed grout for small projects, such as the tile mirror shown on p. 218, but for most jobs it's best to buy latex-modified grout in powder form and then mix it with water. Regular masonry grout also comes in many more colors than premixed grout, allowing you to choose one that closely matches or contrasts the tile color.

There are two types of masonry grout: Unsanded grout is made for joints that are 1/8 in. wide or narrower. Sanded grout is used to fill joints that are wider than 1/8 in. There's also a new generation of specialty grouts, such as Laticrete®'s PermaColor® Grout, which can be used to fill joints ranging from 1/16 to 1/2 in. wide.

There's a third type of grout worth mentioning, called epoxy grout. It's a two-part product that includes an epoxy resin and a hardener. When the two components are mixed, they create a syrupy-thick liquid that cures through chemical reaction. The resulting grout joints are incredibly strong, virtually waterproof, and highly resistant to staining, cracking, and most household chemicals.

However, epoxy grout isn't very DIY friendly. It must be mixed to exact proportions, and is expensive and difficult to apply. Epoxy isn't water soluble, so you must clean up with a solvent, such as paint thinner. And, if you don't get all the epoxy cleaned up before it hardens, it's nearly impossible to remove.

Sealers

The last step of most tiling jobs is to apply a clear silicone-based sealer to the grout joints. The exception is epoxy grout, which doesn't require sealing. Sealing makes grout much less porous, which increases its stain and mildew resistance. And although it's not necessary to seal glazed tile, many natural stone tiles should also be sealed.

Some sealers come with a built-in brush for easy application. Otherwise, just use a small artist's brush to spread the sealer onto the joints. Apply two coats of sealer, allowing the first coat to fully dry before applying the second. And to maintain a sufficient level of protection, reapply the sealer annually. For a stone wall or floor, use a 3-in.-wide foam brush or small sponge and seal the grout joints and the stone tiles simultaneously.

After the grout has fully cured, seal the grout joints with a clear penetrating sealer. If the tile is natural stone (as here), you'll need to seal the entire surface.

CHAPTER THREE

TILING A KITCHEN FLOOR

TILING A KITCHEN FLOOR IS ARGUABLY THE MOST POPULAR of all tiling projects, which isn't surprising when you consider that glazed tile is an ideal surface for today's busy kitchens. It resists stains, spills, and splashes and can withstand years of soapy scrubbings and stampeding people and pets.

Although glazed ceramic tile is still used on floors, we upgraded to glazed porcelain tile for this kitchen because it's much denser, harder, and stronger than ceramic tile. The dark-gray 12-in. x 12-in. tiles are reminiscent of natural slate but feature a subtle mottled pattern that lends a more contemporary look to the room. The tiles were set in latex-modified thinset mortar, as is customary with porcelain tiles. However, before laying the tile we had to fix the plywood subfloor, which was too thin to support the tile.

Ordinarily, we would have reinforced the subfloor with another layer of plywood or cement backerboard (see pp. 66–70), but that would have raised the new floor too much. So, we covered the subfloor with an uncoupling membrane that's only ⅛ in. thick. Besides stiffening the floor, the membrane has the added benefits of providing waterproof protection for the subfloor and helping to prevent cracked tiles and fractured grout joints. The membrane installs easily, but must be installed according to strict guidelines, so, if you opt to use the membrane, follow our instructions carefully.

Prepping the Subfloor

The first step is to carefully remove any existing flooring without damaging the plywood subfloor beneath. In this kitchen, there was an old vinyl-tile floor to scrape up; the residual flooring mastic was stuck securely to the subfloor, so we were able to mortar right over it.

To properly support a tile floor, the subfloor must be at least 1¼ in. thick. In this kitchen, the subfloor was only ¾ in. thick. Rather than build it up with more plywood or backerboard, we installed a ⅛-in.-thick uncoupling membrane, called Ditra. Made by Schluter Systems, the membrane is designed to provide the necessary support without dramatically raising the floor height. A continuous piece of crack-isolation fabric is adhered to the underside of the membrane. The fabric prevents cracks in the subfloor from passing through the membrane to the tile and grout.

The Ditra uncoupling membrane is adhered to the subfloor with latex-modified thinset mortar. Once the mortar cures, the dimples in the top surface are filled with unmodified thinset, which is mortar that doesn't contain a latex additive. After the topcoat of mortar hardens, the tiles are set onto the membrane using latex-modified thinset. Switching back and forth between latex-modified and unmodified mortar may seem tedious and unnecessary, but it's required by the manufacturer and produces the best results.

Mixing modified mortar

Pour about 3 qt. of water into a clean 5-gal. bucket, and then slowly add approximately one-half of a 50-lb. bag of latex-modified thinset mortar. Blend the mortar and water using a ½-in. electric drill and metal mixing paddle. Mix for five minutes until the mortar is silky smooth and lump free. If the blend is too thin and soupy, add a little dry mortar and mix again. If it's too dry and stiff, sprinkle in a bit more water.

Once the mortar is mixed to the proper consistency, lift the mixing paddle out of the mortar but not completely out of the bucket. Run the drill at high speed to fling any excess mortar off the paddle and into the bucket. Now, submerge the mixing paddle into a bucket of clean water. Squeeze the drill's trigger to rinse any remaining mortar off of the paddle. Allow the mortar to slake, or rest, for about five minutes, then mix it again briefly for just a minute or two.

> **TIP** Vinyl flooring installed prior to the early 1980s may contain asbestos, which is a carcinogen. Before removing a vinyl floor, have an asbestos abatement specialist test the old flooring and mastic. If either one contains asbestos, hire a professional abatement contractor to remove the vinyl floor.

Mortar Mixing Tip

How do you know when thinset mortar is mixed to the correct consistency? Here's one foolproof method: After thoroughly mixing the mortar, lift out the mixing paddle and hold it over the bucket. If the mortar is properly mixed, it should hang onto the paddle before very slowly dropping off in large, wet blobs, as shown here.

If the mortar quickly drains off the paddle, it's too thin and watery. Add more dry mortar and mix again. If the mortar stubbornly sticks in place and doesn't drop off the paddle at all, then it's too thick and must be thinned out with a little water.

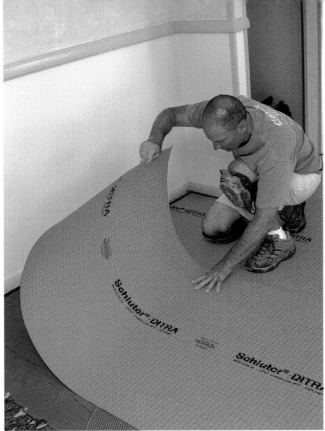

UNCOUPLING MEMBRANE. Ditra membrane is a 39½-in.-wide plastic sheet that's stamped with small square dimples and adhered to the subfloor with latex-modified thinset mortar.

1 **COMBINE WATER AND MORTAR.**

TIP Use a ½-in. corded electric drill to mix thinset mortar. If you don't own one, borrow or rent one. Don't use a cordless drill. The mortar is too thick and you'll likely burn out the drill's motor trying to power the mixing paddle through the heavy-bodied mortar.

2 **BLEND TO A SMOOTH CONSISTENCY.**

3 **RINSE THE MIXING PADDLE.**

Installing the membrane

Beginning in one corner near the base cabinets, spread the mortar across the subfloor with a ³⁄₁₆-in.-deep V-notch trowel. Spread it out 44 in. or so from the cabinets to provide a few extra inches of mortar to accommodate the 39½-in.-wide membrane.

Unroll the uncoupling membrane and slice it to length with a utility knife. Cut it about ¼ in. shorter than necessary so it'll fit into place without buckling. Set the membrane onto the mortared subfloor, placing it ⅛ in. to ¼ in. away from the base (toe kick) of the cabinets. Now firmly press the membrane down into the mortar with a 7-in.-wide flooring roller. Roll over the entire membrane, especially along the edges, to ensure a strong, lasting bond with the mortar.

Use the V-notch trowel to spread another 44-in.-wide swath of mortar onto the subfloor. Cut the next piece of membrane to length and set it down into the wet mortar. It should be butted tightly to the first piece of membrane and not overlapping it. Use the flooring roller to press down the membrane.

Continue to spread mortar and install uncoupling membrane across the floor and up to the opposite wall. Mix up a fresh batch of latex-modified thinset mortar, as needed. As you roll down the membrane closest to a wall, excess mortar will squeeze out. Wipe away the mortar with a damp sponge, being careful not to smear any onto the wall.

1 **SPREAD THE MORTAR. Use a ³⁄₁₆-in.-deep V-notch trowel to spread latex-modified mortar across the subfloor. Tip the trowel up at about a 45° angle.**

2 **SET THE FIRST PIECE OF MEMBRANE. Carefully lay the uncoupling membrane down into the wet mortar. Set it close to the cabinet base and smooth out any trapped air by hand.**

TIP You can walk on the membrane as soon as it's installed, but before doing so, be sure it's in position first. Once the membrane is pressed down into the mortar, it's very difficult to slide or shift into position.

3 **ROLL IT OUT. Use a flooring roller to force the membrane into the mortar. Press down hard on the front handle as you steer the roller around by the rear handle.**

4 **SPREAD MORE MORTAR. Hold the notched trowel at an angle and apply thinset mortar to the subfloor, spreading it out from the edge of the first piece of membrane.**

PORCELAIN TILE FLOOR

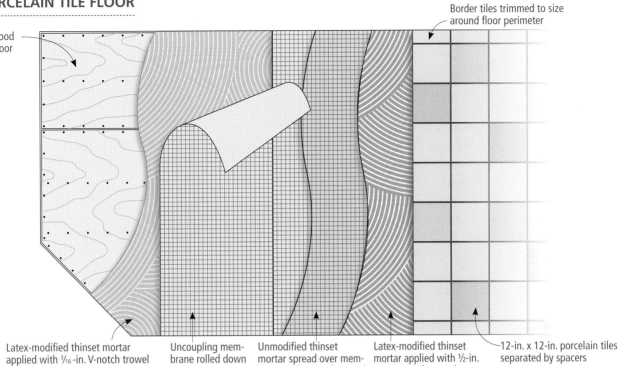

Plywood subfloor

Border tiles trimmed to size around floor perimeter

Latex-modified thinset mortar applied with ³⁄₁₆-in. V-notch trowel

Uncoupling membrane rolled down into mortar

Unmodified thinset mortar spread over membrane with smooth trowel

Latex-modified thinset mortar applied with ½-in. square-notch trowel

12-in. x 12-in. porcelain tiles separated by spacers

TIP A flooring roller provides the best and fastest way to press the uncoupling membrane down into the mortar. This isn't a tool you're likely to own and you'll probably not find one at the local hardware store. However, you should be able to rent one or, if necessary, buy one online for about $25.

5 SET THE SECOND PIECE. Install the next piece of membrane by first setting one end down into the mortar. Then, unroll the rest of the membrane across the floor, making sure that it's butted tightly to the previously installed piece.

TIP Wet mortar is relatively caustic, so when you get it on your hands—and you will—wash it off immediately. And if your hands become irritated and sore, wear rubber gloves while working and apply hand cream at the end of the day.

6 WIPE THE ROLLER CLEAN. As you continue to install the uncoupling membrane, stop occasionally and wipe mortar from the flooring roller with a damp sponge. If you don't, the mortar will harden, making it very difficult to remove later.

Fitting the Membrane around Obstacles

If you need to notch the uncoupling membrane to fit around a floor register or heating vent, don't bother measuring and marking the membrane. Here's a much easier, more accurate method: Cut the membrane to fit the floor space and set it into place. Roll the membrane down into the mortar, then use a utility knife to notch the membrane around the vent hole in the floor.

Use a similar technique to custom-cut the membrane to fit around door casings, doorjambs, and other trim

work: First, cut the membrane about 1 in. or so wider than necessary. Set it into place and press down on the membrane with your hands, forcing it to conform to the door casing or other obstruction. Then use a utility knife to carefully trim the membrane to fit. And remember, you don't have to be super-precise when trimming the membrane to fit, since it can be cut up to ¼ in. short.

NOTCH AROUND VENTS.

TRIM AROUND DOOR CASINGS.

Cutting the membrane to fit

As you work your way across the floor, spreading mortar and installing the uncoupling membrane, you'll eventually have to cut and notch the membrane to fit around obstacles, such as cabinets, islands, doorways, wall corners, and columns.

Start by carefully measuring out to the edge of the previously installed piece of membrane. And measure from at least two places, just in case the floor space is out of square and wider at one end than the other. Use a sharp utility knife to cut the membrane to length first and then to width. And again, to ensure the membrane fits with room to spare, cut it about ¼ in. shorter than necessary.

CUTTING TO FIT. When it's necessary to cut a piece of uncoupling membrane to fit the floor space, measure out to the edge of the previously installed membrane.

TIP To prevent damaging the surface below when cutting the uncoupling membrane to size, always lay the membrane over a sheet of scrap plywood or the subfloor.

USE A SHARP UTILITY KNIFE. The resilient-plastic uncoupling membrane cuts easily with a sharp utility knife. Just be sure to keep your free hand well away from the cut line.

Depending on the size and shape of the room, the final piece of uncoupling membrane might be a long, narrow strip or small rectangular piece. Either way, cut the membrane to fit and then roll it down into the mortar. Once the entire floor is covered with uncoupling membrane, allow the mortar to cure overnight before proceeding.

Mortaring over the membrane

The next step is to spread mortar over the surface of the uncoupling membrane, filling in all the square dimples in the surface. But remember, this time you must use regular unmodified thinset mortar, which does not contain a latex additive.

Start by vacuuming the floor of all dust, dirt, and debris. If you encounter any dried clumps of mortar protruding from the seams or along the walls, chip them off with a putty knife and vacuum them up.

Next, mix up a batch of mortar just as you did before (see pp. 38–39). Pour some mortar onto the floor and spread it across the uncoupling membrane using a large smooth (unnotched) trowel. Hold the trowel at an angle and smear the mortar across the surface, making sure to fill each and every square-dimple depression.

As you swipe the trowel across the membrane, press down hard to scrape away any excess mortar, leaving behind mortar-filled squares. Continue until you've mortared over the entire floor, then stop and allow the surface to harden for 48 hours.

MORTAR OVER THE MEMBRANE. Smear the mortar across the uncoupling membrane with a smooth trowel. Be sure to fill all the square-dimple depressions.

TIP When cutting the uncoupling membrane to size, there's seldom any need to draw lines or snap chalklines. Simply cut along the straight-line layout of the square-dimple grid molded into the surface. The one exception is if you must cut a piece of membrane that's wider at one end than the other. In that case, you'll need to draw or snap a cut line.

Tiling the Floor

With the subfloor properly prepped, the kitchen floor is finally ready for tiling. The 12-in. x 12-in. porcelain tiles are set into a bed of latex-modified thinset mortar and separated by 1/8-in. spacers. Most of the cuts can be made with a manual score-and-snap tile cutter, but you'll need a motorized wet saw to notch tiles to fit around obstructions, including wall corners, cabinets, and floor-mounted heating vents. However, before setting any tile, you must first lay out the tile pattern.

Establishing the tile pattern

The first step to tiling any floor is to determine where in the room you should start tiling to produce the best-looking tile pattern. Establishing the tile pattern is easy in a simple square or rectangular room. But in a kitchen it's more difficult because you have to take into account not only the room size and shape but also how the tiles will align with the cabinets and at thresholds into adjoining rooms. And in our case, the kitchen floor flowed around a peninsula and into a dining room, which was also being tiled.

TIP After measuring the room and determining how much tile you'll need, add an extra 8 to 10 percent to cover waste and mistakes.

It's often best to start laying out the pattern at the main entry into the kitchen since that's the key focal point as you enter and exit. But you also want to make sure that you don't have a full tile along one wall and a tiny sliver of tile at the opposite wall. Optimally, the cut tiles at opposite walls should be exactly the same size, which is virtually impossible to achieve in a kitchen because of the complexity of the layout.

The next-best layout, which is much more achievable, is to have the border tiles be at least one-third to one-half as wide as a full tile. For instance, if you're installing 12-in. x 12-in. tiles, adjust the pattern so the border tiles along the walls are at least 4 in. to 6 in. wide. Now, the tiles at opposite sides of the room might not be the same width, but at least they won't be narrow slivers. The bottom line is that you'll have to make a few compromises to achieve the best-looking, most balanced pattern.

In our kitchen, we balanced the tile pattern on a walkway that runs between the kitchen peninsula and dining area. And we adjusted the pattern so that the cut tiles around the perimeter of the spaces—kitchen and dining room—were at least 4 in. wide. The first step to establishing a pleasing tile pattern is to do a dry layout of two perpendicular rows of tiles. Set a row of tiles down onto the prepped subfloor. Put spacers between the tiles to

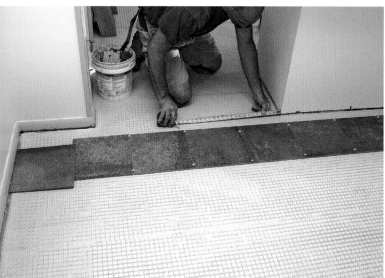

DO A DRY LAYOUT. Create a pleasing tile pattern by first laying down a row of tiles—without mortar. Here, we aligned the tiles with the center of a walkway.

SNAP A CHALKLINE. Establish the first row of tiles by snapping a chalkline onto the subfloor. Measure carefully to ensure the line is parallel with a nearby wall.

DRAW A PERPENDICULAR LINE. Set the edge of a carpenter's framing square on the chalkline, then draw a layout line onto the subfloor that's perpendicular to the chalkline.

ESTABLISH THE STARTING POINT. Snap a second chalkline across the first line to create a perfectly square intersection. This represents the starting point for tiling the floor.

simulate the grout joints. Now slide the tiles right or left to see how they—and, more importantly, their joints—align with the cabinets, wall corners, and thresholds. Lay down a second row of tiles in the opposite direction, perpendicular to the first row. Again, shift the tiles, as necessary, to achieve a near-balanced pattern.

If you're balancing the pattern on a doorway or walkway, as we did, measure and mark the center of the space. Then, align the tile pattern on the center point. If that layout produces a sliver of tile along one wall, shift the pattern to the left or right by the distance of one-half a tile. Once satisfied with the pattern, measure from a nearby wall at one end of the room to the first row of tiles. Mark a pencil line onto the subfloor alongside the tile. Move down to the opposite end of the room, mea-

sure off the same wall the same distance, and mark a second line. Mark the location of the second row of tiles with a single line, drawn at the point where it intersects the first row of tiles.

Remove all the tiles and snap a chalkline along the first two marks, creating a perfectly straight line that's parallel with the wall. Now set a framing square on the chalkline, aligning it with the mark that indicates the location of the second row of tiles. Draw a line onto the subfloor that's perpendicular to the chalkline. Flip the square over and draw a second perpendicular line on the opposite side of the chalkline. Snap a second line along the framing-square lines to create a layout line that's perpendicular to the first chalkline. The intersection of the two chalklines represents where to start tiling.

Starting tiling

Use the drill and mixing paddle to mix up a fresh batch of latex-modified thinset mortar. Dump some mortar onto the subfloor near the layout chalklines snapped earlier. Use a ½-in. square-notch trowel to spread mortar from one of the chalklines out across the subfloor. Hold the trowel at an angle and be careful not to obscure the line with mortar; you'll need to see the line when installing the first row of tiles. Set the first tile into place with its edge flush on the chalkline and then follow the sequence shown in the photos beginning at right.

> **TIP** Stack the boxes of tiles in an adjacent room, not in the kitchen where they'll be in the way. And when you start laying tile, work from three or four open boxes to ensure a nice random mix of tiles of varying colors, shades, and patterns.

1 **SPREAD MORTAR FOR THE FIRST TILES.** Start spreading thinset mortar out from the chalkline using a ½-in. square-notch trowel. Be careful not to cover up the line with mortar.

2 **SET THE FIRST TILE INTO PLACE.** Check to be sure the edge of the tile is aligned perfectly flush with the chalkline and then press it down into the mortar.

3 **CUT TILES TO FIT AS NECESSARY.** Use a score-and-snap tile cutter to cut tiles to size. Here, the next tile was trimmed to 45° to match the angle of the base cabinets.

4 **ALIGN THE SECOND TILE WITH THE FIRST.** Slip the cut tile into place beneath the overhanging face frame of the cabinet. Press it down and slide it within ¼ in. of the toe kick (tiles don't have to fit tight up against the toe kick).

5 **SPREAD MORE MORTAR.** Use the ½-in. square-notch trowel to apply more thinset mortar to the subfloor, holding the trowel at about 45°. Don't spread any more than 10 sq. ft. of mortar at any one time.

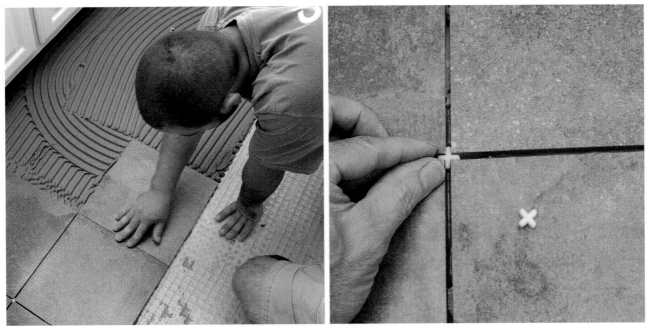

6 **TILE ACROSS THE FLOOR.** Continue to install two rows of tiles across the subfloor, making sure the tiles in the outer row align perfectly flush with the chalkline.

7 **INSERT SPACERS.** Install three or four tiles, then go back and slip ⅛-in. spacers between the tiles. Push the tiles together to create consistent ⅛-in. wide joints.

8 **TIP THE TROWEL ON END AT THE WALL.**
Spread mortar up to the wall, then use the toe of the notched trowel to pull the mortar away from the wall, leaving behind perfectly formed ridges. This tiptoe technique allows you to get close to the wall without hitting your knuckles.

Keep the Mortar Fresh

It's important to set tile into freshly troweled mortar. Therefore, don't spread more mortar than you can tile over in about 15 minutes. As a general rule, only apply 10 sq. ft. of mortar at any one time. If the mortar is troweled out and exposed to the air for more than 15 minutes or so, a crust may form on its surface, which can prevent the mortar from bonding permanently to the tiles. If you notice that mortar has crusted over, scrape it up and discard it, then apply a fresh bed of mortar.

TIP There are a handful of essential tools required for tiling a floor, but few are as important as a good pair of kneepads. The best and most comfortable kind has wide straps and a thick rubber pad that's covered by a hard plastic shell. This type of kneepad costs a bit more than an all-rubber kind, but the level of comfort and protection it offers are well worth the extra money.

9 **FINISH THE FIRST TWO ROWS.** Install the last full-width tiles in the first two rows. Press the tiles down into the mortar, then insert the ⅛-in.-wide rubber tile spacers.

10 **START THE TOE-KICK ROW.** Measure from the cabinet's toe kick out to the edge of the nearest full-width tile. Then subtract ¼ in. to ⅜ in. to account for the grout joints.

11 **INSTALL THE CUT TILE.** Cut the tile to width using the manual tile cutter and slip the cut tile into place. Press it down into the mortar, then insert a spacer. Slide the tile away from the toe kick to create the proper grout joint.

12 **CLEAN AS YOU GO.** After installing three rows of tile, use a damp sponge to wipe the surface clean of any mortar that may have squeezed out of the joints. It's important to clean as you go because once the mortar dries it'll be difficult to remove without scratching the tile.

Tiling around obstacles

Mix more latex-modified mortar, as needed, and continue to work your way out from the cabinets and across the kitchen floor. Depending on the floor you are working on, you may need to cut tiles to fit around cased openings or heating registers.

When you reach a cased opening, which is simply a doorway with no door, trowel mortar across the open threshold and install several full-width tiles before cutting any tiles to fit around the opening. To notch a tile to fit the doorway, start by holding the tile in position, ⅛ in. away from the adjacent tile in the same row. Mark a cut line onto the tile ⅛ in. away from where the tile meets the trim on the inside edge of the doorway.

> **TIP** Working around doorways takes a little bit more time, so spread slightly less mortar than you did when laying tiles out in the open floor space.

Now shift the tile forward and within ⅛ in. of the tile in the previous row. Mark the tile where it butts against the trim on the wall. Extend the two pencil marks to outline the notch that must be cut from the corner of the tile.

Cut out the notch on a wet saw and then install the notched tile, making sure to maintain the ⅛-in. gap from

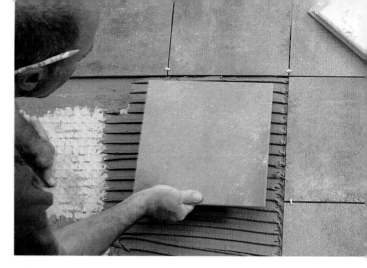

WORK ACROSS THE KITCHEN FLOOR. Continue to lay tiles, two rows at a time. Spread mortar with a ½-in. notched trowel and use the wood tapping block to flush up any uneven tiles.

the adjacent tiles and the doorway trim. Insert tile spacers and continue installing full-width tiles across the subfloor, using the rubber mallet and tapping block to even out any misaligned tiles.

> **TIP** After notching a tile on the wet saw, check the cut at the inside corner of the notch. Often there's a small nib of tile remaining where the two cuts didn't quite come together. To make sure the nib doesn't interfere with setting the tile into place, snip it off with tile nippers.

Tapping Tiles into Alignment

The goal of any tile installation is to get all the tiles aligned perfectly flush and even and on the same plane. This is particularly important when tiling a floor because you'll feel any misaligned tiles underfoot. Unfortunately, achieving 100% perfect alignment isn't always possible because tiles aren't always perfectly flat, exactly square, or even the same size. These slight imperfections make it difficult to get an entire floor of tiles all on the same-exact plane. However, there is a simple tool that can help with this problem and it's little more than a block of wood.

The tapping block shown here has a rubber-coated surface and sharply beveled end. To detect misaligned tiles, simply slide the block across the floor, leading with the beveled end. The sharp edge of the bevel will catch on any tiles that are even slightly out of alignment. To even out the tiles, set the block into place and lightly tap it with a rubber mallet. If you set the block over the intersection of four tiles, as shown, you can even them all up simultaneously.

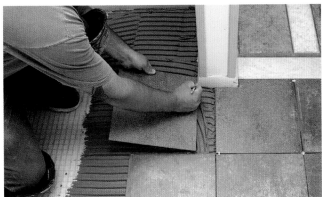

1 MARK THE SIDE OF THE TILE. Hold the tile to be notched in position ⅛ in. from the neighboring tile in the same row. Mark the tile ⅛ in. from where it meets the trim.

2 MARK THE TOP OF THE TILE. Slide the tile to within ⅛ in. of the tile in the previous row. Make a mark on the tile where it intersects the wood trim on the face of the wall.

3 CUT ALONG THE FIRST PENCIL LINE. Set the tile on the wet-saw table and align the first pencil line on the tile with the saw blade. Turn on the saw and cut along the line.

4 CUT ALONG THE SECOND PENCIL LINE. Rotate the tile 90° and slowly saw along the second pencil line. Cut up to, but not beyond, the first line to notch out the corner of the tile.

5 SET THE CUT TILE INTO PLACE. Fit the notched-out corner around the doorway; insert spacers to maintain ⅛-in. grout joints between the tiles.

If there are heating registers in the floor, you'll need to notch tiles to fit around the ducts (the process is similar to notching tiles around a cased opening). Start by removing the registers to expose the sheet metal ducts below. Next, measure from the edge of the nearest tile to the wall. Subtract ¼ in. from that measurement and cut a full-width tile to size. Note that cutting the tile ¼ in. short allows for a ⅛-in. grout joint along the wall and between the notched tile and the adjacent row of tiles. Notch and install the tiles as shown in the photo sequence below.

Complete tiling the floor by cutting and installing tile along the last wall. Then place a chair, table, or other barrier in each doorway to prevent people or pets from entering the kitchen. Allow the mortar to cure overnight before grouting the floor.

TIP Each time you cut a tile on the wet saw, dry the tile with a towel before installing it. A dry tile will form a stronger bond with the mortar than a wet one because excess water can dilute and weaken the mortar.

Notching tiles around a duct

1 **MEASURE THE WIDTH OF THE TILE.** Measure the distance between the wall and the nearest row of floor tiles. Subtract ¼ in. from that measurement and then cut a tile to match.

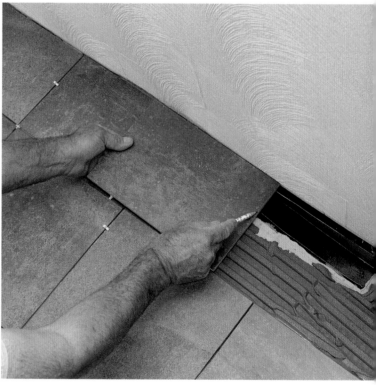

2 **MARK THE END OF THE TILE.** Hold the cut tile in place and make a pencil mark onto the tile ¼ in. away from where its end intersects the front edge of the sheet metal duct.

Take Two: Resetting Tiles

Do-it-yourselfers might be surprised to learn that professional tile contractors regularly pull up a recently set tile to make adjustments. Often there's a low spot in the subfloor and you must add more mortar than normal to raise the tile. Other times, there may be a slight hump in the subfloor and less mortar is needed to press the tile down into proper alignment.

Regardless of the reasons, be aware that sooner or later you'll likely have to pry up a tile and use the trowel to add or scrape away some mortar. This is often the only way to keep the offending tile even and level with its neighboring tiles.

3 **MARK THE FRONT OF THE TILE.** Reposition the cut tile so that its end is ⅛ in. away from the adjacent tile in the same row. Mark the tile ¼ in. from the end of the duct.

4 **OUTLINE THE NOTCH.** Use a layout square to draw pencil lines along each mark, outlining the corner notch onto the tile.

5 **CUT ALONG THE FIRST LINE.** Set the tile onto the wet saw and align the pencil line with the saw blade. Turn on the saw and cut along the line.

6 **CUT ALONG THE SECOND LINE.** Turn the tile 90° and cut along the remaining pencil line. Cut up to, but not beyond, the first line to notch out the corner of the tile. If there's a nib of tile left in the inside corner, snip it off with the nippers.

STANLEY

7 **SET THE NOTCHED TILE INTO PLACE.** If the tile doesn't fit easily around the outside of the duct, return to the wet saw and trim the notch a little larger.

8 **SPREAD MORTAR ON THE OTHER SIDE.** Use the notched trowel to apply thinset mortar to the subfloor on the opposite side of the heat duct. Rake the mortar with the toe of the trowel.

9 **SET THE SECOND TILE.** Cut and notch a second tile, then press it into place on the opposite side of the duct. Again, be sure the tile sits around the duct, not on top of it.

1. CUT THE TILE.

2. BACK-BUTTER THE TILE.

3. POSITION THE TILE.

4. PRESS THE TILE TO THE TOE KICK.

Tiling Toe Kicks

The recessed space at the bottom of kitchen cabinets is called the toe kick because it allows you to stand close to the counter without bumping your toes. In most kitchens, toe kicks are covered with plywood and then painted or stained to match the cabinets. And while there's nothing wrong with plywood toe kicks, tiling the floor provides the perfect opportunity to upgrade the toe kicks by tiling them, too.

Tile will protect the toe kicks from water damage and staining and make them easier to scrub clean. And by extending the tile across the floor and up the toe kicks, you'll create a smooth, visually pleasing transition between the floor and cabinets, as shown above left.

To tile a toe kick, start by measuring the height of the recessed space, which is typically about 4 in. Next, use a manual tile cutter to cut strips of tile ½ in. shorter than the height of the toe kick. Cutting the tiles short makes them easier to install. Then, use a notched trowel to spread mortar onto the back of the tile. This technique, known as back buttering, is much easier than trying to spread mortar onto the narrow, recessed face of the toe kick.

Tip the back-buttered tile at an angle and slide it into position beneath the cabinet. Firmly press the tile to the toe kick, aligning its ends with the tile joints in the floor. There's no need to put spacers beneath the toe-kick tiles; allow them to sit right on the floor tiles. Continue to install narrow pieces of tile to the toe kick around all the base cabinets. Allow the mortar to cure overnight before grouting the joints.

Grouting the Joints

The next step is to fill the ⅛-in.-wide spaces between the tiles with cement-based grout. Now, ordinarily you'd use sanded grout to fill joints wider than ⅛ in. and nonsanded grout for joints ⅛ in. wide or narrower. Here, however, we used a specialty grout from Laticrete called PermaColor, which can be used to fill joints ranging from ¹⁄₁₆ in. to ½ in. wide. It's also stain-, water-, and mildew-resistant.

PermaColor Grout is available in more than three dozen colors. For our kitchen, we chose a color called Platinum because it matched the darker tones in the tile.

Prepping for grouting

Begin by using a utility knife or narrow slotted screwdriver to remove all the rubber spacers from between the tiles. As you pry up the spacers, be careful not to chip or scratch the tile. And the spacers are reusable, so save them for your next tiling project.

Next, go around the room and inspect each grout joint. If you find any that are completely filled with mortar, scratch out the mortar with a utility knife. It's important to remove the excess mortar to create a void for the grout. Again, be careful not to mar the tiles as you scratch out the mortar. Vacuum the floor clean of all dust and dirt.

Add one pint of water to a small bucket, then pour in about 3 lb. of grout. Mix well with a margin trowel until the grout is the consistency of thick yogurt: smooth, creamy, and slightly firm. If the grout is too thin and soupy, add a bit more grout and mix again. If the grout is too thick and dry, mix in a few drops of water. Allow the grout to slake for five minutes, then mix again for a few seconds right before grouting. The slaking process provides the necessary time for all the ingredients and chemicals in the grout to coalesce and become fully hydrated.

1 **REMOVE THE RUBBER SPACERS. Before grouting the floor, take a utility knife and pry up all the rubber spacers from between the tiles. Be careful not to scratch the tile.**

2 **SCRATCH OUT EXCESS MORTAR. If there are any joints filled with mortar, use a utility knife to scratch out the mortar to make room for the grout.**

3 **MIX UP A SMALL BATCH OF GROUT. Use a margin trowel to mix together 1 pt. of water and approximately 3 lb. of tile grout.**

TIP A margin trowel is an ideal tool for mixing grout because it has a very stout, rigid blade that doesn't flex under pressure. And its blade has straight sides and a square nose that excel at scraping grout from the sides and bottom of the bucket.

Applying the grout

The tool commonly used to apply tile grout is a rubber grout float, which is basically a handle attached to a rubber pad. However, be sure to use a high-quality float that has a dense, durable rubber pad. Cheap floats have soft, spongy pads that compress too easily, making it virtually impossible to force the grout into the joints.

> **TIP** If the grout in the bucket starts to stiffen up as you're working, don't add more water. Simply grab the margin trowel and mix the grout for about 30 seconds.

2 GROUT THE PERIMETER TILES. Use the toe of the rubber float to push grout into the tile joints around the perimeter of the room.

> **TIP** It's important to swipe the float at an angle across the tile joints. If you work parallel with the joints, the trailing edge of the float has a tendency to pull the grout out from between the tiles.

Scoop some grout out of the bucket and plop it onto the floor near the cabinets. Grout goes a long way, so you only need a handful or two to start. Take the float and smear the pile of grout across the floor, just to flatten it out a little. Now, hold the float at about 45° and swipe it across the floor, forcing the grout down into the tile joints.

Work in small areas, grouting just three or four tiles at a time. Once the joints are filled, hold the float at 90° with its long edge flat against the floor. Now pull the edge of the float along the tiles to scrape any excess grout from the surface. And don't forget to grout the toe kicks before moving too far out into the room.

1 GROUT THE FIELD TILES. Hold the rubber grout float at approximately 45° and swipe it across the floor, forcing the grout down into the ⅛-in. joints between the tiles.

3 CONTINUE TO FILL THE JOINTS WITH GROUT. Stop occasionally and use the rubber float to scrape excess grout from the surface of the tiles.

When you reach the border tiles at the perimeter of the room, use the end or nose of the float to press the grout into the joints. Don't worry if you accidentally get some grout on the wall or baseboard; it's virtually impossible to avoid. Just be sure to clean off the grout with a damp sponge before it hardens.

Continue to apply grout as you work your way across the kitchen floor. And mix fresh grout, as you need it. Once you've grouted the entire floor, rinse the bucket, rubber float, and margin trowel clean of all grout. Then wait 20 minutes or so before proceeding.

Cleaning off the grout

At this stage, the joints are filled, but there's grout smeared across every tile. The tool typically used to clean the tiles is a grout sponge, which is simply a large, thick sponge that has rounded edges and corners. (Don't use a regular sponge; its square edges and sharp corners will carve the soft grout from the joints.) However, for this job we used a grouting machine that consists of a water bucket with squeegee rollers, and a sponge float, which is simply a sponge attached to a flat backing plate with handle.

Submerge the sponge float or grout sponge into a bucket of clean water, then wring out the excess water. Next, set the sponge down flat on the floor and wipe at an angle across the grout joints, using light pressure. Don't worry about removing all of the grout during this initial wipe-down. All you're trying to do is clean off most of the excess grout.

Wring out the sponge after every swipe across the floor. After wiping down a large area of tile—say, 30 sq. ft. or so—come back with a clean, damp sponge and wipe the remaining grout from the surface. Again, the grout is still soft, so be sure to wipe at an angle across the tile joints. Continue in this manner, using the two-step sponging method, to clean grout from all the tiles.

Now wait for an hour or two for the grout to "set up" or stiffen. If it's a rainy or humid day, wait an additional hour. Then, use a dry cotton cloth to buff any residual grout haze from the tiles. Let the grout harden for two or three days, then apply a clear silicone-based grout sealer to make the grout more stain- and water-resistant.

TIP When cleaning the surface of the tile, be sure the sponge is damp, not soaking wet. A sopping wet sponge will drip water into the joints, diluting and weakening the grout.

TIP You can walk on the floor during the grouting process; just be sure to step in the center of the tiles and not on the joints.

1 **CLEAN OFF THE GROUT.** To remove the excess grout from the floor, wipe down the tiles with a sponge float. This initial pass will remove most but not all of the grout.

2 **MAKE A SECOND PASS OVER THE FLOOR.** Use a damp sponge float to lightly wipe off all the remaining grout from the surface of the tiles. After an hour or two, buff off any surface haze with a dry cloth.

CHAPTER FOUR

TILING A TUMBLED-MARBLE BATH FLOOR

WHEN COMPARING DIFFERENT types of flooring materials, none can match the widespread popularity and historical success of natural stone. Stone floors have been used throughout the millennia and are prized to this very day for their natural beauty and remarkable durability. How long has stone been used for flooring? Well, consider this: Prior to laying down stone slabs, most floors were dirt.

Today, you can find stone tiles cut from marble, slate, granite, and limestone in an almost infinite number of colors, textures, patterns, and sizes. In this chapter, I'll show how to upgrade a bathroom floor by installing 12-in. x 12-in. Turkish tumbled-marble tiles over cement backerboard. Tumbled marble has a slightly rougher, more rustic appearance than standard polished marble tiles, which have sharp, crisp edges and square corners. The result is a bath floor that looks both classic and casual.

In this chapter, I'll also show how to remove a toilet, repair a rotted plywood subfloor, and install an electric radiant-floor heat mat. (This last step is optional and can easily be omitted from the tiling sequence.)

Prepping the Subfloor

There's a considerable amount of prep work to do before setting the cement backerboard, including prying off the existing baseboard molding, removing the toilet, and tearing up the old floor.

In some cases, you may be able to lay cement backerboard directly over the existing floor but only if it and the subfloor are in good condition. Unfortunately, most bathroom floors have some water damage. In the bathroom shown here, water splashed out of the tub over the years had seeped under the vinyl floor and rotted the plywood subfloor. Before installing cement backerboard, we had to tear out the existing vinyl floor and replace the damaged sections of the subfloor.

Removing the baseboard moldings

Start by removing any transition moldings from the doorways and baseboard moldings from around the perimeter of the room. If you plan to reinstall the moldings after tiling, remove them carefully to avoid damaging them. It's also a good idea to label each piece with a sequential number or letter so it'll be easier to reinstall them later to their original positions.

Removing a toilet

When tiling a bathroom, it's necessary to first remove the toilet so you can tile the subfloor beneath it. Don't be tempted to tile around a toilet; you have to remove it. Fortunately, this isn't a difficult job, even for novice do-it-yourselfers.

Start by closing the shut-off valve behind the toilet to stop the flow of water. Flush the toilet and hold down the handle for a minute or so to allow as much water as possible to drain from the tank. Remove the top of the tank and use a large sponge to sop up any water remaining in the bottom of the toilet tank.

Fill a 5-gal. bucket at least halfway with water. Then, in one quick motion, dump all the water into the toilet bowl. The pressure and weight of all the water rushing into the bowl will force out most of the standing water. Then use a small disposable plastic cup to scoop out as much of the remaining water from the bowl as possible. Remove the last bit of water from the toilet with a large sponge. Wring out the sponge and repeat several times until you've sopped up all the water.

TIP If you're going to save the baseboard moldings to reinstall them later, use end-cut nippers or locking pliers to pull the finishing nails out from the back of the moldings. If you hammer the nails through from the rear, the nail heads will splinter the face of the molding.

1 **REMOVE ANY TRANSITION MOLDINGS.** Pry the metal or wood transition molding from the doorway's threshold. (If it's a marble threshold, loosen it with a hammer and ½-in. cold chisel.)

2 **REMOVE ANY BASEBOARD MOLDING.** Use a thin flat bar to pry the molding off the walls. Place a wood shim behind the bar to protect the wall surface.

Disconnect the toilet's water-supply line from the shut-off valve and then pry off the plastic caps from each side of the toilet's base to expose the closet bolts. Use a wrench to remove the hex nuts from the bolts.

Next, spread a tarp or thick blanket on the floor in front of the toilet. Remove the top of the tank from the toilet. Rock the toilet back and forth from side to side to break the wax seal with the closet flange (floor drain). Straddle the toilet and grab each side of the bowl close to the tank. Bend your knees, keep your back straight, and lift straight up. Set the toilet down onto the tarp. Finally, plug up the closet flange with an old towel or rag to seal out sewer gasses and prevent anything from dropping down into the drainpipe.

TIP Removing a two-piece toilet is much easier if you first unbolt the tank from the bowl. That'll reduce the weight of the toilet by more than one-third.

 DISCONNECT THE WATER-SUPPLY LINE. Use a wrench to disconnect the compression fitting that attaches the water-supply line to the shut-off valve. Be sure to close the valve first.

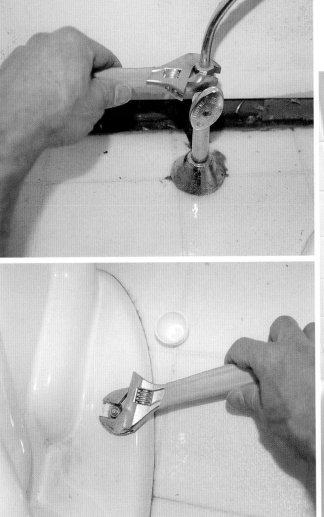

2 **REMOVE THE NUTS THAT HOLD DOWN THE TOILET.** Pop off the plastic caps on each side of the toilet base to reveal the closet bolts. Use a wrench to remove the hex nut from each bolt.

3 **LIFT THE TOILET.** Rock the toilet back and forth to break it free from the wax seal below. Then lift the toilet and gently set it down onto a tarp or thick blanket.

Removing the old flooring

To remove vinyl-sheet flooring, use pliers to grab hold of the flooring in the corner of the room (but first read the tip about asbestos in vinyl flooring on p. 38). Pull the flooring up and away from the corner. Most sheet-vinyl flooring is glued down only around the room's perimeter, so it comes up pretty easily. However, if the flooring is adhered to the entire subfloor, or if you're removing glued-down vinyl tiles, then you'll have to use a floor scraper. Both manual and electric floor scrapers are available at tool-rental dealers.

After loosening one corner, use a utility knife to score the flooring every 16 in. to 20 in. Don't worry about cutting all the way through the flooring; just score the surface. When you pull on the flooring, it'll rip along the scored line.

Roll up and discard the old flooring and sweep the room clean. Then, inspect the room perimeter for areas where vinyl flooring adhesive may have squeezed out from under the flooring. Use a stiff-blade putty knife to scrape up these dried ridges of glue. If you don't remove these obstructions now, they'll interfere with the setting of the cement backerboard. Vacuum the subfloor clean.

Repairing the Subfloor

After removing the old flooring, inspect the subfloor for damage. Pay particular attention to the areas around the perimeter of the room, along the plywood seams, and close to the tub and toilet. If the subfloor is damaged or compromised in any way, take the time now to fix it.

> **TIP** Never lay marble tile—or any other flooring for that matter—over a structurally unsound subfloor. The poor condition of the subfloor will continue to deteriorate and eventually require an expensive structural repair.

Cut out the damaged plywood

When repairing a subfloor, keep in mind that it will likely be made up of two layers of plywood or oriented-strand board (OSB). In older homes, the subfloor might be composed of solid-wood boards, with or without plywood on top.

Use a circular saw to cut out the damaged section of plywood subfloor. Adjust the saw to cut only through the top plywood layer; ½ in. or ⅝ in. deep is usually sufficient.

1 **START AT THE CORNER. Pry up one corner of the old vinyl floor and then grab onto it with pliers. Firmly pull up on the flooring to peel it off the plywood subfloor.**

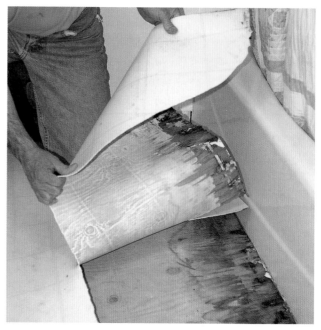

2 **THEN REMOVE IN WIDE STRIPS. Score the vinyl flooring with a utility knife, then rip it out in wide strips. This is easier than trying to remove the entire sheet in one piece.**

> **TIP** If you need to remove vinyl-sheet flooring from a large room, use a hook-blade utility knife. Simply slide the sharpened hook under the flooring and pull. It'll quickly slice through the flooring without cutting into the subfloor below.

If possible, position the cut so it runs down the center of a floor joist. And be sure to cut well beyond any rot and into sound, dry wood. Extract all nails and screws from the cut piece of plywood, and pry it up.

Next, cut a slightly narrower section of plywood from the bottom layer of subfloor. Again, cut beyond the rotted section and only deep enough to go through the plywood. Cutting the patches to different widths ensures that new plywood pieces will overlap and form a strong, rigid joint. If you sawed through both plywood layers along the same line, you'd create a weak spot where the subfloor would flex, causing tiles to crack and pop loose.

If the plywood extends under the bathtub, cut it free with a reciprocating saw or an oscillating multi-tool. Remove all the nails or screws holding down the bottom plywood layer, then pry it up to reveal the floor joists below.

Next, cut 2x4 blocking to fit between the floor joists, a distance that's typically about 14½ in. wide. The blocking provides extra support for the new plywood patches. Install a 2x4 block every 12 in. to 16 in., and fasten each one to the joists with 2½-in.-long drywall screws.

TIP Before sliding the plywood patch into place, mark the positions of the 2x4 blocking and floor joists onto the adjacent subfloor. That way, you'll know where to drive the screws once the plywood patch is set into place.

Patching the subfloor

1 **CUT OUT THE TOP ROTTED SECTION.** Cut through the top layer of plywood first and well beyond the damage.

2 **CUT THE BOTTOM LAYER.** After removing the top layer, cut a slightly narrower strip of plywood subfloor out of the bottom layer. Again, cut beyond the rotted area.

3 **CUT AROUND THE BATHTUB.** If the plywood subfloor extends under a bathtub, vanity cabinet, or other immovable object, cut it free with a reciprocating saw.

4 **INSTALL BLOCKING.** To provide proper support for the plywood patches, cut and install 2x4 blocks between the floor joists.

Cut the bottom plywood patch to fit. (Be sure to use exterior-grade plywood, which is made with water-resistant glue.) Apply a thick bead of construction adhesive to the top edges of the floor joists and 2x4 blocks and set the plywood patch into place. Check to be sure the patch is flush with the surrounding subfloor, then fasten the plywood to the 2x4 blocks and floor joists with 1⅝-in. decking screws spaced about 8 in. apart. Now cut the top plywood layer to size and apply construction adhesive to the surface of the bottom layer; screw down the top layer.

Installing Cement Backerboard

Cement backerboard provides an ideal substrate for setting tile. However, if the plywood subfloor is at least 1¼ in. thick, you can skip this step and set the tile directly on the plywood.

In this bath, the subfloor was composed of two layers of ½-in. plywood, so we added a layer of ¼-in.-thick cement backerboard to obtain the recommended thickness of 1¼ in. Regardless of the subfloor thickness, you should always consider installing backerboard; it'll create a rock-solid substrate and offer superior adhesion for the mortar.

5 **SET THE BOTTOM PATCH IN PLACE.** Apply construction adhesive to the top edges of the floor joists and 2x4 blocks, and then set into place the new ½-in. plywood subfloor patch.

6 **SECURE THE TOP PATCH.** Spread construction adhesive over the bottom patch, and then use 1⅝-in. decking screws to fasten down the top, wider patch.

Cutting Backerboard

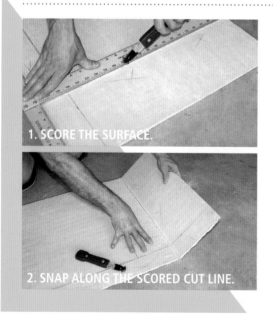

1. SCORE THE SURFACE.

2. SNAP ALONG THE SCORED CUT LINE.

There are a few different ways to cut cement backerboard, including using a circular saw, jigsaw, or electric shears (see p. 22), but the simplest, safest method is to use a carbide-tipped scoring tool. This simple hand tool consists of little more than a plastic handle fitted onto a flat steel blade that's armed with a super-sharp tungsten-carbide tooth. Here's how to use a scoring tool:

Measure and mark the backerboard, making it about ⅛ in. smaller than necessary. Align a T-square or other long straight-edge with the cut mark. Draw the scoring tool along the edge of the T-square to scratch a groove into the surface. Score the line two or three more times to deepen the groove.

With the scored line facing up, hold down the backerboard with one hand and then slowly pull up on the end of the sheet until it snaps in two. The scored edge usually breaks off cleanly, but if it's a little ragged, pare it smooth with a utility knife.

TUMBLED-MARBLE FLOOR

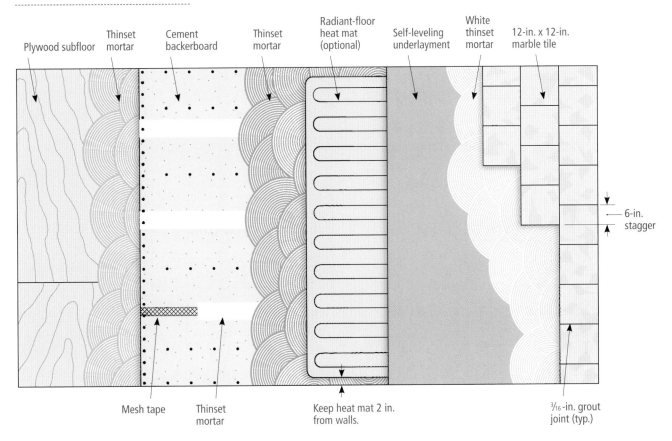

Plywood subfloor · Thinset mortar · Cement backerboard · Thinset mortar · Radiant-floor heat mat (optional) · Self-leveling underlayment · White thinset mortar · 12-in. x 12-in. marble tile

6-in. stagger

Mesh tape · Thinset mortar · Keep heat mat 2 in. from walls. · $^3/_{16}$-in. grout joint (typ.)

Installing the backerboard

Cement backerboard must be set down in a bed of thinset mortar to provide maximum support for a tile floor. Many do-it-yourselfers, and even some professional contractors, often skip this step and screw the backerboard directly to the plywood. Don't be tempted by this shortcut. You may save a little time up front, but you'll pay the price down the road when the floor flexes and tiles start cracking.

Mix up a batch of latex-modified thinset mortar and pour some onto the subfloor. Use the smooth (unnotched) edge of a ¼-in. notch trowel to spread the mortar across the plywood. Then, use the ¼-in. notched edge of the trowel to rake the mortar, creating a series of ridges. Spread the mortar about 1 in. beyond the edges of the backerboard sheet.

> **TIP** Cement backerboard contains silica dust, which can irritate lungs and nasal passages. Wear a dust mask or respirator when cutting backerboard, and never cut it indoors.

1 SPREAD THE MORTAR. Use a smooth trowel to spread the thinset mortar across the subfloor and then switch to a notched trowel to create ridges.

Lay the backerboard into the mortar, and then use a hammer and 2x4 block to tap the backerboard down into the mortar. Secure the backerboard to the subfloor with 1¼-in.- or 1⅝-in.-long backerboard screws. Drive screws every 4 in. around the perimeter edges, and space them 8 in. apart throughout the "field" or center of the sheet.

Cut the next piece of backerboard to fit beside the first piece. Apply mortar to the plywood subfloor with the notched trowel, extending it slightly beyond the edges of the sheet. Set the backerboard into the thinset, making sure to leave a ⅛-in. gap between it and the first sheet.

Fasten the sheet to the subfloor with backerboard screws. Again, follow the same fastener pattern as before: 4 in. apart around the perimeter edges and 8 in. apart throughout the field.

TIP A cordless impact driver provides the best and easiest way to drive the screws, but if you don't own one you can use a standard cordless drill/driver.

2 **SET THE FIRST SHEET.** Lay the first sheet of backerboard onto the subfloor and tap it down into the mortar with a hammer and 2x4 block.

3 **SET THE SECOND SHEET.** Apply more thinset mortar to the subfloor, then install the next backerboard sheet. Leave a ⅛-in. gap between the two sheets.

TIP Most backerboard sheets have the fastener pattern stamped into their surface, providing a visual guide that shows exactly where to drive in each screw.

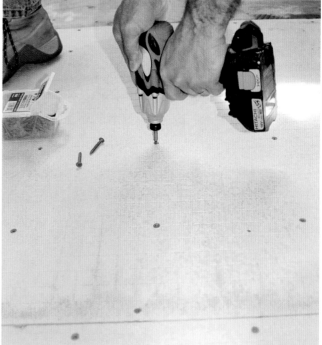

4 **FASTEN THE BACKERBOARD TO THE SUBFLOOR.** Use a cordless impact driver to drive 1¼-in. or 1⅝-in. backerboard screws.

Setting Backerboard in a Toilet Alcove

1. SCRAPE AWAY THE OLD WAX SEAL.

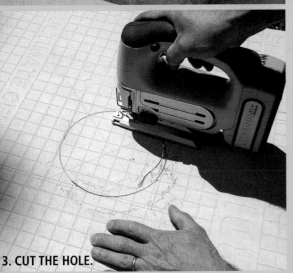

2. MEASURE AND MARK THE LOCATION OF THE CLOSET FLANGE.

3. CUT THE HOLE.

If you're tiling a bathroom floor, you'll have to install cement backerboard around the toilet's floor drain, which is called a closet flange. And if the shut-off valve protrudes from the floor, as most do, you'll also have to notch the backerboard to fit around the valve. Fortunately these cuts are easily made with a jigsaw fitted with a metal-cutting blade.

Start by using a stiff-blade putty knife to scrape the old wax seal from the closet flange. Next, use a pencil compass to draw a circle onto the backerboard to represent the diameter and position of the closet flange. To ensure the hole fits with room to spare, make the circle about ¼ in. larger than the outside diameter of the flange.

Cut the circle from the backerboard using a jigsaw fitted with a metal-cutting blade. Plunge-cut the blade through the backerboard on the inside of the circle. Then use moderate pressure to guide the saw around the circle to cut the hole. If necessary, also use the jigsaw to notch the edge of the sheet to fit around the shut-off valve.

Spread thinset mortar onto the subfloor around the closet flange. Be careful not to get any mortar on the flange or into the holes in the flange. Set the backerboard down into the thinset and secure with backerboard screws. Keep the screws at least 2 in. away from the edge of the hole; driving the screws any closer will fracture the backerboard.

4. SCREW DOWN THE BACKERBOARD.

Taping the joints

The final step to installing cement backerboard is to cover all the seams with adhesive-backed fiberglass mesh tape and thinset mortar. Again, this step is often skipped, but that's a big mistake. Taping the joints is critical because it transforms all the individual sheets of backerboard into one monolithic, seamless slab.

1 **TAPE THE JOINTS. Cover the joints between the sheets of backerboard with adhesive-backed mesh tape. Center the 2-in.-wide tape over the seams.**

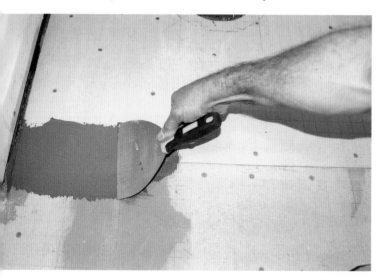

2 **APPLY MORTAR. Use a 6-in.-wide drywall knife to spread a very thin layer of thinset mortar over the taped joints. Allow the taped seams to cure overnight.**

Installing a Radiant-Floor Heat Mat

If you want to upgrade the bathroom's heating system, now's the time to install an electric radiant-floor heat mat. If not, then skip ahead to tiling the marble floor. The nice thing about setting the heat mat between the backerboard and marble tile is that the entire floor will absorb and then radiate heat, creating a warm and cozy floor.

> **TIP** If you are planning to install a heat mat, check with a licensed electrician or authority having jurisdiction (AHJ) to make sure the installation will comply with any applicable codes or regulations.

The heat mat is typically laid in thinset mortar, more mortar is immediately spread on top, and then the tiles are set. For this bathroom installation, however, we added a step to improve the performance of the radiant heat: pouring self-leveling compound over the mat to create a perfectly smooth, level surface for laying the tile and to provide a bit more thermal mass for radiating heat.

Setting the mat

Mix up a batch of latex-modified thinset mortar and spread mortar onto the backerboard with a ¼-in. notched trowel; spread only enough mortar to set one-half of the heat mat. Lay the radiant-floor heat mat down into the mortar, and press down with a rubber grout float. Carefully fold the second half of the heating mat over the first half—don't crease it—then spread mortar onto the backerboard. Press the mat into the mortar with the grout float.

Use a utility knife to cut a small slit in the heat mat and pull through the metal floor-sensing probe that's attached to the mat. Be very careful to cut between two electrical cables. And be sure the probe doesn't cross or come in contact with one of the electric cables woven into the mat. If it does, it'll send the wrong temperature reading to the thermostat.

Allow the mortar to cure overnight and then mix up a batch of self-leveling compound according to the package directions. The compound should have the consistency of a thin milkshake. Start in the room corner farthest from the door and pour the compound directly onto the floor. If mixed to the correct consistency, the compound will float out smooth and seek its own level. If necessary, use a steel float to help spread the compound.

TIP Heat mats are available in standard sizes and can also be ordered custom-made. The mat comes with a thermostat and floor-sensing probe that relays the floor temperature to the thermostat.

1 **LAY THE HEAT MAT INTO THE MORTAR.** Be careful not to crease or crush the electrical cables contained within the mat.

2 **FIRMLY PRESS THE MAT INTO THE MORTAR.** Using a rubber grout float, work out from the center to squeeze out trapped air and wrinkles.

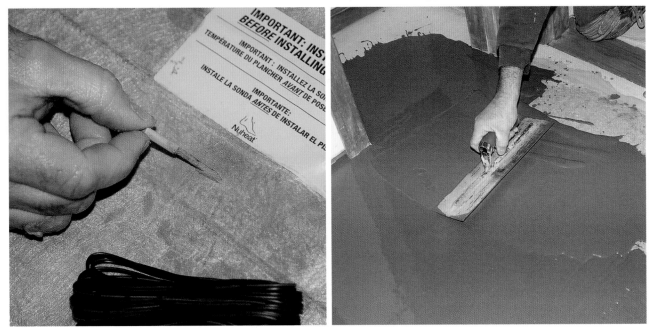

3 **LOCATE THE PROBE.** Cut a slit in the heat mat between two electrical cables and pull through the heat-sensing probe. Rest the probe on top of the mat.

4 **POUR AND SPREAD LEVELING COMPOUND.** Once the mortar beneath the heat mat has fully cured, slowly pour self-leveling compound over the entire mat. Use a steel float to help spread the compound.

Hooking up the thermostat

The radiant-floor heat mat must be connected to a dedicated electrical circuit, which is a circuit that provides power only to the heat mat. Hire a licensed electrician to connect the circuit to the main electrical panel. The electrician can also do the rest of the heat-mat installation, including pulling a new electrical cable and running wires from the heat mat to the thermostat location; you could also do this work yourself (always following the manufacturer's instructions) if you are comfortable running electrical wires.

> **TIP** Install the radiant-floor heat mat so that it extends to within 6 in. or so of the toilet's closet flange. That way, the floor around the front of the toilet will be toasty warm.

1 **PULLING WIRES.** A nylon string or fish tape is used to pull the wires from the radiant-heat floor mat up the wall and out the hole for the electrical switch box.

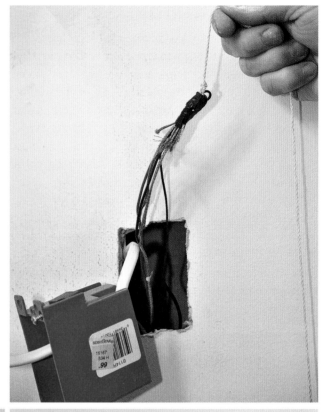

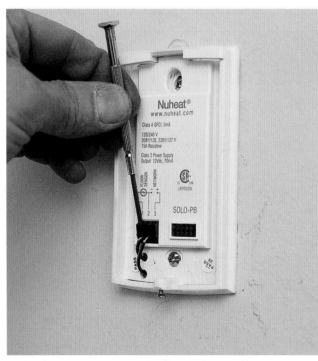

2 **MAKING THE CONNECTIONS.** After making the electrical connections inside the switch box, the thermostat is mounted on the wall and the floor-sensing wires are attached to the screw terminals.

3 **ATTACHING THE FACEPLATE.** The faceplate is hooked onto the thermostat, pressed flat, and then secured by tightening the tiny screw on the bottom.

Installing Marble Tile

Most of the tools and materials required for putting down a marble floor are identical to laying any tile floor, with two important exceptions: Marble, and all other natural stone tiles, can't be cut with a manual score-and-snap tile cutter; you must use a motorized wet saw to make all the cuts. If you don't own a wet saw, you can rent one by the day.

The other important difference is that marble tiles must be set in white thinset mortar. Using standard gray mortar can cause the marble to warp and crack.

Laying out the tile pattern

Ordinarily, it's a good idea to balance the tile pattern on the width of the room so that the tiles in the first and last rows are the same size. However, for a bathroom or similar space, it's best to balance the pattern on the most visually dominant area, in this case, the space between the vanity cabinet and the bathtub.

Start by checking to see if the tile fits beneath the door casings and doorjambs. If not, you'll have to trim them to accept the new floor. Next, hold a framing square against the end wall and centered between the tub and vanity. Draw a perpendicular layout line along the edge of the square and onto the floor. Now stretch a chalkline down the center of the floor. Align the string with the perpendicular line marked on the floor, then snap the chalkline. This line represents the center of the tile layout.

1 **CHECK THE FIT.** Set a tile beside the doorway. If necessary, use a handsaw to trim the bottom ends of the casings and jambs to allow the tile to slip underneath.

3 **SNAP A CHALKLINE.** Stretch a chalkline across the room, aligned with the perpendicular pencil line. Snap the chalkline to mark the center of the tile layout.

2 **ESTABLISH THE CENTERLINE.** Hold a framing square against the end wall and centered on the main floor area. Draw a line along the square and onto the floor.

Start tiling

Mix up a batch of white latex-fortified thinset mortar and, starting at the centerline, spread about 4 sq. ft. of mortar onto the floor with a ¼-in. notched trowel. Place the edge of the first tile right on the chalk line and press it down into the mortar. Set the next couple of tiles in the same the row, using the chalk line as a guide. Then use the notched trowel to spread more mortar.

Lay the tiles in the adjacent row, but this time, stagger the joints by 6 in.—the distance of one-half tile—to create an offset pattern. And to maintain consistent grout joints, be sure to insert ³⁄₁₆-in. rubber spacers between the tiles. Continue setting tiles down the center of the room, working out in both directions from the chalkline. Use the wet saw to trim tiles to fit along the tub and walls and against any cabinets.

> **TIP** Keep boxes of tile right outside the door of the room you're working in. If you put them in the room, you'll be constantly moving them out of the way.

1 **START TILING.** Set two tiles into the mortar, positioning them on the chalkline. Use a notched trowel to spread more white mortar onto the floor.

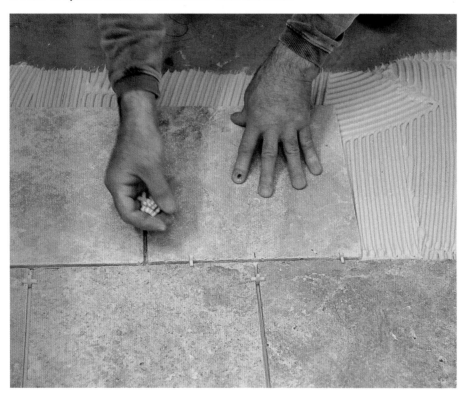

2 **STAGGER THE TILES BETWEEN ROWS TO CREATE AN OFFSET PATTERN.** Insert ³⁄₁₆-in.-thick spacers between the tiles to create consistent grout joints.

> **TIP** Press tiles down into the mortar with a slight twisting motion; that'll ensure a good, lasting bond with the backerboard.

Tiling around a Closet Flange

If you're tiling a bathroom, you'll need to cut a round hole in the tile to fit around the toilet's closet flange. Depending on the tile pattern, you may need to cut the hole in one tile (as we did here) or in two, three, or even four tiles. It all depends on how the tile pattern falls at the flange. Regardless of how many tiles you need to cut, the wet saw provides an easy way to make the circular cutout.

Hold the tile in place and mark the position of the closet flange onto the tile. Next, set a plastic flange extension ring onto the tile and use it as a template to trace the circular cutout. If you don't have an extension ring, use a pencil compass.

To cut the hole, start by holding the rear edge of the tile tight against the wet saw's sliding table. Then, slide the front edge of the tile forward into the spinning blade. Make the first cut along the edge of the circle. Continue to make small cuts into the tile, slowly removing material, but never cutting beyond the circular outline.

Once you've cut away part of the tile, make several long, closely spaced cuts across the diameter of the circle. Then saw across the previous cuts to remove large pieces of tile. Now saw away at the tile a little at a time until the circle is formed. The edge of the hole will be a little rough, but that's okay; it'll be hidden beneath the toilet.

Before spreading any mortar, lay the tile over the closet flange to make sure it fits with a little room to spare. If necessary, return to the wet saw and enlarge the hole. Spread thinset mortar onto the floor around the closet flange, then set the tile into place.

1. MARK THE POSITION OF THE CLOSET FLANGE.

2. MAKE THE CUTS AND SET THE TILE.

Finish tiling

Continue setting tiles across the floor, making sure to follow the 6-in.-offset pattern established earlier. Use the notched trowel to spread only about 4 sq. ft. of mortar at a time. That way, you won't have to rush to set the tiles before the mortar begins to harden.

Marble, like all natural stone, is very porous. To prevent staining and water spotting, use a sponge or white cotton cloth to apply a coat of penetrating sealer to the tiles. And be sure to use a sealer specifically formulated for natural stone, not just a masonry sealer. Allow the sealer to dry overnight before grouting.

TIP Draw cut lines and reference marks onto the marble tiles with a pencil, not a pen or felt-tip marker. Ink will soak into the porous marble, making it virtually impossible to remove.

1 **TILING ALONG A VANITY CABINET. Slip each tile underneath to the recessed toe kick. Be sure the mortar extends all the way to the toe kick so that the entire tile is bonded to the floor.**

TIP Don't open the boxes of tile until you need them. At the end of the job, unopened boxes can be returned to the store for a refund or credit.

2 **TILING AROUND A DOORWAY. Use the wet saw to notch tiles as necessary to fit around doorways. Press the tile down into the mortar, then slide it underneath the door casings. Be sure to install the casing tiles first before setting the adjacent tiles; otherwise, the adjacent tiles will be in the way.**

3 **CUT THE LAST ROW. Tile across the room and toward the open doorway. Cut the last tile to fit, then set it into the mortar. Allow the mortar to dry overnight.**

4 **SEAL THE TILES. Apply a liberal coat of clear penetrating sealer to the marble tiles. Be certain to use a sealer that's specifically formulated for natural stone.**

Grouting

The final tiling step is to fill in the joints between the tiles with grout. In this case, the grout joints were wider than ⅛ in., so we used sanded grout. (For joints ⅛ in. or narrower, use nonsanded grout.) Be sure to use polymer-modified tile grout, which contains acrylic additives that make the grout much more water- and stain-resistant. Mix up a small batch of grout (see p. 33), and then use a rubber float to smear the grout across the tiles.

> **TIP** Cementitious masonry products, such as thinset mortar and tile grout, can irritate the skin of some people. Protect your hands by wearing rubber gloves when mixing, spreading, and cleaning up mortar and grout.

1 **SCRAPE AND FILL.** Tilt the float on edge and scrape the tile to remove excess grout. Then pull the excess grout forward and press it down into the next joint.

> **TIP** Use a high-quality silicone or siliconized caulk, not grout, to fill gaps between the marble tile and the bathtub, cabinets, and moldings. Grout can't expand and contract with changes in humidity. Caulk will remain flexible without losing its grip.

2 **SPREAD THE GROUT.** Smear the grout diagonally across the floor with a rubber grout float. Force the grout deep into each and every joint and surface crevice.

Cleaning the tile

After grouting, wait 15 to 30 minutes before attempting to clean the tiles. You must wait long enough so that you can wipe the tiles clean without disturbing the grout. However, wait too long and the grout will harden on the tiles. Be aware that grout will dry much faster on a hot, dry day than on a cool, humid one. I like to wait 15 minutes and then use a damp sponge to clean one or two tiles. If the sponge wipes the grout from the joints, I stop and wait another 10 to 15 minutes.

For this job, we used a grouting machine to clean the tile, which is simply a large water bucket fitted with squeegee rollers. If you don't own a grouting machine, or can't rent one, simply use a large grout sponge and plastic bucket filled with clean water.

To use the machine, start by soaking the sponge float in the water bucket, then press it across the rollers to squeeze out excess water. The rollers remove most of the water, but the float is usually still a bit too wet. So, hold the sponge over the bucket and press your hand across the sponge to squeeze out the remaining water.

Hold the float or grout sponge flat against the floor, apply moderate downward pressure, and wipe the tiles clean. After each pass, rinse the float or sponge in the water bucket.

Continue to work your way across the floor, one section at a time, until all the tiles are clean. Allow the floor to dry for an hour or two, then buff the tiles with a dry, soft cloth. Work carefully around the tile joints; the grout will be stiff but not yet fully cured. Wait a few days for the grout to harden, then apply a coat of penetrating sealer to all the grout joints.

2 SQUEEZE OUT MORE WATER. Hold the sponge float over the bucket and use your hand to squeeze out any remaining water. The sponge must be damp, not soaking wet.

1 SOAK AND SQUEEZE. If using a grouting machine, dunk the sponge float into the bucket, then roll it across the three squeegee rollers to press out the excess water.

3 WIPE THE TILES CLEAN. Glide the sponge float across the floor to wipe away any remaining grout from the surface of the tiles. Rinse the sponge after each swipe.

Installing the Toilet

1. INSTALL TWO CLOSET BOLTS.

2. CAULK THE CLOSET FLANGE.

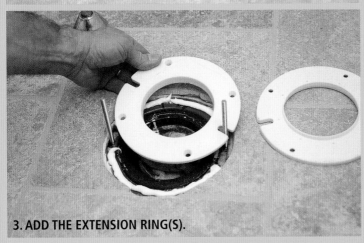

3. ADD THE EXTENSION RING(S).

After tiling a bathroom floor, you'll find that the new floor is higher than the toilet's closet flange. To ensure a watertight seal with the toilet, the flange must be flush with or slightly higher than the tile. To remedy this situation, raise the level of the closet flange with a closet-flange extension kit.

Take the two closet bolts that come with the extension kit and insert them into the slots on either side of the closet flange. Check to be certain the T-shaped head of each bolt is trapped in the slot.

Apply a thick bead of adhesive caulk around the entire top surface of the closet flange. Note that during this phase, the drainpipe is still plugged up with a cloth.

Place one of the extension rings onto the closet flange. Press down on the ring to set it into adhesive caulk. Check to make sure the ring is flush with or slightly above the surface of the marble tile. If it's still too low, install another extension ring, using adhesive caulk to stick it to the first ring.

Once the extension ring is in place, tip the toilet over onto its back and press a wax bowl ring around the discharge opening on the bottom of the toilet. Now you can set the toilet and reconnect the water supply. (Important: Don't forget to remove the rag from the toilet's drainpipe!)

Finishing Up

Once the floor is tiled and grouted, there are a few more steps to put the bathroom back together. You'll need to install baseboard and transition molding, reinstall the toilet, and possibly trim the door(s) to fit.

Before installing baseboard molding, go around the room and locate each wall stud. Once you find a stud, mark its position by putting a small strip of masking tape on the floor right in front of the stud. Cut the baseboard molding to length and nail it to the wall.

> **TIP** If you're working in a bathroom, nail up the baseboard around the toilet alcove prior to installing the toilet. That's a whole lot easier than trying to work around the toilet.

At the threshold to the room, you'll need to install some sort of transition molding to connect the new marble floor to the floor of the adjoining room or hallway. In this case, we made an oak threshold and beveled it to accommodate the thickness of the marble. However, you can buy stock oak, aluminum, and marble thresholds at most home centers and lumberyards. Cut the oak threshold to length, apply some construction adhesive to the floor, and then nail down the threshold. Set a marble threshold with white mortar.

1 ADD TRIM. Nail baseboard molding to the wall around the room perimeter. Mark the location of each wall stud with a strip of tape pressed onto the floor.

2 INSTALL TRANSITION MOLDING ACROSS THE DOORWAY. Here, an oak threshold was beveled to ease the transition from the marble floor to the oak floor in the hallway.

Trimming doors to fit

1 **MEASURE ON THE DOOR JAMB.** Chances are good that you'll need to trim the bottom ends of the doors to clear the new marble floor. Put a piece of ½-in. plywood next to the door jamb (the plywood represents the space beneath the door). Measure up to the bottom of the lowest hinge.

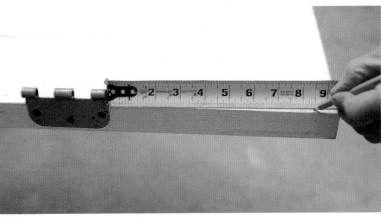

2 **TRANSFER THE MEASUREMENT TO THE DOOR.** Measure down from the lowest hinge and mark the door. Use a T-square or combination square to draw a cut line across the door.

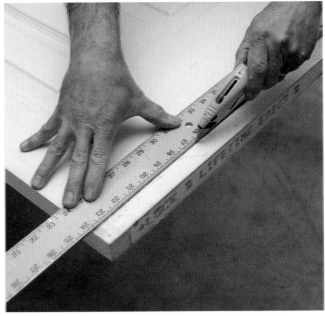

3 **SCORE THE CUT LINE.** Hold a straightedge guide on the cut line, then use a sharp utility knife to cut along the straightedge and through the top door layer.

4 **TRIM THE BOTTOM OF THE DOOR.** If necessary, clamp a straightedge in place to produce a perfectly straight cut.

CHAPTER FIVE

TILING A WOOD-PLANK PORCELAIN FLOOR

THE NATURAL BEAUTY AND APPEARANCE of hardwood flooring is now available in a tile product known as wood-plank porcelain. These 6-in.-wide x 36-in.-long porcelain tiles come in a wide range of colors and feature realistic wood-grain patterns and textures. And unlike traditional wood flooring, porcelain tiles won't ever squeak, scratch, or need refinishing.

Wood-plank porcelain is installed with the same tools and materials used to lay other porcelain floor tiles (see pp. 36–59). In this chapter, I'll show how to set porcelain planks in thinset mortar over a poured-concrete slab. Similar techniques can be used to lay the tile planks over plywood, cement backerboard, and other tile-ready surfaces.

It's worth mentioning that individual porcelain planks do look a lot like real wood—the ones we installed resemble weathered barn boards—but the completed tile floor isn't going to fool anyone into thinking it's a traditional hardwood floor. First, all the planks are identical in width and length. The wood-grain patterns molded into the tiles are repeated, but there are enough different patterns that they're not noticeable in the finished floor. Then there are the grout joints in between, which are a dead giveaway. And porcelain tile is hard and cold, as compared with natural wood. However, porcelain planks are perfect for creating a floor that's reminiscent of hardwood but much more durable and easier to maintain.

Prepping the Surface

A poured-concrete slab provides a near-perfect substrate for setting tile. It's flat, smooth, and, most important, rock-solid and stable. Any flex or instability in the substrate can cause grout to crack and tiles to pop loose, but there are no worries about flex with a concrete-slab floor.

However, it's still important to clean and prep the slab before setting any tiles. Start by sweeping the room with a broom, working from the walls and corners in toward the room center. At this point, don't worry about getting every speck of dust; just sweep up all the loose dirt and debris.

Next, take a stiff-blade putty knife or steel trowel and slowly scrape it across every inch of the floor. When you encounter an obstruction, such as a dried glob of joint compound, construction adhesive, or paint, scrape it loose. If necessary, use a hammer and cold chisel to remove particularly stubborn obstructions. Once the concrete slab is scraped smooth, vacuum the floor to remove all dirt and debris.

> **TIP** When scraping smooth the concrete floor, be sure to wear safety glasses to protect your eyes from flying bits of debris.

Depending on the size of the concrete slab, its surface might be divided into sections by expansion joints or control joints, which help prevent and limit cracking in the slab. These joints, just like joints in cement backerboard (see p. 70), must be treated to prevent them from causing the tiles to crack or pop loose. Here, we covered the joints with liquid waterproofing membrane (see p. 30) and crack-isolation fabric.

The crack-isolation fabric comes in a 36-in.-wide roll. Use scissors to cut enough 6-in.-wide strips to cover all the expansion and control joints in the room. Then, take a paint stick and stir the liquid waterproofing membrane for at least two minutes. Apply the waterproofing membrane and crack-isolation fabric as shown in the photos on the facing page. The treated joints are ready for tiling once they're dry to the touch, which typically takes 30 to 60 minutes.

1 **PREP THE SURFACE. Before setting any tile, use a steel trowel or putty knife to scrape the floor smooth and clean of any joint compound, construction adhesive, or paint.**

2 **VACUUM THE FLOOR. Broom-sweep and then vacuum the floor of all dust, dirt, and debris. Pay particular attention to the room corners and along the base of the walls.**

Covering joints in the slab

1 **APPLY THE MEMBRANE.** Use a 3-in.-wide disposable paintbrush to apply a coat of liquid waterproofing membrane to one of the joints in the slab. Brush it out—centered on the joint—to at least 7 in. wide along about 40 in. or so of the joint.

2 **APPLY THE FABRIC.** Immediately press a 6-in.-wide strip of crack-isolation fabric down into the wet membrane. Smooth out all wrinkles and air bubbles.

3 **BRUSH ON A SECOND COAT.** Apply a second coat of waterproofing membrane over the fabric, spreading it slightly onto the concrete floor. Be sure that 100% of the fabric is sealed with waterproofing membrane.

4 **FINISH THE JOINT.** Treat the remainder of the control joint in the same way, making sure to set the fabric between two wet coats of membrane. Repeat to seal all remaining floor joints.

Setting the First Rows

Measure the length of the room to determine where to start setting the first row of full-width tiles—that is, tiles that don't need to be cut narrower. For this project, we balanced the 6-in.-wide tiles in the room so there would be a 2½-in.-wide strip of tile at the beginning and ending walls. Balancing the tile pattern will typically require cutting tiles in the first and last rows, but it does eliminate any chance that the last row will be a narrow strip of tiles.

Once you've determined your starting point, snap a chalkline onto the floor. Double-check your measurement to make sure the chalkline is perfectly parallel with the starting wall. If the line is askew, you'll end up with tapered pieces of tile along the walls, a telltale sign of a poorly laid-out tile job. In the room shown here, our beginning "wall" was actually a sliding patio door. So, we snapped the chalkline at a position where we could install three full-width rows before we had to trim the tile along the door's threshold.

Also, measure the width of the room to see if you can start the first row with a 36-in.-long full-length plank or if you must cut it shorter. It's important to stagger the end joints between the tiles from one row to the next, but you don't want to end— or start—a row with a piece of tile that's shorter than about 12 in. (according to the tile manufacturer's recommendation). If necessary, cut the first plank in a row to ensure that the last plank won't be too short.

1 **ESTABLISH A STARTING POINT. Snap a chalkline onto the floor to establish a starting point for the first row of tiles. Double-check to make sure the line is parallel with the walls.**

2 **SPREAD THE MORTAR ONTO THE FLOOR. Here, we used a ¾-in. x ¾-in. round-notch trowel, as recommended by the tile maker.**

3 **SET THE FIRST TILE INTO THE MORTAR. Press down and then slide it even with the chalkline. Check the tile for level before setting the next tile.**

WOOD-PLANK TILE FLOOR

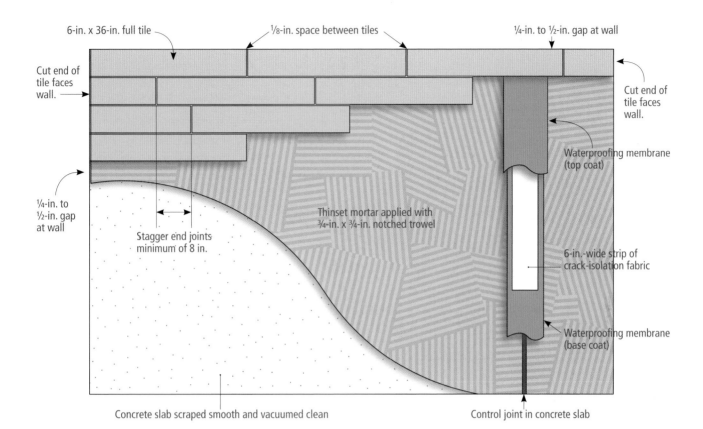

6-in. x 36-in. full tile

⅛-in. space between tiles

¼-in. to ½-in. gap at wall

Cut end of tile faces wall.

Cut end of tile faces wall.

Waterproofing membrane (top coat)

¼-in. to ½-in. gap at wall

Stagger end joints minimum of 8 in.

Thinset mortar applied with ¾-in. x ¾-in. notched trowel

6-in.-wide strip of crack-isolation fabric

Waterproofing membrane (base coat)

Concrete slab scraped smooth and vacuumed clean

Control joint in concrete slab

Spreading the mortar

To adhere wood-plank porcelain tiles to the concrete floor, use fortified thinset mortar, which is mixed with water. For this particular porcelain plank, the tile manufacturer recommended using a ¾-in. x ¾-in. round-notch trowel, which produced a coverage rate of about 40 to 45 sq. ft. of tile for each 50-lb. bag of mortar. Mix the mortar in a 5-gal. bucket, using a ½-in. electric drill and paddle mixer, following the directions on pp. 38–39. Let the mortar rest (or slake) for five minutes so the ingredients can coalesce. Then, mix it again briefly just once more.

Scoop some mortar from the bucket using the trowel and dump it onto the floor. Hold the trowel at approximately 45° and rake the mortar across the floor. Be sure to press down hard so that the teeth of the trowel scratch along the concrete floor. When done properly, the trowel will produce perfectly formed ridges of mortar divided by lines scraped down to the concrete.

Spread the mortar up to within ⅛ in. or so of the chalkline, being careful not to obscure the line. And only mortar an area that you can comfortably tile in 15 to 20 minutes. For most do-it-yourselfers, that's typically about 10 to 12 sq. ft. at a time.

Setting the tiles

Press the first tile down into the mortar with a slightly shifting motion, and then slide it flush with the chalkline. Check the tile for level in two directions: Place a 24-in. level lengthwise on the tile, and then lay a 9-in. torpedo level across the width of the tile. Adjust the tile, if necessary, until it's level.

Use a manual score-and-snap tile cutter to cut the first tile in the next row to length (see the sidebar on p. 88).

Cutting Tiles by Hand

To cut a tile on a manual score-and-snap tile cutter, first draw a pencil line onto the tile indicating where to cut. Set the tile onto the cutter's table and hold it tight against the fence.

Align the cutting wheel with the pencil mark, and then lower the handle to press the cutting wheel down onto the tile. Push the handle forward while pressing down hard. The hardened-steel wheel will score the glazed surface of the tile. Now pull down on the cutter's second handle to snap the tile in two. Note that some manual tile cutters have only one handle, which is used to both score and snap the tile.

1. LOWER THE CUTTING WHEEL TO SCORE THE SURFACE.

2. PULL DOWN ON THE SECOND HANDLE TO SNAP THE TILE IN TWO.

Press the cut tile into the mortar to start the second row, then install another full-length tile. Feel along the joints between the tiles with your fingertips to ensure they're flush and even. Slip ⅛-in.-thick rubber spacers in between the tiles to create consistent grout joints.

4 **SET THE SECOND ROW. After starting a row with a cut tile, install a full-length tile. Press down the 36-in.-long porcelain plank, making sure not to disturb adjacent tiles.**

5 **INSERT TILE SPACERS. To create uniform grout joints, insert ⅛-in.-thick rubber spacers between the tiles. Place two spaces at each end and four or five along each long edge.**

> **TIP** Rather than setting cross-shaped spacers down flat between the tiles, stand them upright. That'll make it much easier to remove them later.

Continue installing full-width tiles to complete each row. When necessary, cut the last tile in each row to fit within about ½ in. of the wall. Baseboard molding will eventually hide the gaps. And remember to always place the cut end of a tile against a wall, never against the end of another tile.

In our installation, we worked back to the starting wall, which, again, was a sliding patio door, and then began laying tiles out toward the room's center. However, rather than pulling out the wet saw to rip the tiles to fit along the threshold, we chose to wait until the end of the project and cut tiles for both ends of the room at the same time. If you have a similar situation, be sure to scrape up the mortar from in front of the starting wall before it hardens.

Use the notched trowel to spread more thinset mortar across the floor. Again, apply only enough mortar that you can tile over in about 20 minutes. As you install each porcelain plank, pay close attention to the end-butt joints from one row of tiles to the next. Stagger the joints by at least 8 in. (though we found 12 in. to 16 in. looks better).

6 **WORK BACK TOWARD THE EDGE. After setting the first two rows, we worked back toward a patio door, which had an alcove that was too shallow to accept two full-width rows of tile.**

7 **CUT TO FIT. If necessary, cut the last tile in the row to fit within ½ in. of the wall. Baseboard molding will sit on top of the tile, effectively hiding the gap.**

8 **STAGGER THE JOINTS. Continue to set full-length porcelain planks across the rows, making sure to stagger the end-butt joints by a minimum of 8 in. from one row to the next.**

TIP When you're not spreading mortar or if you take a rest break, drape a damp towel over the mortar bucket to prevent the thinset from drying out.

Once you've pressed down the tile, slide it up against the adjacent plank to squeeze out any excess mortar from the grout joint. When doing so, be careful not to shove any of the previously installed tiles out of position. Run your fingers across the joint to ensure the tiles are even, then wipe off the excess mortar with a damp sponge. Now slide the tile back a little—without pressing down—and insert ⅛-in. spacers between the tiles. Carefully push the tiles together to maintain consistent grout joints.

Installing tiles in this manner may seem a bit tedious, pressing them down and sliding them back and forth, but here's why it's important: First, pushing the tiles together allows you to detect even the slightest height differences between tiles, which can be challenging when setting 3-ft.-long porcelain planks. And second, this technique provides an easy, effective way to squeeze out excess mortar, which then leaves more space for grout.

9 PRESS AND SLIDE. Press the tile down into the mortar, and then slide it up against the adjacent plank. Feel the joint to confirm that the tiles are flush with one another.

10 WIPE OFF EXCESS MORTAR. Use a damp sponge to wipe off any mortar that squeezes up from between the joints. Don't press down too hard, though, or you'll disturb the tile. Then insert ⅛-in. spacers between the tiles.

What's with All the Ridges?

Spreading thinset mortar with a notched trowel is a widely accepted practice, but did you ever wonder why that's necessary? Well, it turns out that the raised ridges of mortar created by the notched trowel play an important role in adhering the tile to the substrate.

When a tile is pressed down into the mortar, the raised ridges are compressed and the air in between is squeezed out, creating a vacuum that holds the tile firmly in place. That's why it's best to rake the mortar in relatively straight, parallel lines, as shown here. Sweeping the trowel through the mortar in semicircular or wavy swirls will trap air, which can adversely affect the mortar's bond strength.

Tiling across the Room

Once you've laid the first three or four rows, simply repeat the same step-by-step process as you work your way across the room and toward the ending wall.

We discovered the most manageable approach was to spread a swath of thinset mortar wide enough to accommodate two rows of tiles, an area a little over 12 in. wide. And again, to work at a leisurely pace, don't mortar an area much larger than about 12 sq. ft. at any one time.

One of the challenges of setting such long, narrow tiles is getting each one to align perfectly with the adjacent tiles. It's inevitable that sooner or later you'll press a tile down a little too low. When that happens, slip the trowel at least 1 in. under the end—not edge—of the offending tile and lift up. It may take 5 to 10 seconds, but keep applying constant upward pressure and the tile will eventually pull free. Use the trowel to apply a small amount of mortar beneath the tile. Then press the tile back into place, leveling it even with the adjacent tiles.

> **TIP** For tile to bond permanently to mortar, the mortar must be moist. If you notice that a dry shell has formed on the surface of the mortar, scrape it up and spread out some fresh mortar. Never set tile onto mortar that has started to cure. Note that this problem is exacerbated on hot, dry days, or when the heat is on in the room.

1 TILE ROWS IN TWOS. Work your way across the room, tiling two rows at a time. Use the notched trowel to spread mortar out about 12 in. from the previously laid rows.

2 RESET A LOW TILE. If a tile is too low, carefully pry it up using the end of the trowel or a stiff-blade putty knife. Be careful not to chip the end of the tile plank.

3 ADD MORTAR AND RESET. Raise one end of the tile, but don't lift the entire plank out of position. Spread some mortar beneath the raised tile, then press it back down into place.

Installing the Last Row

Chances are good that you'll have to cut the last row of tiles down in width to fit against the ending wall. However, a manual tile cutter doesn't have the capacity to rip 36-in.-long planks. You must use an electric wet saw, which, if you don't own, you can rent by the day.

Wet saws have diamond-impregnated abrasive blades that easily slice through porcelain planks. A small water pump delivers a continuous stream of water over the blade to help cool the blade and eliminate dust.

To rip a tile plank to the proper width, start by marking the cut line along the entire length of the plank. Unlike a tablesaw, a wet saw doesn't have a rip fence that can be locked in place to establish the width of cut. Instead, hold the tile flat against the wet saw's sliding table and advance the tile into the spinning blade. Cut slowly and follow the line as closely as possible. Don't worry if the cut isn't perfectly straight. It'll be hidden by the baseboard molding.

And when you must notch a porcelain plank to fit around a wall corner or doorway, form the notch in two passes on the wet saw. First, make a rip cut along the length of the tile, stopping as you reach the corner of the notch. Slide back the table until the tile is free of the blade. Then, rotate the tile 90° and cut across the tile to complete the notch. Be very careful when installing a notched plank because it's easy to snap off the narrow end of the tile.

Grouting the Joints

Cement-based tile grout is used to fill the gaps between the porcelain planks. It comes in powder form and is mixed with water, similar to thinset mortar. As explained in chapter 2, there are two basic types of grout: sanded and nonsanded (or unsanded). For this porcelain-plank installation, we could have used nonsanded grout (which is made for joints that are ⅛ in. wide or narrower), but instead, we tried a new all-purpose grout made by Laticrete, called PermaColor grout. It's specially engineered to fill joints ranging from 1/16 in. to ½ in. wide.

We mixed the grout by hand in a small bucket using a margin trowel, but you could use a drill with mixing paddle as well. Add only enough water to hydrate the grout, then mix it to the consistency of creamy peanut butter: ultra-smooth and lump-free. After mixing, allow the grout to rest (or slake) undisturbed for five minutes.

Notching the last row

1 RIP THE TILE TO WIDTH. Making long rip cuts on a wet saw is a little tricky, so be sure to hold the tile firmly against the sliding table and push it slowly into the blade.

2 **NOTCH THE TILE, AS NECESSARY.** To cut a notch into a tile, use the wet saw to first make the rip cut. Then rotate the plank 90° and cut across its width to form the L-shaped notch.

3 **SET THE NOTCHED TILE INTO PLACE.** To avoid cracking the tile, support the narrow end and gently press it into the mortar using light pressure.

Scoop a small pile of grout onto the floor and then use a rubber grout float to smear the grout across the tile. Tip the float up on its long edge and wipe across the floor, forcing the grout down into the joints between the tile planks. Don't worry about being too neat at this stage; just concentrate on packing the joints full of grout.

After grouting about 12 to 16 sq. ft. of floor, go back to where you started grouting. Now, put both hands on the grout float, tip it up onto its edge, and with great pressure scrape the tile clean of any excess grout. Be sure to scrape at an angle across the joints to prevent the float from pulling the grout from between the tiles. Continue in this manner until you've grouted the whole floor.

Next, fill a bucket with water and use a grout sponge to wipe clean the surface of the tile. Dunk the sponge into the bucket, and then wring out the excess water. It's important that the sponge is damp, not wet. A wet sponge will dilute and weaken the grout. Wipe the sponge at an angle across the grout joints, using light pressure. If you push down too hard, you'll scrub the grout out of the joints. Wring out the sponge after each and every swipe across the floor. And refill the bucket with clean water every 15 to 20 minutes. Look closely to ensure there's no grout stuck in the wood-grain texture.

After wiping the floor clean, allow the grout to "set up" or harden for an hour or two. If it's a very wet or humid day, you may have to wait an additional hour. Then, use a dry cotton cloth to lightly buff any residual grout haze from the surface of the tiles. Allow the grout to cure overnight, and then install baseboard molding around the perimeter of the room. Finally, to help make the grout more stain resistant, apply a clear silicone-based grout sealer (see p. 35).

1 **MIX AND APPLY.** Mix some tile grout and water in a plastic bucket. Allow the grout to slake for five minutes, then scoop a small pile onto the floor with a margin trowel.

2 **START WITH THE FLOAT FLAT.** Use a flat rubber grout float to forcefully smear the pile of grout perpendicularly across the floor. Spread the grout across four or five rows of tile.

3 **TIP THE FLOAT ON EDGE.** After spreading out the grout, tip the float up onto its edge and swipe it across the floor, forcing grout down into the joints between the tile planks.

4 **USE THE TOE AT THE PERIMETER.** When grouting close to walls, around doorways, and other tight spaces, it's easier to use the end, or toe, of the float to force in the grout.

5 **SCRAPE OFF THE EXCESS.** After packing the tile joints with grout, use the edge of the float to scrape the floor clean of any excess grout. Work at an angle across the joints.

6 **SWITCH TO A SPONGE.** Wipe off the remaining grout with a damp grout sponge. Use light pressure so you don't disturb the grout, and wring out the sponge frequently.

7 **INSTALL MOLDING AS NECESSARY.** Allow the grout to cure overnight, then install baseboard molding and shoe molding, which will cover the space between the tile floor and drywall.

CHAPTER SIX

TILING A SHOWER

INSTALLING NEW TILE around a shower stall is a relatively simple yet effective way to enhance the overall look and functionality of a bathroom. However, in this chapter I'll show a shower upgrade that goes beyond a simple retile job. It's a total shower reconstruction that includes removing an existing cast-iron bathtub, installing new cement backerboard to the walls, building and tiling a new shower pan (floor), and tiling the shower walls and ceiling. The result is a custom-built shower showpiece that measures a spacious 30 in. wide by 60 in. long.

Now, we did have to call in a plumber to reposition the drainpipe, slope the subfloor toward the drain, and install a new shower valve, but the rest of the work is do-it-yourself doable. The updated tile design includes 12-in. x 24-in. tiles on the lower wall sections and 13-in. x 13-in. tiles on the upper wall sections and ceiling. A double row of 2-in. x 2-in. mosaic tiles separates the lower and upper wall sections.

If your bathroom has a functional shower, you can, of course, skip the steps on removing the tub and building the shower pan and start with covering the walls with backerboard. I also include step-by-step instructions for properly waterproofing the walls prior to tiling and tips for cutting around the shower valve and ceiling light fixture.

Demolition

If you're doing a total shower upgrade, there's a fair amount of demolition work to do before you can start tiling, but it goes surprisingly fast. In this standard-size bathroom, we stripped off the old wall tile and drywall, busted out the tub, and cleaned away all the debris in about three hours. However, it's important not to rush or be overly aggressive. The secret to safe demolition is to work carefully and methodically. And protect yourself with eye goggles and a dust mask. Finally, be sure to turn off the water to the bathroom before proceeding.

Removing the old tile

Start by using a hammer and stiff-blade putty knife to remove any existing tile from the shower walls. Set the tip of the putty knife in the grout joint between two tiles. Strike the putty knife with the hammer, then pry back to loosen one tile. Once you've removed the first tile, the rest of the tiles come off pretty easily. Simply slip the putty knife behind the tiles, tap it with the hammer, and pry the tiles off the wall.

> **TIP** Use a framing hammer for demolition work. Its straight claw is better at prying and chopping tasks than the curved claw of a traditional nail hammer.

If there are tiles on the ceiling above the tub, start by using the hammer and putty knife to loosen the first couple of tiles. Then, use the claw of the framing hammer to pry off the tiles, one at a time; use the putty knife to scrape any remaining mortar from the ceiling. If you're planning on retiling the ceiling, apply a skim coat of latex-modified thinset mortar across the ceiling now. This thin layer of mortar will provide a much better tile-mounting surface than the old drywall.

Next, strip off the existing drywall from the walls to expose the studs.

> **TIP** It's better to clear away demolition debris in several smaller buckets, rather than one large trash can. A large can filled with tile and wallboard will be extremely heavy and difficult to carry, especially if you must go down a flight of stairs.

Removing a bathtub

If you're removing a cast-iron tub (as shown in the sidebar on the facing page), use a sledgehammer to bust out the tub. This approach might seem a bit extreme, but it's the only practical way to remove the tub, which would be too difficult and heavy to remove in one piece. (If the tub is made of acrylic, you can cut it out with a reciprocating saw.)

REMOVE THE OLD WALL TILE. Strip the old tiles off the bathroom walls with a hammer and stiff-blade putty knife. Drive the putty knife behind the tiles, and pry outward.

> **TIP** Demolition work is dirty, dusty, and potentially dangerous. Always wear work gloves, eye goggles, hearing protection, and a dust mask. A hardhat can offer added protection when working overhead.

Demolishing a Cast-Iron Bath Tub

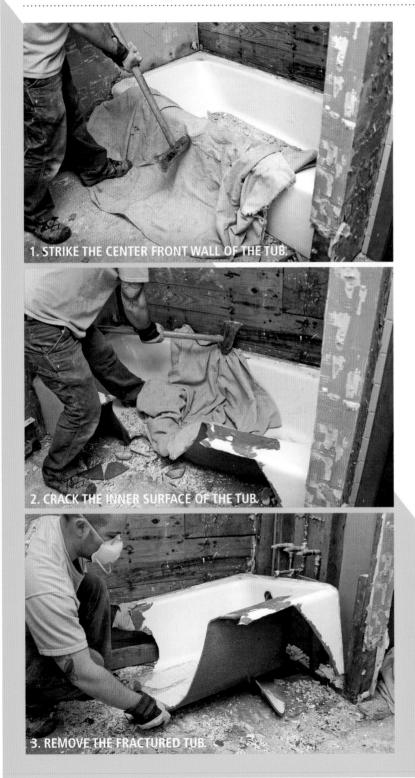

1. STRIKE THE CENTER FRONT WALL OF THE TUB.

2. CRACK THE INNER SURFACE OF THE TUB.

3. REMOVE THE FRACTURED TUB.

Begin by draping a thick canvas drop cloth or quilted moving pad over the front edge of the tub. The thick fabric will prevent the hammer blows from bouncing off the tub, but more important it'll contain flying shards of porcelain and iron.

To demolish the tub, use a 6-lb. to 10-lb. sledgehammer. Stand outside the tub and swing the sledgehammer like a golf club. Strike the outer, center surface of the tub just above the floor, then strike it again about 6 in. higher. Continue hitting the tub, moving up 6 in. with each blow until the tub cracks.

Now step one foot inside the tub and repeat the process to crack the inner surface of the tub. Again, strike the center of the tub wall, starting low and moving up after each impact.

Reposition the drop cloth to cover the back surface on the opposite side of the tub, directly across from the cracked front wall. Strike the inner wall several times, starting low and moving up with each blow until the tub wall cracks vertically. Then, with an overhand swing, bring the sledgehammer down onto the top edge to crack the tub in half.

Carry away the smaller pieces of the fractured tub, then slide out and remove the larger halves. Sweep and vacuum the floor clean of all dust and debris.

Prepping the Shower Subfloor

With the tub out of the way, the next step is to build the new shower pan, starting with the curb—the raised threshold that defines the outer edge of the shower pan. The curb supports the shower enclosure and, more important, creates a dam that keeps the water inside the shower (see the drawing on p. 111).

If necessary, this is also the time to patch the subfloor and call in the plumber to reposition the drainpipe and install a new shower valve.

Building the curb

Cut three pressure-treated 2x4s to span the length of the shower stall. If you removed a standard-size tub, this dimension will be about 60 in. long. Set in place one 2x4, parallel with the back wall, and fasten to the subfloor with 3-in.-long drywall screws.

Use a caulking gun to apply a thick bead of construction adhesive along the length of the 2x4, then set the next 2x4 on top. Fasten the two 2x4s together with 3-in. screws. Also, drive two screws at an angle through each end of the 2x4 and into the wall studs to help stabilize the curb and prevent it from rocking side to side. Repeat the process for the third and final 2x4.

1 **SCREW DOWN THE FIRST 2X4. Create the curb by first fastening a pressure-treated 2x4 to the subfloor in front of the shower alcove. Secure the 2x4 with 3-in.-long screws spaced 10 in. to 12 in. apart.**

TIP Note that we cut the cleats and patch from ½-in.-thick plywood because the existing subfloor was ½ in. thick. If your subfloor is thicker, use the appropriate thickness plywood to make the cleats and patch.

2 **ADD THE SECOND 2X4. Apply a bead of construction adhesive and then set a pressure-treated 2x4 on top of the first 2x4. Hold the edges flush, then fasten the top 2x4 with 3-in. screws.**

3 **FASTEN DOWN THE THIRD 2X4. Apply construction adhesive between the second and third course, and then secure the final 2x4 in the stack.**

Patching the subfloor

After the tub is removed, there will be a large hole in the subfloor where the tub trap was located. You must patch this hole before building the shower pan, but don't install the patch until the new plumbing work has been completed. The plumber will need to access the existing drainpipe through the hole when relocating the shower drain. In this case, the new drain was placed in the center of the shower pan. If you're installing a linear drain, it'll be located along one edge of the pan.

To patch the hole, start by cutting two cleats from ½-in.-thick CDX plywood to support the patch. Make each cleat about 4 in. longer than the width of the hole, and 2 in. narrower than one-half the hole length (see the photo below).

Slip each cleat into the hole and pull it tight against the underside of the subfloor; secure with 1¼-in. drywall screws. Measure the hole in the subfloor and cut a ½-in. CDX plywood patch about ⅛ in. smaller. Run a thick bead of construction adhesive lengthwise down the center of each cleat. Set the plywood patch into place and secure it with 1¼-in. screws. Vacuum the subfloor clean of all dust and debris.

Next, cover the subfloor with 15-lb. felt underlayment (also called builder's paper). The asphalt-saturated felt adds an extra layer of wear protection and prevents chafing between the plywood subfloor and the rubber shower-pan liner, which will be installed next. Don't staple or nail down the felt; just cut it to fit and lay it over the subfloor.

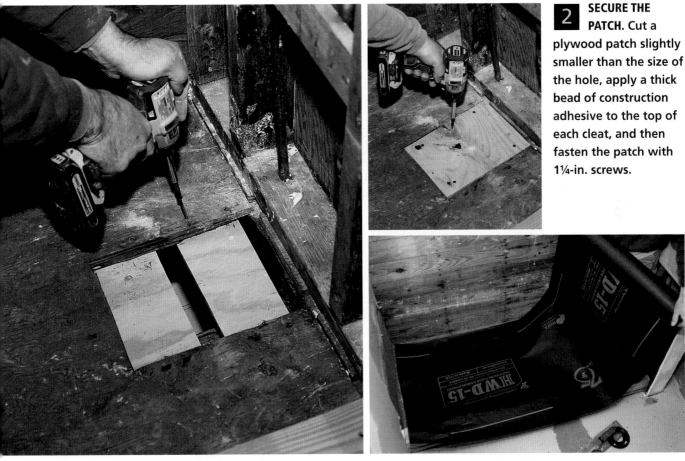

2 **SECURE THE PATCH.** Cut a plywood patch slightly smaller than the size of the hole, apply a thick bead of construction adhesive to the top of each cleat, and then fasten the patch with 1¼-in. screws.

1 **SCREW IN TWO CLEATS.** Cut two plywood cleats to span the hole in the subfloor. Fasten the cleats to the subfloor with 1¼-in. screws.

3 **COVER THE FLOOR WITH FELT UNDERLAYMENT.** Trim the underlayment to fit snugly within the confines of the shower pan.

Lining the Shower Pan

The next step is to install the thick rubber liner that forms a waterproof base for the shower. Shower-pan liners are available at most home centers, tile stores, and plumbing-supply shops. They come on large rolls and are sold by the linear foot. Gently set the rubber liner down into the shower pan, making sure it extends at least 8 in. up the three shower walls and wraps completely up and over the curb.

Neatly fold the corners of the liner so that they lie perfectly flat against the walls. This technique is similar to wrapping a gift box. Fold the liner back against itself, then press it flat to the wall. Do not cut the liner to make it lie flat. The liner must stay intact to form a waterproof barrier.

Secure the rubber liner to the wall with 1-in. galvanized roofing nails. Place the nails about 1 in. down from the top edge of the liner and spaced 12 in. to 16 in. apart (or drive one nail into each stud). Drive the nails perfectly flush with the liner. Wrap the liner up and over the curb, but don't nail it in place just yet.

> **TIP** Before installing the shower-pan liner, inspect it to ensure there are no holes, rips, or gouges. Even the smallest pinhole will render the liner unusable. Hold the liner up to the sun or a bright light for help in finding any flaws.

1 **SET THE LINER INTO THE SHOWER PAN.** Check to be certain that the liner extends at least 8 in. up the walls and wraps over the curb.

Tileable Shower Pans

An alternative to building a mortared pan is to install a prefabricated, ready-to-tile shower pan. Made from resilient plastic, these preformed pans automatically provide the proper drainage slope and waterproofing to ensure a leak-proof installation. Once the pan is connected to the drainpipe, you can immediately begin setting tile; no need to screed mortar or wrestle with a rubber liner.

Tileable shower pans are available in a wide range of stock sizes and shapes, and some manufacturers will even custom-make the pan to fit your space. The only drawback to prefab shower pans is that they typically cost three to four times more than a traditional mud-and-liner pan.

2 **FOLD THE CORNERS.** At each corner of the shower, carefully pinch and fold the liner back against itself. Press the liner flat against the wall and tight to the corner.

3 **SECURE THE LINER WITH SHORT ROOFING NAILS.** Position the nails 1 in. down from the top edge of the liner, which is above the water line.

Sealing the drain

Locate the shower drain by pressing down near the center of the liner. When you feel the four bolt heads protruding from the drain, use a utility knife to cut a very small slit through the liner directly over each bolt head. Press down to force the bolt heads through the liner. Then, use a knife to cut the liner from the circular drain hole. Be sure to cut around the inside diameter of the drain, not the outside.

Now pull back the liner to expose the shower drain and apply a thick bead of silicone sealant around the top surface of the drain flange. Lay the rubber liner back down over the shower drain. Push the bolt heads through the slits cut earlier and press the liner down into the silicone.

Apply shower-pan liner adhesive from the edge of the hole outward, covering an area about 7 in. in diameter. Wait 30 seconds or so for the adhesive to become tacky, then set the drain's metal locking flange over the bolt heads. Rotate the flange counterclockwise to trap the bolts in the four slots. Alternately, tighten each bolt with a wrench to secure the flange to the shower drain.

Sealing the shower drain

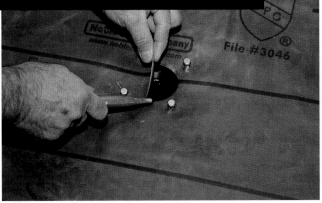

1 **CUT THE DRAIN HOLE IN THE LINER.** Note that you must also cut a small slit for each of the four hex-head machine bolts.

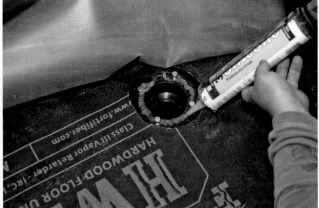

2 **APPLY SEALANT.** Carefully fold back the shower-pan liner and use a caulking gun to apply a thick bead of silicone sealant around the shower drain flange.

3 **SWAB ADHESIVE AROUND THE DRAIN HOLE.** Using the applicator wand, liberally spread the adhesive well beyond the drain hole.

4 **SET THE METAL LOCKING FLANGE OVER THE DRAIN.** Rotate the flange to trap the bolts within the four slots. Tighten the bolts with a wrench.

Now carefully wrap the rubber liner up and over the curb. Press the liner down tightly into the corners along the inside of the shower pan and outside along the bathroom floor. Secure the liner by driving roofing nails through the outer surface of the curb. Do not nail into the top of the curb or through the inner surface on the shower pan side. If the liner extends out onto the bathroom floor, use a utility knife to trim it flush along the outside bottom of the curb.

> **TIP** If you get any silicone sealant on your hands or tools, immediately clean it off with a white cloth dipped in mineral spirits (aka, paint stripper).

Installing Cement Backerboard

Cement backerboard provides a near-perfect surface for mounting tiles, especially in wet areas such as shower stalls. It's flat, hard, stable, and extremely water-resistant. The shower walls are covered with ½-in.-thick cement backerboard, fastened with 1¼-in.-long backerboard screws.

We used a cordless impact driver to install the screws, but a cordless drill/driver could be used as well. And we rented a pair of electric shears to cut the backerboard. There are a few different ways to cut backerboard, including using a circular saw, but shears cut cleanly and quietly with a minimal amount of dust.

TILE SHOWER

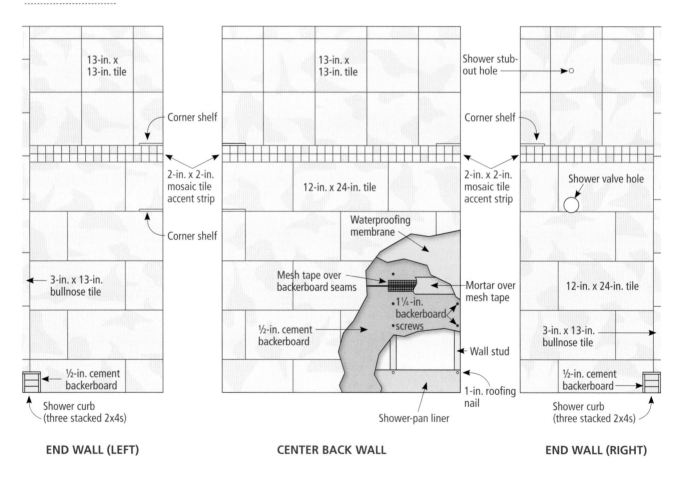

END WALL (LEFT) **CENTER BACK WALL** **END WALL (RIGHT)**

Attach backerboard to the walls

Backerboard comes in 3-ft. x 5-ft. sheets. Measure and cut the sheets to size using the electric shears. Push the first piece of backerboard tight to the ceiling and then screw it to the back wall of the shower. Drive the screws slightly below the surface. If any screw heads protrude, even just a little, they'll interfere with setting the tile.

Set the next backerboard sheet directly below the first sheet. Then, drive two or three screws partway into the wall between the sheets to act as spacers. Screw the backerboard sheet to the lower wall section, then remove the spacer screws. Keep the screws 8 in. up from the shower floor to avoid piercing the rubber liner.

Install backerboard to the end wall opposite the shower valve in the same way.

> **TIP** Wear a dust mask when cutting and scraping backerboard. The silica dust contained in cement backerboard can irritate your lungs.

1 **CUT THE BACKERBOARD SHEETS TO SIZE.** Here, we're using electric shears, which are available from most tool-rental stores.

2 **FASTEN TO THE WALL.** Be sure to drive the heads of the 1¼-in. backerboard screws just below the surface.

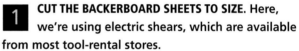

3 **SPACE THE SHEETS.** Drive screws in between the backerboard sheets to create the proper spacing. Fasten the sheet to the wall, then remove the spacer screws.

Working around the shower valve

It takes a bit more time—and patience—to install backerboard to the remaining shower wall. That's because it's necessary to cut holes around the shower valve and the shower stub-out, which is the pipe that supplies water to the showerhead.

Start by cutting the backerboard sheet to size and then cut the valve hole as shown in the photos at right.

Now measure and mark the center point of the shower stub out onto the backerboard sheet and trace the outline onto the sheet. The stub-out hole is usually only about 1 in. or so in diameter, so there's no need for a template—just draw the circle freehand. Score and tap out the stub-out hole just as you did for the shower valve hole.

Carefully set the backerboard sheet against the wall. Feed the shower stub out through the upper hole, and then press the larger hole over the shower valve. If the valve hole fits too tightly, enlarge it with the utility knife. Screw the backerboard to the wall studs, then reattach the mud ring to the shower valve.

2 **TRACE AROUND THE RING. Measure the wall to find the center of the valve, then transfer those dimensions to the backerboard. Hold the mud ring against the backerboard, directly over the center point of the shower valve, and trace the outline.**

3 **USE A SHARP UTILITY KNIFE TO SCORE THE OUTLINE. Make several passes with the knife around the circle until you've cut ⅛ in. deep.**

1 **USE THE RING AS A TEMPLATE. Unscrew the plastic rough-in mud ring from the shower valve. Put the screws back in the valve so you don't lose them.**

4 **TAP AROUND THE SCORED LINE WITH A HAMMER. The backerboard will start to fracture and eventually break free, revealing the hole. Trim the edge of the hole smooth with the utility knife.**

5 **INSTALL THE BACKERBOARD.** Hold the backerboard in place and slip the stub-out through the upper hole. Then press the bottom of the sheet over the shower valve.

6 **SCREW THE MUD RING BACK ONTO THE SHOWER VALVE.** Leave the plastic ring in place until you're ready to tile around the valve.

Tape the joints

To help prevent cracking and water penetration, you must finish the joints between the backerboard sheets with mesh tape and thinset mortar. This crucial step is often skipped because people incorrectly think that the tile-setting mortar will fill and waterproof the joints between the backerboard sheets. It will not. The long-term success of the tile installation is reliant upon finishing the joints with tape and mortar. Do not skip this step.

Start by using a damp sponge to wipe down the joints between the backerboard sheets. Allow the surfaces to dry, then cover the horizontal seams with adhesive-backed, rotproof fiberglass mesh tape. Cut the tape to length with scissors or a utility knife.

1 **TAPE THE JOINTS.** Cover the seams between the backerboard sheets with adhesive-backed fiberglass mesh tape. Center the 2½-in.-wide tape on the seam and firmly press it against the backerboard.

Also apply mesh tape to the seams along the ceiling and in the corners of the shower. Use your fingertips to firmly press the tape into the corners, making sure it overlaps evenly onto each wall.

Now screw 4½-in.-wide strips of backerboard to the inside and outside surfaces of the curb. Cut another 4½-in.-wide strip of backerboard and screw it to the top of the curb. Then apply fiberglass mesh tape to the two corner seams along the top of the curb. Also, tape the joints between the ends of the curb and the shower walls, and the vertical seams where the backerboard sheets meet the existing bathroom walls. As a general rule, tape any joint that has even the slightest possibility of getting wet.

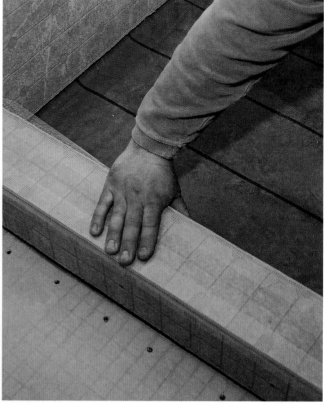

3 **TAPE THE CORNER JOINTS ALONG THE TOP OF THE CURB.** Firmly press the tape to the backerboard, centered over the corner.

2 **SCREW BACKERBOARD TO THE CURB.** On the inside, keep the screws about 1 in. down from the top of the curb so they're well above the water line.

TIP Before covering the screw heads with mortar, use the 5-in. drywall knife to scrape smooth the area around each screw head. This is necessary because backerboard tends to mushroom up around the screw heads, creating raised rings of cement dust.

Mortar the joints

Mix up a batch of latex-modified thinset mortar (see p. 39) and apply the mortar to all the taped joints with a 5-in.-wide drywall knife. Use enough pressure to force the mortar through the tape and into the joint between the backerboard sheets. Now go over the same joint with a 12-in. or 14-in. smooth trowel. Firmly press on the trowel to flatten the joint and remove any excess mortar.

Now use the putty knife to cover each screw head with a thin layer of mortar. Press hard on the putty knife to avoid creating a hump of mortar. Then, apply mortar to the top and both sides of the shower curb. Allow the mortar to cure overnight before proceeding.

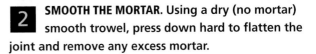

1 **APPLY THE MORTAR. Use a 5-in. drywall knife to apply thinset mortar to the taped joints. Force the mortar deep into the seam between the backerboard sheets.**

2 **SMOOTH THE MORTAR. Using a dry (no mortar) smooth trowel, press down hard to flatten the joint and remove any excess mortar.**

3 **COVER EACH SCREW HEAD. Spread the mortar well beyond the screw, creating a patch that's at least 4 in. in diameter.**

4 **MORTAR THE CURB. Spread mortar onto the top and inside and outside surfaces of the shower curb. Be sure to cover the entire curb in mortar, not just the taped joints.**

Building the Shower Floor

The floor of the shower is made from a mixture of three parts masonry sand and one part Portland cement. (For this shower, we mixed three 5-gal. pails of sand with one 5-gal. pail of Portland cement in a wheelbarrow.) Pour in about 1 pt. of water and mix well with a garden hoe. Add a bit more water and mix again until the cement has the texture of damp sand: It clumps together when squeezed but crumbles easily.

> **TIP** You can save some time—and elbow grease—by renting an electric cement mixer to mix the sand and Portland cement. Set up the mixer outdoors and be sure it's plugged into a GFCI-protected electrical outlet.

Unscrew the shower drain to raise it 1½ in. above the rubber shower liner. Cover the strainer with masking tape to keep out any cement. Spread a little pea gravel around the drain to prevent cement from plugging up the weep holes in the metal locking flange.

Place a 2-ft. level on top of the drain, hold it level, then mark where the bottom edge of the level contacts the shower liner on the back wall of the shower. Measure up ½ in. from the mark and draw a short level line. This reference line represents the height of the cement along the walls of the shower pan.

Next, set a self-leveling laser level on top of the strainer and project a laser line onto the shower liner on the back wall. Adjust the laser until it's perfectly aligned with the reference line. Now dump some cement into the shower pan and pack it down tightly with a 12-in. smooth trowel. Add a little more cement and repeat until it's built up to the laser line. Rotate the level, as necessary, to project a level line onto the end walls and inside surface of the curb. Then, use the trowel to smooth the cement flush with the laser line. The cement around the drain will be too high, but don't worry about that for now. Concentrate on creating a level line around the perimeter of the shower pan.

Next, use a 2-ft. level as a screed to create the proper slope. Set one end of the screed on top of the strainer and hold the other end even with the line of cement along the walls. Swing the screed in an arc to scrape away cement from the high spots around the strainer.

Once you've established the proper slope, use a wet sponge to drip water over the entire shower pan. The surface should be wet but not overly saturated. Lightly glide the smooth trowel over the shower pan to create a glass-smooth surface . Now unscrew the strainer, raising it an amount equal to the thickness of the tile. Allow the cement in the shower pan to cure overnight.

How Much Should the Shower Pan Slope?

Shower floors typically slope toward the drain ½ in. per ft., though a slope of ¼ in. per ft. is also acceptable. In fact, a ¼-in. slope is recommended for people with limited mobility because it's slightly less steep. Here, we formed the shower pan with 1½ in. of cement at the drain and 2 in. along the walls (see the drawing on the facing page).

To ensure that the shower floor slopes toward the drain, we used a laser level to establish a level line around the shower pan, and then used a 2-ft. level as a screed to scrape the mortar to the proper slope. If you don't own a laser level, use a 4-ft. level to establish the high point of the slope.

1 **SPREAD THE CEMENT.** Set a self-leveling laser on the shower drain, then use a smooth trowel to spread cement even with the level line projected on the walls.

SHOWER FLOOR DETAIL

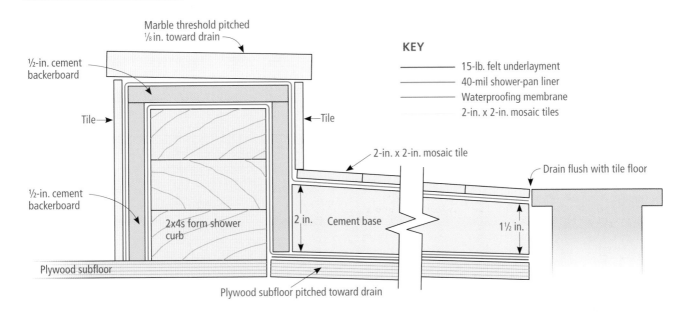

Marble threshold pitched ⅛ in. toward drain

½-in. cement backerboard

Tile

½-in. cement backerboard

Plywood subfloor

2x4s form shower curb

2 in.

Cement base

Plywood subfloor pitched toward drain

Tile

2-in. x 2-in. mosaic tile

Drain flush with tile floor

1½ in.

KEY

15-lb. felt underlayment
40-mil shower-pan liner
Waterproofing membrane
2-in. x 2-in. mosaic tiles

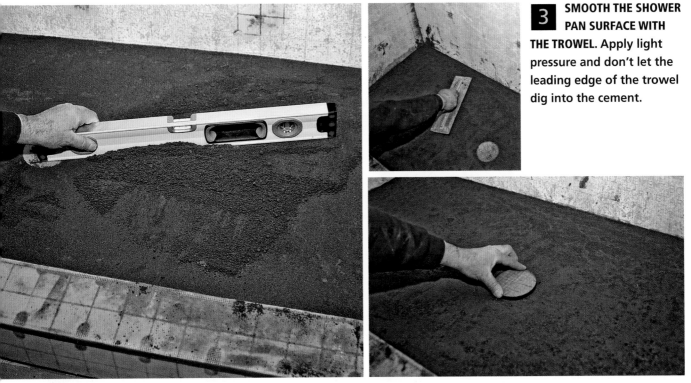

3 **SMOOTH THE SHOWER PAN SURFACE WITH THE TROWEL.** Apply light pressure and don't let the leading edge of the trowel dig into the cement.

2 **SCREED THE CEMENT TO THE CORRECT SLOPE.** Set the level on the strainer and raise the other end even with the level line at the walls.

4 **UNSCREW THE STRAINER.** Turn the strainer counterclockwise to raise it above the shower floor the thickness of the tile, which is typically between ¼ in. and ⅜ in.

Waterproofing

There's one more important step to complete before you begin tiling: waterproofing the walls and shower pan as an extra level of protection against water damage (you don't need to waterproof the ceiling). We used a liquid waterproofing membrane that rolls on as easily as paint. And as a bonus, the rubbery liquid also serves as a crack-isolation membrane. If any cracks develop in the backerboard or shower pan, they won't telegraph through to the tile.

Prepping the surface

Start by using a masonry rubbing stone to smooth the taped joints between the backerboard sheets. This tool is nothing more than a coarse stone fitted with a handle. Scrub the mortared joints with the rubbing stone to grind off hardened mortar ridges and to smooth any rough spots. Remove dust by wiping down the entire shower with a damp sponge.

Applying the waterproofing

Apply the waterproofing membrane to the wall with a short-nap paint roller. Start near the top of the wall and work your way down. Roll the membrane onto each of the three shower walls, then coat the top and sides of the shower curb. Use a paintbrush to apply waterproofing membrane to the wall corners and other areas you can't reach with the roller. Next, roll the liquid membrane onto the floor of the shower.

Wait for the waterproofing membrane to dry and then roll on a second coat. It usually takes 10 to 15 minutes for the surface to dry, depending on the air temperature and relative humidity. However, you'll know it's time to roll on the second coat: The first coat changes from bright blue to dark green. Allow the second coat to dry thoroughly before proceeding.

1 **PREP THE SURFACE. Smooth the mortared joints between the backerboard sheets with a masonry rubbing stone. Don't own a rubbing stone? Use a brick.**

Shower Pan Simplified

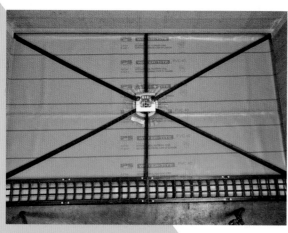

Courtesy Mark E. Kirby, Mark E Industries, Inc.

The most challenging part of building any shower floor is creating the proper pitch, or slope, toward the drain. If the pitch is too shallow, water won't drain properly. If it's too steep the floor will be uncomfortable, and even dangerous, to stand on. Fortunately, there's an easy way to create the appropriate slope, even if you've never built a shower floor.

The easy-to-install Quick-Pitch® System consists of a plastic center ring that snaps onto the drain, and several float sticks that radiate out from the ring. The plastic float sticks are tapered—taller along the walls, shorter at the drain—so they automatically provide the proper pitch. Simply spread cement even with the tops of the float sticks and you're done. The center ring and float sticks remain cast in the cement floor.

2 **WATERPROOF THE WALLS.** Spread the liquid waterproofing membrane onto the walls with a paint roller. Be sure to coat the entire surface.

3 **WATERPROOF THE SHOWER FLOOR LAST.** Roll the liquid membrane across the entire surface. Be careful not to leave behind any drips or puddles.

Tiling the Back Wall

Before setting any tile, establish the tiling pattern by measuring and marking the walls for each tile course. Here, we installed 12-in. x 24-in. tiles to the lower wall sections, a double row of 2-in. x 2-in. tiles, and then 13-in. x 13-in. tiles up to and across the ceiling (see the drawing on p. 104).

Ordinarily, it's best to balance the pattern so that the tiles around the perimeter of the wall are approximately the same size. However, in a shower it's more important that the tiles in the lowest course—the ones closest to the water—are at least half the width of a full-size tile. That's because a narrow strip of tiles along the water line is much more likely to leak. In this shower we adjusted the pattern so that the tiles in the lowest course were 6 in. high.

Tile the back wall of the shower, first, followed by the two narrower end walls. Next, tile the ceiling and shower floor; save the curb for last.

Setting the first full course

Begin by attaching 1x4 ledger boards to the shower walls to support the first full-size course of tiles. Measure the width of the back wall and mark its center point on the wall directly above the ledger board. Then use a 4-ft. level to draw a perfectly plumb line at the center mark. This vertical line represents the center of the tile pattern.

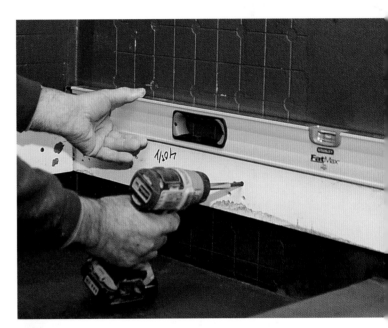

1 **FASTEN 1X4 LEDGER BOARDS TO THE THREE SHOWER WALLS.** Be certain each ledger is perfectly level.

TIP It's important that all three ledgers are level but equally important that they're level with each other. Level across from the end-wall ledgers to the middle of the ledger on the back wall. If necessary, adjust the ledgers to ensure perfect alignment.

Mix up a fresh batch of latex-modified large-format tile mortar and set the first full course of tile as shown in the photos below. After completing the first course, hold a 4-ft. level across the face of the tiles to ensure they're all on the same plane. If any tiles are protruding, tap them into alignment. If a tile is sunken in too far, pry it from the wall, add more mortar, and reinstall it. It's important to get the first course perfect because any irregularities will affect all subsequent tile courses.

> **TIP** If you're installing glazed ceramic or porcelain tiles, cut them with a manual score-and-snap tile cutter. If you're working with stone tile, use a wet saw.

Setting the next two courses

The second tile course is installed the same as the first, with one main difference: The first tile is centered over the vertical centerline; it doesn't butt up to the line as the first-course tiles did. Set the first tile in place, and then install tiles to the left and right of this center tile as before. Remember to slip ⅛-in.-thick spacers beneath the tiles to separate them from the tiles in the first course.

Cut tiles to fit as necessary at each end of the row. After completing the second course, hold a 4-ft. level against the face of the tiles to ensure they're all on the same plane. Repeat to install one more course of 12-in. x 24-in. tiles.

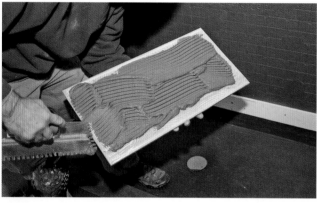

2 **BACK-BUTTER THE FIRST TILE.** Use a ¼-in.-wide x ⅜-in.-deep square-notch trowel to apply mortar to the back of the tile.

3 **SPREAD MORTAR ONTO THE WALL.** Use the smooth, unnotched edge of the trowel to skim-coat the wall. This skim coat creates a second bonding surface for the tile and enhances its adhesion to the waterproofing membrane.

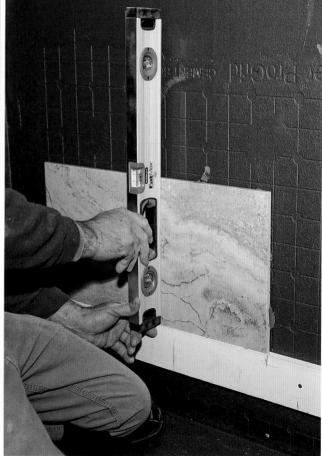

4 **SET THE FIRST TILE.** Set the tile on the ledger, then press it to the wall. Align the end of the tile with the vertical centerline on the wall. Check the tile for plumb with a level.

 TIP Skim-coating the wall with mortar creates a second bonding surface for the back-buttered tiles but only if you press the tile into place immediately after applying the skim coat. If the skim coat dries before the tile is installed, it serves little benefit.

5 **CONTINUE THE FIRST COURSE.** Install tiles to the left and right of the center tile. Insert ⅛-in. rubber spacers in between the tiles to create the proper-width grout joint.

6 **CUT TILES TO FIT.** Use a manual cutter to trim tiles to fit as necessary at each end of the first course. Draw the cutting wheel across the tile, then push down to snap the tile.

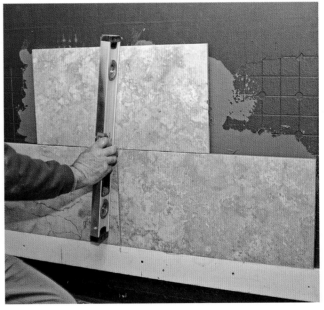

7 **SET THE END TILE.** Back-butter the cut tile, set it on the ledger at the end of the row, then press it into place. Be sure to leave a ⅛-in. space between the tiles.

8 **STAGGER THE SECOND COURSE.** Center the 24-in.-wide tile directly over the joint between the two tiles below, which positions the tile at the precise center of the shower wall. Check for plumb with a 2-ft. level.

Tiling the End Walls

If you're following our design, tile the narrow walls at each end of the shower with the same 12-in. x 24-in. tiles used on the back wall. And trim the outer edges of each end wall with 3-in.-wide x 13-in.-long bull-nose tiles. Bull-nose tiles have one rounded edge that lends a clean, finished look to the tiled walls.

Installing the first course

Measure the width of the end wall and mark its center point on the wall. Use a level to draw a perfectly plumb centerline onto the wall. Repeat for the opposite end wall.

Trowel a mortar skim coat for the first course onto the end wall. Set the tiles, starting with the bull-nose tile and working toward the inside corner, as shown in the photos below.

Tiling the end walls

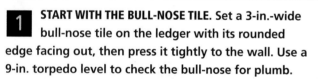

2 **SET THE NEXT TILE.** Cut a tile to fit between the bull-nose and the wall centerline, minus ⅛ in. for the grout joint. After pressing the tile to the wall, check it for plumb.

1 **START WITH THE BULL-NOSE TILE.** Set a 3-in.-wide bull-nose tile on the ledger with its rounded edge facing out, then press it tightly to the wall. Use a 9-in. torpedo level to check the bull-nose for plumb.

3 **TILE TO THE CORNER.** Cut a tile to fit between the shower corner and wall centerline, minus ⅛ in. for the grout joint. Set the tile on the ledger and press it to the wall. Slip ⅛-in. spacers between the tiles, including the bull-nose piece.

4 **CHECK FOR ALIGNMENT.** To see if the tiles are straight and properly aligned, hold a 4-ft. level across the face of the tiles. Adjust any tiles that are out of alignment.

Installing the next two courses

Start the second course by installing a full-size tile. Set the tile ⅛ in. away from the bull-nose tile, and press it to the wall. Slip a ⅛-in. rubber spacer under each end of the tile. Next, cut a tile to fit into the shower corner. Again, remember to subtract ⅛ in. for the grout joint.

Install the next course in the same manner, and then move to the other side of the shower and install three tile courses—with bull-nose trim—to the opposite end wall.

Tiling around the Shower Valve

The next step is to cut a circular hole in the tile to fit around the shower valve. Depending on where the valve falls within the tile pattern, you may need to cut the hole in more than one tile. In our installation, the valve fell almost entirely within one tile in the fourth course.

Cutting the hole

Measure and mark the center point of the shower valve on the tile. Then use the plastic mud ring from the valve to trace the outline of the mud ring onto the tile.

Use a wet saw to make a deep V-shaped cut into the tile (you could also make the cut with a right-angle grinder). The V-cut removes most of the waste and provides space for maneuvering the blade. Next, make a series of closely spaced cuts across the hole. Space the cuts about ½ in. apart and be careful not to saw beyond the pencil outline. Then saw across the previous cuts to trim away most of the waste. Finish by using a pair of tile nippers to trim off the jagged points from around the inside of the hole.

> **TIP** Be sure to wear eye goggles when using tile nippers as protection from flying bits of tile.

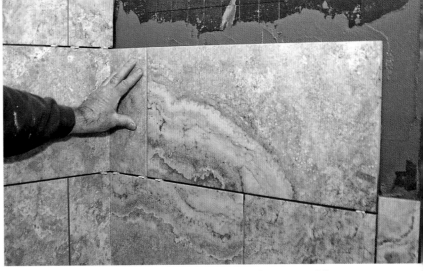

WORK YOUR WAY UP THE WALL. Start the second course with a full-size tile and then cut a piece of tile to fit into the shower corner. Be sure to allow for the ⅛-in. grout joint.

1 **ROUGH OUT THE SHOWER-VALVE HOLE.** First, make a V-cut within the circular outline and then, as shown here, make a series of closely spaced kerf cuts across the hole. Cut across the kerfs to trim away most of the waste material.

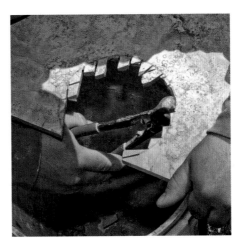

2 **CLEAN UP THE HOLE.** Use tile nippers to carefully snip off all the jagged points from the inside of the hole. Don't worry if the hole is a little rough around the edge; it'll be concealed by the valve's escutcheon plate.

Back-butter the tile, skim-coat the wall, and then press the tile into place. Check to be sure the hole fits comfortably around the valve and that the tile is ⅛ in. from the bull-nose tile.

3 **INSTALL THE TILE.** Gently press the tile to the wall, checking to make sure the hole fits around the shower valve and doesn't overlap it.

In-Shower Shelving

1. MORTAR THE BACK EDGES.

2. SET THE SHELF.

Adding storage shelves to a shower provides a convenient place to store shampoo bottles, bars of soap, and razors. But hanging a ready-made shelf or storage rack on the wall always looks like an afterthought, instead of a thoughtful design detail.

The solution is to integrate the storage into the tile job by installing corner shelves. The semicircular shelves come in a range of colors and are typically made of natural stone or a resilient resin that resembles stone. Choose a shelf that closely matches the color of the shower tile and install it during the tiling sequence.

In an average-size shower, consider installing at least three shelves: two in the back corner of the shower, spaced about 16 in. apart, and one in the front corner near the showerhead.

To install a corner shelf, use the trowel to apply a thick bed of thinset mortar along each back edge of the shelf. Then press the shelf into the corner and let it rest on the tile course below. Wipe away the excess mortar with a damp sponge. Notch the tiles in the next course to fit up and over the corner shelf.

Mosaic Accent Strip

This shower has a decorative accent strip around all three walls, which serves to visually separate the lower four courses of 12-in. x 24-in. tiles from the 13-in. x 13-in. tiles that will be installed later. The 4-in.-tall strip is composed of two rows of 2-in. x 2-in. tiles. The mosaic tiles shown here complement the shower-wall tiles; they're of similar color and pattern. However, you could create a much bolder design by choosing mosaic tiles that contrast the color of the wall tiles.

Installing the mosaic tiles

To create the 4-in.-tall accent strip, cut two rows of tiles from a sheet of 2-in. x 2-in. mosaic tiles. Place the mosaic sheet face down and slice through the mesh backing with a utility knife to produce a strip that's two tiles wide and six tiles long. Each 12-in. x 12-in. mosaic sheet yields three such strips.

Mix up a fresh batch of latex-modified thinset mortar. Apply the mortar to the wall with the notched trowel, then use a putty knife to flatten the ridges. Set the first accent tile strip into place, then press it to the wall using a rubber float. Be aware that the 2-in. x 2-in. mosaic tiles are thinner than the wall tiles, so only press them in until

the two surfaces are flush. And allow the mosaic tiles to rest right on top of the tile course below; don't install rubber spacers beneath the accent strip.

Continue installing mosaic-tile strips across the back wall of the shower. Leave a space between each strip that's equal to the grout joints between the mosaic tiles. When the accent strips are properly spaced, they'll appear to be one long continuous strip, not several shorter ones butted end to end.

Repeat to install mosaic accent strips to each end of the shower. Then install two more corner shelves, one in the back corner of the shower and one in the front, near the showerhead.

> **TIP** If you decide to use glass tiles for the mosaic accent strip, be sure to set the tiles in white thinset. Standard gray thinset will show through and change the color of the glass tiles.

2 **SET THE STRIPS.** Set the first mosaic-tile strip into place, then press it to the wall with a rubber float. Allow the strip to rest directly on the tile course below (no spacers).

1 **CUT THE ACCENT STRIP.** Use a sharp utility knife to slice a double row of accent tiles from a sheet of 2-in. x 2-in. mosaic tiles. Each 4-in.-wide strip contains 12 tiles.

3 **FINISH THE BACK WALL.** Continue installing mosaic strips across the back wall of the shower. Use a damp sponge to clean mortar from the surface of the strips, pressing lightly to avoid disturbing the double row of tiles.

Tiling the Upper Walls

The upper wall sections are covered with 13-in. x 13-in. tiles, which are installed in the same manner as the 12-in. x 24-in. tiles on the lower wall: Each tile is back-buttered and the walls are skim-coated with mortar.

However, there is one key difference: The 13-in. x 13-in. tiles are aligned in straight rows, not staggered as they were with the 12-in. x 24-in. tiles. This straight-line pattern mirrors the alignment of the 2-in. x 2-in. tiles in the mosaic accent strip.

Installing 13-in. x 13-in. tiles

Measure the width of the back wall and draw a vertical line down the center of the wall. Use the notched trowel to apply mortar to the back of a 13-in. x 13-in. tile and set the tile in the middle of the wall, making sure it's centered precisely over the centerline. Set the tile on top of the mosaic accent strip—no spacers needed—and press it to the wall. Check the tile for plumb.

Continue to install tiles out in both directions from the center tile. After setting four tiles, lay a 4-ft. level across the top of the tiles to ensure the course is level.

TILE THE UPPER WALL. Set the first tile in the middle of the back wall and then install tiles out in both directions. Check for level, and, if necessary, slip small plastic wedges beneath the tiles to level up the course.

Notching Tiles around Shelves

NOTCH THE TILE, THEN CHECK ITS FIT.

If you're installing corner shelves in your shower (see p. 118), you'll need to notch each end tile to fit over the shelf. Hold the end tile in place and mark where the top of the shelf meets the edge of the tile. Extend the mark across the face of the tile, stopping 1 in. from the opposite edge.

Now use the wet saw to cut along the line, stopping 1 in. from the edge. Rotate the tile 90° and make the short perpendicular cut at the 1 in. mark to form the notch. Dry-fit the tile into the corner, making sure the notch fits around the shelf. Once satisfied with the fit, back-butter the tile, skim-coat the wall with mortar, and set the tile into place. Repeat to notch the end-wall tile to fit around the corner shelf.

Cutting the hole for the shower stub-out

Now you can install the last course of full-size 13-in. x 13-in. tiles to the three shower walls (including the bull-nose tiles along the vertical edges of the two end walls). This course goes up quickly because there's only one obstruction: the shower stub-out. Cut the hole for the stub-out as shown below.

1 **MARK FOR THE STUB-OUT.** Hold a tile on top of the stub-out and ⅛ in. away from the adjacent tile. Mark where the left and right sides of the pipe meet the tile edge (left). Then hold the tile to the left of the stub-out, ⅛ in. above the tile below, and mark where the top and bottom of the pipe intersect the tile (right). Use a square to extend the lines across the tile, outlining the location of the stub-out.

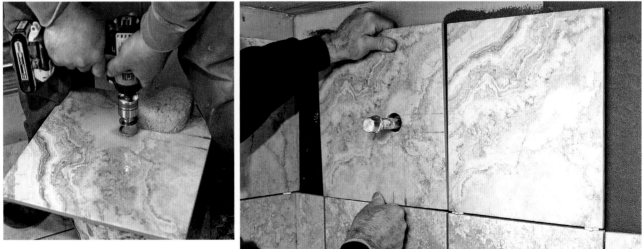

2 **BORE THE STUB-OUT HOLE.** Use a 1⅛-in.-dia diamond-grit hole saw to bore a hole through the saw. Flood the surface with water from a sponge to keep the saw from overheating.

3 **DRY-FIT THE TILE.** Set the tile over the stub-out to ensure it fits properly; the slightly oversized hole allows for a little adjustment. Then back-butter the tile, skim-coat the wall, and press the tile into place.

Tiling the Ceiling

If you're planning to tile the ceiling, measure the ceiling depth from the back wall out to the edge of the shower area. Then establish a pattern that accepts 13-in. x 13-in. tiles and a row of bull-nose tiles along the outer edge. In this case, we cut 3-in.-wide tile pieces to fit along the back edge of the ceiling, tiled across the ceiling with two courses of 13-in. x 13-in. tiles, and then set 3-in.-wide bull-nose tiles at the outer edge of the shower ceiling.

Also, it's important to set the ceiling tiles in high-strength thinset that's formulated for overhead application. Here, we used Laticrete 255 MultiMax™ mortar, which costs a bit more than standard thinset mortar but is tenaciously strong. The mortar contains Kevlar fibers that dramatically increase its bond strength, while reducing weight.

And since the ceiling was skim-coated earlier (see p. 98), there's no need to trowel on any more mortar. Simply back-butter the tiles and press them into place.

1 **TILE THE CEILING.** Press the 13-in. x 13-in. tiles to the shower ceiling, keeping them perfectly aligned with the grout joints between the tiles mounted on the back wall.

2 **FILL IN WITH 3-IN.-WIDE TILE.** Cut narrow pieces of tile to fit at the top of the back wall and along the back edge of the shower ceiling. Space the tiles ⅛ in. apart.

TIP When laying out the ceiling pattern, remember that the bull-nose tiles along the ceiling must align perfectly with the vertical rows of bull-nose tiles on the end walls.

3 **SET BULL-NOSE TILE ALONG THE OUTER EDGE.** Maintain ⅛-in. grout joints between the bull-nose tiles and the neighboring ceiling tiles.

Tiling around a light fixture

If your shower has a recessed light in the ceiling, as ours did, you'll have to cut a large hole in the tile to accommodate the fixture. In our shower, the light fixture spanned a grout joint, so we had to cut two tiles. Measure and mark for the fixture and cut the hole with the wet saw, just as you did earlier for the shower valve (see p. 117).

Note that it's important to cut the hole slightly larger than the outside diameter of the fixture but smaller than the flange on the trim kit. That allows you to remove the fixture should it ever need replacing, and yet the trim kit will conceal the edge of the hole.

> **TIP** If you're planning to install a recessed light in the shower, it's important to buy one that's designated as a "wet" or "shower-rated" fixture. These fixtures are specially designed for use in wet areas and include shower trim kits that block out moisture. Light fixtures rated for "damp locations" aren't suitable for use above a shower or tub.

TILE AROUND A CEILING LIGHT FIXTURE. Cut one or two tiles as necessary and then back-butter and set. Be sure the tile doesn't cover any part of the light fixture.

Tiling the Shower Floor

The floor of this shower is tiled with the same 2-in. x 2-in. mosaic tiles used earlier to create the 4-in.-wide accent strip. Here, however, the tiles are installed in full 12-in. x 12-in. sheets.

1 **SPREAD THE MORTAR.** Apply latex-modified thinset mortar to the shower floor using a 3/16-in. V-notch trowel. Spread only enough mortar to cover 2 to 3 sq. ft. of floor. (Note that you don't need to back-butter the shower-floor tiles.)

2 **INSTALL THE FIRST SHEET IN THE CORNER.** Use a rubber float to gently press the 12-in. x 12-in. mosaic-tile sheet down into the mortar.

3 **SET THE SECOND SHEET NEXT TO THE FIRST.** Be sure the grout joints between the sheets are exactly the same width as the space between the individual 2-in. x 2-in. tiles.

Tiling around the drain

When you reach the shower drain, hold the sheet in place over the drain and identify the three or four 2-in. x 2-in. tiles that overlap the drain. Cut those tiles from the sheet with a utility knife. Now press the sheet into the mortar with the cutout space wrapping around the drain.

Take one of the tiles cut from the sheet and hold it in place over the drain. Mark the tile where it overlaps the drain. Use a spare shower-drain strainer as a template to trace the semicircular cut line onto the tile. Don't have a spare strainer? Use a pencil compass adjusted to the exact radius of the shower drain.

Take the tile over to the wet saw and remove most of the waste with a single straight cut across the tile. Then grip the tile with both hands and hold it against the spinning blade. Carefully move the tile back and forth to slowly grind away the tile and smooth the edge of the curved cut.

Wipe the tile dry with a towel, then set it into place beside the shower drain. Use the same marking and cutting method to fit the remaining 2-in. x 2-in. tiles around the drain. Continue to install full 12-in. x 12-in. sheets to the rest of the floor.

Tiling around a shower drain

1 **REMOVE TILES TO FIT.** Cut a few 2-in. x 2-in. tiles from a mosaic-tile sheet so that the sheet fits comfortably around the shower drain.

2 **MARK TILES FOR CUTTING.** Hold a tile over the shower drain and mark where the tile overlaps the drain: at the top, right corner and along the bottom edge.

3 **DRAW THE CURVE.** Use a shower-drain strainer as a template to connect the two marks on the tile. Or, use a pencil compass to draw the curved cut line.

4 **SET THE CUT TILE INTO PLACE.** Adjust its position to maintain the proper-width grout joint between it and the adjacent tiles.

After installing the final mosaic-tile sheet, use the rubber float to gently press down the entire floor. This final step flattens high spots and ensures that all the tiles are flush and even. That's important because even tiny surface irregularities will feel uncomfortable with bare feet. Allow the shower floor to harden overnight before proceeding.

Finish tiling the walls

Unscrew and remove the 1x4 ledger boards and prepare to install the lowest course of wall tiles. Measure the space between the shower floor and the bottom edge of the first course of wall tile. Subtract ⅛ in. for the grout joint. Use the wet saw to cut 12-in. x 24-in. tiles to the proper width.

Next, skim-coat the wall with mortar, then back-butter the tile. Press the tile to the center of the wall. Let the tile rest directly on the shower floor, which will create the proper ⅛ in. grout joint at the upper edge. Install the remaining tiles to the back wall of the shower. At each end wall, you'll need to notch tiles to fit over the shower curb, as shown in the photos on the facing page.

Tiling the Curb

The final tiling step is to cover the inner and outer surfaces of the shower curb with tile. You can tile the top of the curb as well, but here's a better option: Cover the top of the curb with a ¾-in.-thick marble threshold. The marble slab creates a seamless surface that's impervious to water penetration.

We topped the curb with a standard 6-in.-wide marble threshold, which is available at most lumberyards and home centers. Just be aware that because the threshold is made of light-colored stone, it must be adhered to the curb with white thinset mortar.

FINISH TILING THE FLOOR. Continue to install full mosaic-tile sheets to the shower floor. Use a rubber float to lightly press each sheet into the mortar bed.

1 TILE THE BOTTOM COURSE. Set the first tile in the middle of the back wall, straddling the joint in the course above. Rest the tile on the shower floor, then press it to the wall.

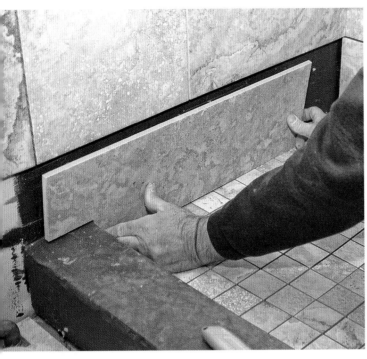

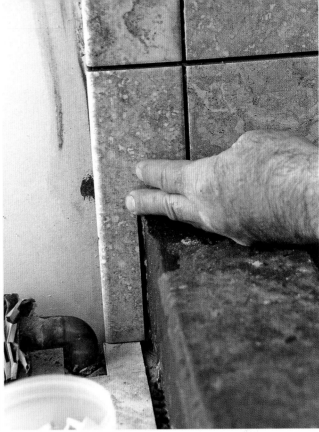

2 **NOTCH AROUND THE CURB.** Before spreading any mortar, dry-fit the notched tile to make sure it fits properly.

3 **NOTCH THE BULL-NOSE TILE** to fit around the outer corner of the curb. Check to be sure that all the grout joints align.

Tiling the inner surface

Place a self-leveling laser level inside the shower and project a level line across the top of the curb. If the curb is out of level, which is common, adjust the laser line until it's flush with the high end of the curb.

Hold a 13-in. x 13-in. tile in place against the inner surface of the curb and mark where the laser line crosses the tile. Repeat to mark the remaining tiles in the course. Cut the tiles to size, back-butter them with mortar, and press each one against the inner surface of the curb.

If the curb isn't level, the tiles at the low end will protrude above the curb, but that's okay. It's more important that the top edge of the tile course is level, not the curb itself. Space the tiles ⅛ in. apart, then hold a 4-ft. level across the face of the tiles to make sure they're flush and perfectly aligned.

1 **TILE THE INNER CURB.** Cut strips of tile to fit along the inner surface of the shower curb. Adhere with thinset mortar.

Tiling the outer surface

Move the laser level outside the shower stall and project a level line across the top of the curb. Adjust the laser until the line is perfectly flush with the tops of the tiles adhered to the inner surface of the curb. Now raise the laser line 1/8 in.

Hold a tile in place against the curb and mark where the laser line intersects the tile. Cut the tile on the mark. Apply mortar to the back of the tile, then press it to the curb. This tile is now 1/8 in. higher than the tiles on the inner surface of the curb, providing just the right amount of pitch to ensure that water runs off the marble threshold and back into the shower.

Install the remaining tiles in a similar manner, making sure to mark the cut line according to the laser projection. Use a 4-ft. level to confirm that all the tiles are properly aligned and flush with one another. Allow the mortar to cure overnight before setting the marble threshold.

Setting the curb threshold

Measure the length of the curb, then subtract 1/8 in., which allows the threshold to fit without binding. Cut it to length with the wet saw.

Mix a batch of white thinset mortar and spread it across the top of the curb. Add more mortar, as necessary, to build it up 1/4 in. or so above the top edge of the tiles. Set the threshold down on top of the curb.

Now lay a 4-ft. level on the threshold to confirm that it's level. If it isn't, insert small plastic wedges underneath it. Then, set a 2-ft. level or 9-in. torpedo level across the threshold to make sure it's out of level by 1/8 in. and pitching down toward the shower. Allow the mortar to cure overnight.

2 **MARK THE OUTER TILES FOR CUTTING. Project a level line across the tile with a laser level. Mark the tile where indicated by the laser line and cut the tile to size on the mark.**

3 **CHECK THE ALIGNMENT. After installing the tiles to the outer surface of the curb, hold a 4-ft. level against the tiles to confirm that they're in line and perfectly flush.**

4 **MORTAR THE CURB.** Spread a thick bed of white thinset mortar across the top of the curb. Build up the mortar to ¼ in. or so above the top edge of the tiles.

5 **SET THE MARBLE THRESHOLD ONTO THE CURB.** Center the 6-in.-wide marble slab so that it overhangs the sides of the curb equally.

Grouting the Tiles

Unsanded grout is typically used to fill ⅛-in.-wide grout joints, but here, we used an all-purpose grout called PermaColor that can fill joints ranging from ¹⁄₁₆ to ½ in. wide. Made by Laticrete, the grout is also highly resistant to staining and mildew growth.

Before spreading the grout, remove all the rubber spacers from between the tiles and vacuum the entire shower stall—curb, floor, walls, and ceiling—of all dust and dirt.

Grouting the ceiling

Mix up a batch of grout with a margin trowel (see p. 33) and then use the trowel to scrape some grout onto a rubber grout float. Hold the float upside down and smear grout across the bull-nose tiles at the outer edge of the ceiling. Force the grout deep into the joints, then use the edge of the float to scrape the excess grout off the ceiling.

Continue to apply grout in this manner, filling each and every joint. When working close to a wall or in a corner, use the narrow end, or toe, of the float to force in the grout. The toe of the float provides better leverage when grouting in tight, narrow areas.

TIP Grouting tile goes pretty quickly, but rushing can lead to mistakes. Work methodically and be sure to fill each inch of every joint. If you miss grouting even a tiny section, water will seep behind the tiles and eventually ruin the wall.

Grouting the walls

Start grouting the walls near the ceiling and work your way down to the floor, but don't grout the walls one at a time. Instead grout the upper sections of all three walls, then work on the middle sections, and finally the bottom sections. This side-to-side, top-down strategy eliminates having to repeatedly reach up and then squat down.

Use the rubber float to force grout into the joints, one tile at a time. Fill the joints around two to three tiles, then scrape off the excess grout and repeat the process. Pay particular attention when grouting the mosaic-tile accent strips; they require quite a bit of grout to fill.

Grouting the shower floor

The shower floor, like the mosaic-tile accent strips, has a lot of joints to fill. Be sure to mix up a fresh batch of grout, if necessary, before starting. Apply a good amount of grout to the floor, then swing your arm in an arc to smear a wide swath of grout across the floor. Use the toe of the float to fill the joints in the corners and along the walls. And be sure to pack grout around the shower drain. Tip the float on edge and scrape it across the tile to remove all the excess grout.

Finally, grout the shower curb, including all the vertical spaces between the tiles and the long horizontal joint beneath the marble threshold. Wait 20 to 30 minutes for the grout to firm up before wiping the tiled surfaces clean of all remaining grout.

Cleaning off the grout

Starting on the ceiling, lightly wipe a damp grout sponge diagonally across the tiles. The grout is still relatively soft, so be careful. And don't try to remove all of the grout during this initial wipe down; just clean off most of it.

Rinse and wring out the sponge after every swipe across the ceiling. After cleaning the entire ceiling, use the sponge to wipe all the remaining grout from the ceiling tile. Repeat this two-step sponging method to clean grout from the shower walls and floor.

Wait about two hours for the grout to stiffen. Then, use a dry cotton cloth to buff any residual grout haze from the tiles. Let the grout harden for two or three days, then apply a clear silicone-based grout sealer.

> **TIP** When removing excess grout, scrape the float diagonally across the tile. Otherwise, the float has the tendency to drag the grout out of the joints.

1 **GROUT THE CEILING.** Apply grout to the ceiling with a rubber grout float. Start by grouting the joints between the bull-nose tiles at the outer edge of the ceiling.

2 **WORK TOWARD THE BACK WALL,** forcing grout into each joint. Use the toe of the float to grout close to the wall or in a corner.

4 **GROUT THE SHOWER FLOOR.** To fill the joints in the mosaic-tile shower floor, use the rubber float to smear grout across the tile. And pack grout around the drain, too.

3 **GROUT THE MOSAIC-TILE STRIPS.** Load up the float with plenty of grout to fill the joints in the decorative accent strip. Smear the grout diagonally across the surface of the tiles, and then tip the float on edge and scrape the excess grout from the wall.

TIP For best results when grouting, use a new—or at least, newer—rubber float, which has sharp square edges and corners. The edges of old, used floats are often worn down, rendering them less effective for forcing grout between the joints.

5 **CLEAN OFF THE GROUT.** Use a damp grout sponge to clean excess grout from the ceiling, wall, and floor tiles. Clean grout from the ceiling, walls, and floor with a damp sponge. Wipe diagonally across the joints to avoid disturbing the grout.

CHAPTER SEVEN

TILING A TUB SURROUND

GLAZED CERAMIC TILE is an ideal material to install on the walls around a bathtub. It's waterproof, highly stain resistant, easy to clean, and extremely durable. And tiling a tub surround is well within the capability of the average do-it-yourselfer because, unlike a shower stall, you don't have to build a shower pan or install a drain.

Tiling around a tub is also relatively affordable: You'll need approximately 80 sq. ft. of tile to tile around a standard 5-ft. bathtub. Add another 15 to 20 sq. ft. if you choose to tile the ceiling above the tub.

In this chapter I'll show how to tile a tub surround, starting with a complete demolition of the old tile and drywall. Then, follow step-by-step instructions for installing Kerdi-Board, a brand-new tile substrate made from super-lightweight polystyrene foam. Lastly, I'll show how to tile the walls and ceiling. Here, we chose bright-white glazed-ceramic tile, installing 10-in. x 13-in. tiles on the lower portions of the walls, followed by a decorative chair rail. The upper wall sections and ceiling are covered with 6-in. x 6-in. tiles. And to lend a clean, neat, finished appearance to the bath, we installed 3-in. x 6-in. bull-nose tiles around the perimeter of the surround.

Tile Demolition

Most tile-demo jobs require pounding, prying, and smashing the tiles into pieces. And while this method is effective, it also creates clouds of dust and a mountain of debris. Here, I'll show how to use a reciprocating saw to quickly and neatly cut out the old tile walls.

> **TIP** Be sure to wear all the necessary safety gear during the entire demolition process to protect yourself from injury: eye goggles, dust mask, hearing protection, and work gloves.

Cutting out the existing tiled wall

Use the recip saw with the short-cut blade (see the sidebar on the facing page) to slice the tiled wall into large sections that are approximately 16 in. to 20 in. wide x 24 in. to 36 in. tall. The blade won't be able to saw through the tile itself, but if you guide it along the grout joints, the blade will quickly and cleanly slice through the wall.

After cutting one tub wall into four or more sections, use a flat bar to pry the edge of one section from the wall. Slip your hands behind the tiled wall and give it a good yank. It'll pop free from the studs in one large piece. Continue in this manner to remove the tiled wall sections from the remaining tub-surround walls and ceiling.

Polystyrene Tile Substrate

The next step is to prep the walls for tile by installing a suitable substrate. We could've used cement backerboard (as with the shower in chapter 6) but instead chose Kerdi-Board, a new tile substrate from Schluter that's made from extruded polystyrene. The ½-in.-thick panels are lightweight, easy to cut, and, most important, 100% waterproof.

> **TIP** Once you've completed the demolition phase, consider upgrading the tub and shower system. Now's the perfect time to install a new shower valve, tub spout, and shower head, while the wall studs are exposed and there's plenty of room to cut out the old plumbing.

1 **CUT OUT THE EXISTING TILED WALL. Slice the tiled wall into large sections by steering the short-cut blade along the grout joints.**

2 **PULL THE WALL OFF THE STUDS. It will come off in one large piece with the tiles still stuck to the drywall.**

Recip Saw Prep for Easy Demo

A reciprocating saw is a great tool for demolition work because it can quickly cut through virtually any building material. However, when cutting into a tiled wall, you must be careful that the saw's long blade doesn't slice into electrical wires, plumbing pipes, or wall framing. Here's a clever trick to prevent such damage:

Put an old, used blade in the saw. Plug in the saw, then slowly squeeze the trigger until the plunger is fully extended, pushing the blade out as far as possible. Now, unplug the saw and draw a pencil line onto the blade about 1 in. from the saw shoe. That dimension represents the thickness of the existing tiled wall: ¼ in. of tile, ½ in. of drywall, plus ¼ in. extra.

Remove the blade from the saw and clamp it into a vise with the pencil line flush with the top of the vise jaws. Put on a pair of work gloves and eye goggles, then bend the blade back until it snaps in two. Remove the short tang-end of the blade from the vise and install it into the reciprocating saw. You can now use the saw to slice through the tiled wall without worrying about damaging anything inside the wall cavity.

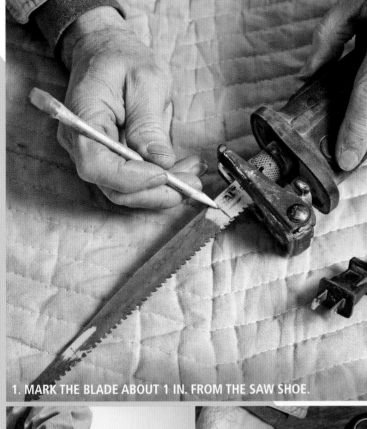

1. MARK THE BLADE ABOUT 1 IN. FROM THE SAW SHOE.

2. BEND THE BLADE UNTIL IT SNAPS.

3. INSTALL THE SHORT END OF THE BLADE INTO THE SAW.

Installing the substrate

You'll need five 4-ft. x 8-ft. sheets of ½-in.-thick Kerdi-Board to sheathe the walls and ceiling of a standard 5-ft. tub surround. Begin by measuring the ceiling and cutting a piece of Kerdi-Board about ¼ in. smaller so it'll fit without binding. You can cut the polystyrene panel with a regular utility knife, but you'll get better results with a snap-off utility knife. Extend the blade out about 2 in. and tighten the knife's locking knob. Cut into the edge of the panel, then firmly press down to slice completely through the ½-in.-thick panel.

Set the ceiling and wall panels into place as shown in the photos below.

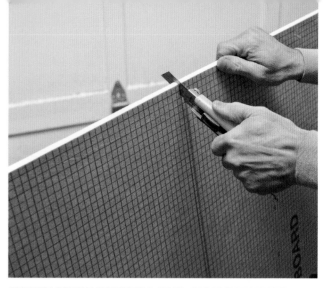

CUT THE SUBSTRATE WITH A SNAP-OFF UTILITY KNIFE. Extend the blade about 2 in. and slice through the polystyrene panel.

> **TIP** When measuring and cutting the polystyrene panels to fit around the tub, it's important to keep the bottom end of the panels ¼ in. above the tub.

1 **SET THE CEILING PANEL FIRST.** Cut a polystyrene panel about ¼ in. smaller than the ceiling above the tub. Raise the lightweight panel and press it against the joists.

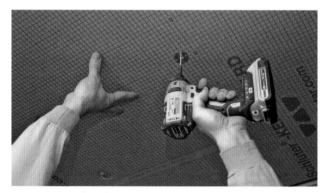

2 **SECURE THE PANEL.** Use a cordless impact driver to fasten the Kerdi-Board to the ceiling joists with metal washers and 1⅝-in.-long screws. Space the screws 12 in. apart along each joist, driving each screw just deep enough to compress the panel's surface and create a shallow circular depression.

3 **FIT THE END PANEL.** Cut the panel to fit tight to the ceiling but ¼ in. above the top edge of the tub. Secure the panel to the wall studs with washers and galvanized screws.

4 **CUT HOLES IN THE PANEL.** Measure and mark the locations of the tub spout, shower valve, and showerhead onto the second end panel. Use the utility knife to cut out the three circular holes.

5 **SCREW THE SHOWERHEAD END PANEL OVER THE PROTRUSIONS.** If it fits too tightly, don't force it. Enlarge the holes with the utility knife.

TIP Polystyrene panels must be fastened every 16 in. along the walls and ceiling. If the wall studs or ceiling joists are spaced farther apart than 16 in. on-center, you'll have to install additional framing to reduce the span.

6 **SHEATHE THE BACK WALL.** Cut two pieces of substrate for the back wall: The lower panel is a full 48 in. wide, and the upper panel is sliced lengthwise to fit. Fasten both panels to the wall studs.

7 **SECURE THE PANEL EDGES.** Screw into the horizontal seam between the two panels on the back wall. Position each screw so that the washer straddles the joint.

Sealing the bottom seams

Before tiling can begin, you must apply a specialized fabric strip, called Kerdi-Band, to all the seams, joints, and screw heads. The 5-in.-wide fabric strip is adhered with thinset mortar and creates a waterproof surface behind the tiles.

Start by using a ½-in. electric drill and mixing paddle to mix up a batch of unmodified thinset mortar. Mix the mortar with water, not a liquid polymer additive. Use a 6-in.-wide putty knife to apply a thin skim coat of mortar to the substrate along the bottom of one end wall. Spread the skim coat about 6 in. high, but be careful not to get any mortar into the ¼-in. gap between the substrate and tub.

Next, use a ¼-in. V-notch trowel or ⅛-in. square-notch trowel to spread a layer of mortar over the skim coat. Then, immediately fill the ¼-in. gap along the top of the tub with Kerdi-Fix sealant, which is a specially formulated waterproofing caulk.

Cut a strip of Kerdi-Band to length and press it into the mortar. Check to be sure that the strip's bottom edge overlaps the caulked joint and is flush with the top of the tub. Embed the Kerdi-Band into the mortar by firmly pressing it down with the putty knife. Scrape away any excess mortar that squeezes out from behind the strip and then wipe down the strip and wall with a damp sponge.

Repeat the above steps to install Kerdi-Band along the bottom of the back wall and remaining end wall of the tub surround. Always start with a skim-coat of mortar, then apply a second mortar coat with the notched trowel. Press down the fabric strip and smooth out any wrinkles with the 6-in. putty knife.

Sealing the screw heads and corner joints

Cut one 5-in.-sq. piece of Kerdi-Band for each exposed screw head. Skim-coat over a screw head, then use the notched trowel to apply a second mortar coat. Press the fabric square into the mortar, making sure it covers the screw head and washer. Embed the fabric with the 6-in. putty knife. Press down firmly to force out any excess mortar. Then smooth the patch with a damp sponge. Repeat to waterproof the remaining screw heads and washers on the walls and ceiling.

Use the same technique to install Kerdi-Band along the horizontal seam between the two panels on the back wall of the tub surround: Trowel on the mortar, embed the fabric strip, and then wipe it down with a damp sponge.

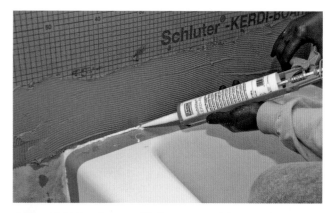

1   **CAULK THE GAP. Fill the ¼-in.-wide gap along the top of the bathtub with Kerdi-Fix, a sealant that helps waterproof the tub walls.**

2   **INSTALL KERDI-BAND. Use a 6-in. putty knife to embed a 5-in.-wide strip of Kerdi-Band into the mortar. Position the strip to overlap the caulked joint along the tub.**

There are five inside corner joints that must be sealed with Kerdi-Band, including the two vertical corner joints and the three horizontal corner joints around the ceiling of the tub surround. In each case, you must cut the Kerdi-Band strip to length and then crease it lengthwise down the center.

Apply mortar to each of the two vertical inside corner joints, then press in the creased fabric strips with the putty knife. Smooth out any wrinkles and then wipe down both joints with a damp sponge. Repeat to install fabric strips along the three ceiling corner joints. Allow the mortar to cure overnight before proceeding.

> **TIP**   When sealing a corner joint with Kerdi-Band, be sure the fabric strip overlaps onto each wall by at least 2 in.

1 **COVER THE SCREW HEADS.** Using a V-notch trowel, spread the mortar across the surface, covering an area that's about 8 in. sq.

2 **EMBED THE KERDI-BAND PATCH.** Use a 6-in. knife to press the patch firmly into the mortar, covering the washer and screw head. Scrape away any excess mortar that squeezes out.

3 **SMOOTH THE PATCH.** Wipe down lightly with a large damp—not wet—sponge. Wring out the sponge often in clean water.

4 **SEAL THE SEAM ON THE BACK WALL.** Straddle the horizontal seam with a strip of Kerdi-Band. Be sure the strip is centered over the seam, then press it down with a 6-in. knife.

5 **SEAL THE CORNER JOINTS.** Seal the two vertical corner joints (and the three joints between the tub walls and ceiling) with strips of Kerdi-Band. Crease the strip down the center and use the knife to embed it into the mortar.

Tiling the Tub Surround

When this home was built, more than 22 years ago, the tub surround was tiled with plain 4-in. x 4-in. white tiles—standard equipment for newly built homes of that period. For this tub remodel, we kept the clean, crisp look of glossy white tiles but updated the design with different-size tiles.

The lower walls are covered with 10-in. x 13-in. bright-white ceramic tiles set in a staggered-brick pattern. A decorative 1½-in. x 8-in. chair rail runs along the top of the 10-in. x 13-in. tiles.

The upper walls above the chair rail are covered with 6-in. x 6-in. tiles set in-line, meaning the grout joints are aligned vertically and not staggered. The 6-in. x 6-in tiles then continue across the ceiling in a diagonal pattern. Finally, the outer edges of the tub surround are neatly trimmed with 3-in. x 6-in. bull-nose tile.

We chose these tiles to create a more attractive, interesting design, but there was also a practical reason: Installing larger tiles greatly reduces the number of grout joints, and that's important in a wet environment, such as a tub surround or shower. Fewer grout joints means fewer places for water to seep in behind the tile.

> **TIP** Whenever possible, buy tile with all the same lot number. Tiles with matching lot numbers were all manufactured on the same day from the same batch of ingredients. Tiles from different lots might be slightly different in color or sheen.

TILE TUB SURROUND

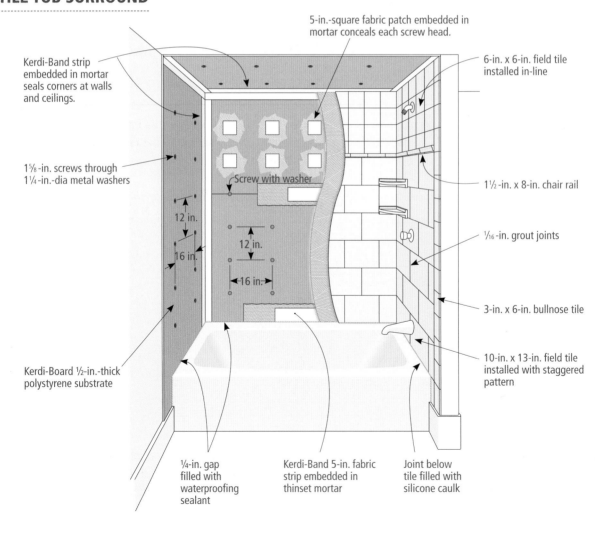

5-in.-square fabric patch embedded in mortar conceals each screw head.

Kerdi-Band strip embedded in mortar seals corners at walls and ceilings.

1⅝-in. screws through 1¼-in.-dia metal washers

Kerdi-Board ½-in.-thick polystyrene substrate

Screw with washer

12 in.

12 in.

16 in.

16 in.

6-in. x 6-in. field tile installed in-line

1½-in. x 8-in. chair rail

1/16-in. grout joints

3-in. x 6-in. bullnose tile

10-in. x 13-in. field tile installed with staggered pattern

¼-in. gap filled with waterproofing sealant

Kerdi-Band 5-in. fabric strip embedded in thinset mortar

Joint below tile filled with silicone caulk

Tiling the rear wall

Mix polymer-modified thinset mortar with water in a 5-gal. bucket, blending the mortar until smooth using an electric drill and mixing paddle. To apply the mortar, use a square-notch trowel that has ¼-in.-wide x ⅜-in.-deep notches along one edge and one end but no notches along the remaining edge and end.

Start by using the trowel's smooth (unnotched) edge to smear a thin skim coat of mortar along the bottom of the rear wall. Spread the mortar about 12 in. high. Then use the notched edge to mortar over the skim coat; this second application is the tile-setting mortar bed.

Press the first full-size 10-in. x 13-in. tile into place with the center of the tile straddling the centerline of the rear wall. Continue to set 10-in. x 13-in. tiles along the edge of the tub, butting the tiles tightly together to create 1/16-in.-wide grout joints; there's no need to insert spacers.

Use a manual score-and-snap tile cutter to cut a tile to fit at each end of the first course. Check to be sure the top edges of all the tiles in the first course are perfectly flush and level. If not, slip tile wedges beneath to even up the tiles.

> **TIP** Skim coating is important because it maximizes the mechanical bond between the mortar bed and the polystyrene substrate. Just be sure to apply the mortar bed before the skim coat dries.

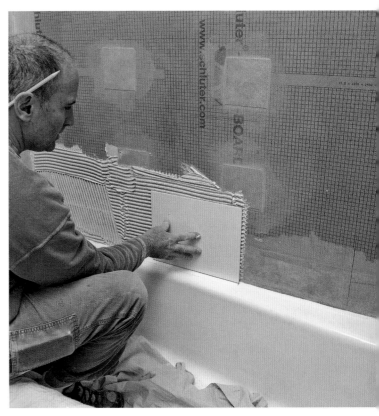

1 **START TILING IN THE CENTER.** Press the first full-size 10-in. x 13-in. tile into place in the center of the rear wall. Set tiles to the left, then spread mortar to the right of center.

2 **CUT END TILES TO FIT.** Use a manual tile cutter to cut a tile to fit at each end of the first course. Score the glazed surface first, then cleanly snap the tile in two.

3 **SET THE END TILES.** Install the cut tile at the end of the course, fitting it within ⅛ in. of the corner. Its cut edge will be hidden by tile on the adjacent end wall.

Smear a skim coat of mortar for the next course onto the polystyrene substrate. Then use the trowel's notched edge to apply the tile-setting mortar bed. Install the first tile in the second course, aligning its left edge with the wall's centerline. Offsetting the tile in this manner creates a staggered brick pattern between the tiles in each course. Install the remaining full-size 10-in. x 13-in. tiles in the second course, working out in both directions from the center. Cut a tile to fit at each end of the course and press it into place (with its cut edge facing into the corner, where it will be hidden).

Install the third course in the same manner as the first course, aligning the middle of the first tile with the wall's centerline. Install the fourth tile course the same as the second course.

TIP Use a 4-ft. level to ensure that each tile course is running perfectly level. If necessary, insert small tile wedges to level up a misaligned tile course.

Tiling the end walls

Next, install four courses of 10-in. x 13-in. tiles to the "wet" wall, which is the end wall that houses the plumbing pipes for the shower valve, tub spout, and shower arm.

Apply mortar along the bottom of the wall. Install the first full-size tile at the top of the tub and 3 in. back from the edge of the wall. Set two or three 3-in. x 6-in. bull-nose tiles along the vertical edge of the wall. Be sure the rounded bull-nose profile of each tile piece is at the outer edge of the wall.

You'll need to drill a hole in the next 10-in. x 13-in. tile to accommodate the pipe for the tub spout. Use a 1⅛-in.-dia. diamond-grit hole saw to cut the hole and then set the tile into place, making sure it fits comfortably around the copper pipe protruding from the wall.

When you reach the shower valve, remove the plastic mud ring from the valve and use it as a template to draw the hole outline onto the tile. Make a series of cuts into the tile with the wet saw, then snip off the waste pieces of tile with tile nippers (as shown in chapter 6). Set the tile into place over the shower valve.

Continue tiling up the wall, installing bull-nose tiles along with the 10-in. x 13-in. tiles, until you've completed four courses.

4 **STAGGER THE SECOND COURSE. Press into place the first tile in the second course. Position the** left edge of the tile precisely on the centerline of the rear wall.

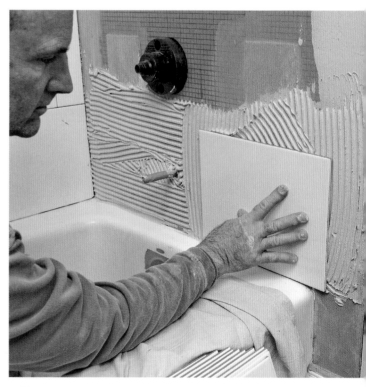

1 **TILE THE WET WALL. Trowel mortar onto the end wall, then press the first 10-in. x 13-in. tile into** place. Note that the tile is positioned 3 in. from the edge of the wall.

2 **INSTALL BULL-NOSE TILES VERTICALLY.** Shift the adjacent 10-in. x 13-in. tile, if necessary, to align the bull-nose tiles flush with the wall.

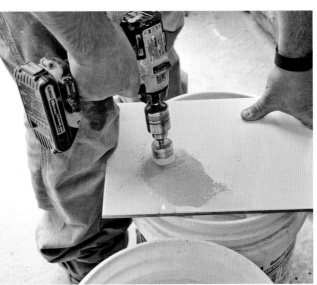

TIP Before drilling a hole with a diamond-grit hole saw, pour a puddle of water onto the tile. The water will help the hole saw cut cooler and cleaner.

3 **DRILL A HOLE FOR THE TUB-SPOUT PIPE.** Cut the hole with a 1⅛-in.-dia. diamond-grit hole saw.

4 **SLIP THE TILE OVER THE SPOUT.** It's okay if the hole is slightly off-centered, as long as the tile can be pushed tight to the wall.

5 **SET THE TILE OVER THE SHOWER VALVE.** Tilt the cut tile into place, checking to make sure it clears the valve. The hole is purposely cut oversized to allow future access to the valve.

Installing the corner caddies

On this tub surround, we installed two ceramic corner shelves, also known as corner caddies. If you're following our design, apply a thick bed of mortar to the back edges of the caddy and press it into place on top of the fourth course. Then install the tiles in the fifth course. Note that the tile at the end of the course will have to be notched to fit over the corner caddy (see the sidebar on p. 120).

Install the fifth tile course, then, if desired, set another corner caddy directly above the first caddy. Again, notch the tiles in the corner to fit around the second caddy.

Install the sixth and final course of 10-in. x 13-in. tiles to the rear wall and wet wall. Then tile the opposite end wall. Start with a full course of 10-in. x 13-in. tiles and continue tiling up the wall, staggering the grout joints.

1 INSTALL A CORNER-CADDY SHELF. Trowel mortar onto the back two edges of the caddy and press it into place.

2 NOTCH THE NEXT ROW AROUND THE CADDY. Set the notched tile into place, making sure to maintain the proper-width grout joints.

3 TILE THE WALL AT THE OTHER END. Using the same process as on the first two walls, start at the tub with full-size 10-in. x 13-in. tiles and stagger the joints up the wall.

Installing the chair rail

Once you've tiled all three walls with six courses of 10-in. x 13-in. tiles, it's time to install the decorative chair rail. Apply a skim coat of mortar onto the wall just above the 10-in. x 13-in. tiles. Spread mortar onto the back of a length of chair rail and press it into place in the center of the rear wall. Continue to install full-length pieces of chair rail, working out from the center.

Next, install full-length pieces of chair rail along the two end walls, and then use the wet saw to cut a 45° miter onto the ends of four pieces of chair rail. Trim the pieces to length and mortar them into the corners. Slip tile wedges beneath the chair rail, if necessary, to hold them level and flush.

Tiling the upper wall sections

Apply mortar to the upper wall sections using the same two-step method as before: Apply a skim-coat of mortar, then trowel on the tile-setting bed of mortar. Press 6-in. x 6-in. tiles into place, aligning them vertically. Use the tile cutter to trim a tile to fit at each end of every course. Install the tiles with their cut edges facing into the corner. Repeat the above steps to install 6-in. x 6-in. tiles to the two end walls.

The tiles that run along the very top of the walls must be trimmed to fit, but don't install these tiles until after you've tiled the ceiling (assuming that you are tiling the ceiling).

> **TIP** Miter-cut the chair rail first, and then square-cut it to length. That way, if the miter doesn't come out perfect, you can recut it. If you cut the chair rail to length first, you can't recut the miter because the chair rail will then be too short.

1 **INSTALL THE CHAIR RAIL. Working out from the center of the rear wall, butt the 1½-in.-tall x 8-in.-long chair rail pieces tightly together.**

2 **MITER THE CORNERS. Cut the chair rail tiles to 45°, then mortar them into the corners to form miter joints. Don't worry about small gaps; they'll be filled with grout.**

TILE THE UPPER WALL SECTION. Press into place the first two courses of 6-in. x 6-in. tiles. Note that these tile courses are aligned vertically; their joints aren't staggered.

Tiling the ceiling

Before tiling the ceiling, install the last of the bull-nose tiles across the ceiling at the outer edge of the tub surround.

Next, use the tile cutter to slice several 6-in. x 6-in. tiles in half diagonally. Smear a skim coat of mortar onto the ceiling, then spread mortar onto the back of one diagonal-cut half tile. Press the tile into place alongside the bull-nose course. Continue in this manner, alternating diagonal half tiles with full-size 6-in. x 6-in. tiles. Work your way across the ceiling, setting 6-in. x 6-in. tiles at 45°. Diagonal-cut the tiles to fit within ⅛ in. of the walls around the perimeter of the ceiling.

Once the ceiling is tiled, cut and install 6-in. x 6-in. tiles to fit along the very top of each wall. Allow the mortar to cure overnight before grouting the joints.

> **TIP** If you're having trouble cleanly cutting the tiles on the diagonal with a manual score-and-snap tile cutter, use the wet saw.

Tiling the ceiling

1 **INSTALL BULL-NOSE TILES ACROSS THE CEILING. If necessary, snap a chalkline to ensure the bull-nose course is perfectly straight.**

2 **TRIM TILES FOR THE CEILING PERIMETER. Cut several 6-in. x 6-in. tiles in half diagonally using the score-and-snap tile cutter.**

3 **SET THE FIRST COURSE. Working out from the bull-nose tiles, set the first course by alternating diagonal half-cut tiles with full 6-in. x 6-in. tiles.**

4 **INSTALL THE FIELD TILES. Tile across the ceiling with full-size tiles set at a 45° angle. Then trim the perimeter edges of the ceiling with diagonal half-cut tiles.**

Grouting the Tile

Since the spaces between the tiles are just ¹⁄₁₆ in. wide, you must use unsanded grout to fill the joints. Buy a bag of polymer-modified tile grout and mix it with water in a small bucket using a margin trowel. Start grouting at the ceiling, then work your way down the walls toward the tub.

Applying the tile grout

Mix the grout until it's smooth and the consistency of thick yogurt. Apply the grout to the ceiling with a rubber grout float. Smear the grout diagonally across the surface, forcing it deep into the joints.

Continue applying grout to the tub walls, making sure to pack it tightly into the joints above, below, and in between the chair rail pieces. When you reach the bottom of the walls, fill each and every grout joint, but don't apply grout to the space along the top of the bathtub; this gap will be filled later with silicone sealant. Wait 20 to 30 minutes for the grout to firm up before proceeding.

Cleaning off the grout

Use a damp sponge to clean off the remaining grout. Wipe the sponge at an angle across the grout joints.

After wiping down the entire tub surround, allow the grout to "set up" or harden for 30 to 60 minutes. Then, use a dry cotton cloth to lightly buff off any remaining grout haze. Let the grout cure for at least 24 hours, then treat each grout joint with clear grout sealer. Finally, apply a thin bead of white 100% silicone sealant along the top edge of the bathtub.

TIP Be sure to wear eye goggles when grouting the ceiling to protect your eyes from any grout that might drop from the rubber float.

2 GROUT THE CHAIR RAIL. Use the end of the float to force grout into the joints between the chair rail. Also, pack grout into the joints above and below the chair rail.

1 APPLY THE GROUT. Use a rubber float to smear bright-white grout across the ceiling. Press firmly on the float to force the grout deep into the tile joints.

3 CLEAN OFF THE EXCESS GROUT. Wipe the damp grout sponge diagonally across the tiled surface to avoid disturbing the grout joints.

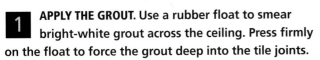

CHAPTER EIGHT

TILING A FIREPLACE WALL

TILE IS A NEAR-PERFECT surfacing material to install around a fireplace. It's durable, easy to clean, available in dozens of colors and patterns, and most important, it's fireproof. Here, we set 12-in. x 24-in. glazed-porcelain tiles around a newly installed gas fireplace. The 16-in.-tall x 60-in.-wide fireplace was built into a wall that was sheathed with ½-in.-thick cement backerboard. However, we didn't just tile around the fireplace, we tiled the entire wall from the hearth all the way up to the cathedral ceiling.

Setting porcelain tile around a fireplace is similar to tiling any wall: The tiles are set in a bed of gray latex-modified thinset mortar that's applied to the wall with a notched trowel. The one significant difference is that for this project we had to use large-format mortar, which is specifically formulated for installing large, heavy tiles. And since there's a TV attached to the wall above the fireplace, we also had to drill holes and cut openings into the tile to accommodate the TV's mounting bracket, and electrical and coaxial cable boxes.

At the end of this chapter, I'll also show how to upgrade a traditional brick fireplace by installing natural slate tiles and an ornate mantelpiece.

Tiling the Hearth

At the base of our gas fireplace, there's an 8-in.-deep x 10-in.-tall plywood "step" that was built to create a hearth. A slab of polished granite was cut to fit the top of the hearth, but before setting the granite, we had to tile the hearth. (If your fireplace doesn't have a hearth, you can skip this step, of course.)

Applying tiles to the hearth face

To establish a balanced tile pattern across the hearth, begin by measuring the length of the hearth and then marking its exact center, which should align with the center of the fireplace.

Next, dry-lay tiles from the center point out in both directions toward each end of the hearth. Place the center point of the hearth between two tiles. And leave a ⅛-in. space between the tiles to simulate grout joints. Now, measure the tiles that extend past each end of the hearth. If they're less than 12 in. wide, which is one-half the length of a tile, shift the tile pattern so that the hearth center aligns with the middle of a 24-in.-long tile, not between two tiles. (See the drawing on the facing page.) That adjustment will produce a balanced pattern with appropriate-size tiles at each end.

Next, use a 4-ft. level to check the top of the hearth for level. If it's not level (ours was not), place a laser level on the floor about 4 ft. from the hearth. Turn on the level to project a level line across the hearth. Adjust the height of the laser until the line is flush with the high end of the hearth.

Hold a tile in place at the center of the hearth and mark where the laser line intersects the tile; this is where you need to cut the tile. Repeat to mark the remaining full tiles across the face of the hearth. Identify each tile with a letter or number to make sure they get installed in the right order. Cut the tiles lengthwise with a motorized wet saw.

Now mix up a batch of latex-modified large format tile (LFT) mortar, blending the mortar and water with a ½-in. electric drill and metal mixing paddle in the usual way (see p. 39). Beginning with the tile that goes in the center of the hearth, back-butter the tile with a ¼-in.-wide x ½-in.-deep square-notched trowel. Set the tile on the floor in front of the hearth, then tip it up and press it tightly into place. Set the next tile beside the first tile with a ⅛-in.-thick rubber spacer between the tiles. Check to make sure the top edges of the two tiles are perfectly aligned. If not, slip a plastic shim beneath the lower tile to raise it flush.

> **TIP** Ordinarily porcelain tile can be cut with a manual score-and-snap tile cutter. But the Italian tiles used for this fireplace were so dense and hard they wouldn't cut cleanly with a manual cutter. Therefore, all cuts—straight and notched—were made with a motorized wet saw.

1 MARK THE TILE CUT LINE. Shoot a level line across the hearth with a laser level. Hold a tile at the center of the hearth and mark where the laser line crosses the tile.

2 CUT THE HEARTH TILES. Use a motorized wet saw to cut each hearth tile along its length. Porcelain tile is dense and hard, so cut slowly with light pressure.

TILE PATTERN LAYOUT

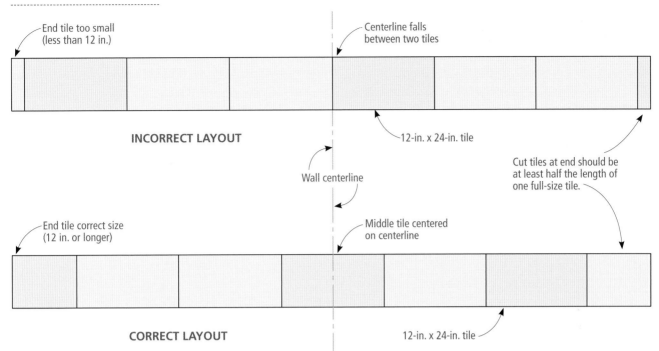

End tile too small
(less than 12 in.)

Centerline falls
between two tiles

INCORRECT LAYOUT

12-in. x 24-in. tile

Wall centerline

Cut tiles at end should be
at least half the length of
one full-size tile.

End tile correct size
(12 in. or longer)

Middle tile centered
on centerline

CORRECT LAYOUT

12-in. x 24-in. tile

3 **SET THE FIRST FACE TILE.** Stand the porcelain tile on edge on the floor in front of the hearth. Then, tip it up and press it tightly against the face of the plywood hearth.

4 **SHIM AS NECESSARY.** If the first two tiles aren't perfectly flush along the top edges, insert a plastic shim beneath the lower tile to raise it into alignment.

5 **MARK AND INSTALL THE SIDE TILES.** Hold a tile against the side of the hearth and mark where it intersects the top of the face tile. Use a wet saw to cut the end tile on the mark and then mortar and set in place, slipping it behind the protruding lip of the face tile.

TIP The secret to mixing smooth, lump-free mortar is to sprinkle mortar into the water just a little at a time. Dumping large amounts of mortar into the water all at once will cause dried clumps of mortar to form, which can remain even after mixing.

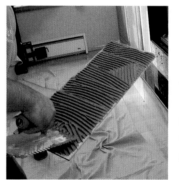

6 **SET THE GRANITE SLAB. Apply a thick bed of mortar across the plywood hearth and then set the slab. Press down firmly, and check to make sure it overhangs each end of the hearth by the same amount.**

Hold a 4-ft. level across the face of the two tiles to make sure they're straight and in line with each other. If a tile is angling out, tap it in with a rubber mallet. If it's tilted in, pull it off the hearth, add more mortar, and press it back into place. Also check each tile for plumb (vertical alignment) using a 9-in. torpedo level. It's important to get the first two tiles perfectly straight and plumb because the other hearth tiles will be aligned with them.

Continue to install full-length tiles across the face of the hearth, working out in both directions from the center. Cut the end tiles ½ in. long so that they will conceal the edges of the tiles that will be installed on the sides of the hearth. Cut and install the side tiles and then allow the mortar to cure overnight before proceeding.

Installing the hearth stone

Because our hearth was out of level, the granite slab will rest on top of the tiles, not on the plywood hearth. We spread a thick bed of latex-modified thinset mortar over the top of the hearth, building it up until it's about ½ in. higher than the top edge of the tiles.

Carefully set the granite slab down into the mortar. Press down and wiggle the slab back and forth to flatten the mortar. Stop when the granite contacts the tile. Use a damp sponge to wipe away any mortar that squeezes out from beneath the slab.

Tiling around the Fireplace

Begin tiling the wall by installing the first course above the hearth. And to maintain a balanced tile pattern, continue to follow the tiling sequence started with the hearth: Work from the center out in each direction, cutting tiles to fit at the ends of the wall.

Note that the gas fireplace shown here has a wide metal frame that gets installed after tiling. The frame runs around the perimeter of the fireplace and extends a few inches past the tile. Therefore, we cut the tiles around the fireplace about ½ in. short, since the frame would eventually cover the gap. If your fireplace doesn't have a frame, cut the tiles to fit within ⅛ in. of the metal or brick firebox, but be careful not to tile over any air vents.

Installing the first tile course

Thinset mortar is pretty tenacious stuff and it'll bond to virtually any clean, dry surface, including wood, concrete, metal, and backerboard. However, the metal panel below

1 **APPLY MORTAR. Trowel thinset mortar onto the fireplace panel and onto the back of the porcelain tile, making sure to cover the entire surface with crisply formed ridges of mortar.**

2 **CHECK FOR PLUMB. Firmly press the tile into the mortar and align its end with the center of the wall. Then, check the tile for plumb using a 9-in. torpedo level.**

TILE FIREPLACE

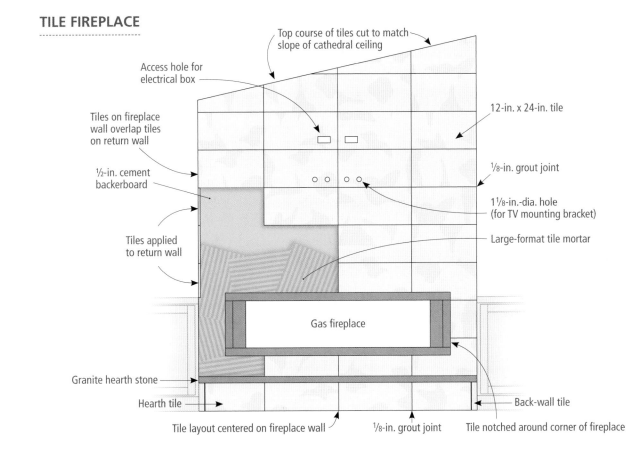

Top course of tiles cut to match slope of cathedral ceiling

Access hole for electrical box

Tiles on fireplace wall overlap tiles on return wall

½-in. cement backerboard

Tiles applied to return wall

12-in. x 24-in. tile

⅛-in. grout joint

1⅛-in.-dia. hole (for TV mounting bracket)

Large-format tile mortar

Gas fireplace

Granite hearth stone

Hearth tile

Tile layout centered on fireplace wall

⅛-in. grout joint

Back-wall tile

Tile notched around corner of fireplace

3 **SET THE SECOND TILE. Press the tile into the mortar with its cut edge up. Then hold a 4-ft. level across the first two tiles to check that they're on the same plane. If not, adjust the tiles by tapping them in or pulling them out.**

this gas fireplace had a slick painted surface. So, to make sure the mortar stuck permanently to the metal, we first scuffed up the surface with an abrasive diamond pad. (We could also have used medium-grit sandpaper.) We then vacuumed the surface clean and wiped it down with a damp cloth to remove any dust.

Measure the space between the top of the hearth and the bottom edge of the fireplace. If a perimeter frame will be installed after tiling, subtract ¼ in. to ½ in. Use a wet saw to cut the first two tiles to size.

Use the notched trowel to apply mortar to the metal panel below the fireplace and to the back of the first tile. Doubling up on the mortar will help ensure a permanent bond to the metal panel. Press the tile into place with its cut edge facing up. Align the end of the tile with the center of the wall, then use a torpedo level to check the tile for plumb. Repeat the process to install the next tile, remembering to slip a spacer between the two tiles. Use a 4-ft. level to make sure the tiles are straight and aligned on the same plane.

Notching the end tiles

Depending on the style of your fireplace, you'll likely need to notch the tile at each end of the first course to fit around the bottom corner of the fireplace. Start by measuring the distance from the last-installed tile to the end of the wall. Subtract ⅛ in. for the grout joint and cut an end tile to fit. Then mark, lay out, notch, and install the end tile as shown in the photos below. Repeat for the end tile at the opposite end of the fireplace, and then cut and install tiles to fit along each vertical end of the fireplace.

> **TIP** When working with dark-colored tiles, it's often difficult to see pencil lines drawn on the tiles. Solve this problem by either using a white marking pencil or by putting a strip of masking tape onto the tile and then drawing the lines onto the tape.

Installing the end tiles

1 MARK THE TILE FOR THE NOTCH. Hold the tile at the end of the first course, ⅛ in. away from the adjacent tile. Mark the top edge of the end tile where it intersects the side of the fireplace. Then, without moving the tile, mark its left end flush with the top of the adjacent tile.

2 CONNECT THE MARKS. Use a framing square or layout square to connect the two marks, outlining the notch on the corner of the tile.

3 CUT THE SHORT LINE. Set the tile on the wet saw and cut along the shorter pencil line.

> **TIP** After making a cut on a motorized wet saw, the tile will be soaking wet. It's important to thoroughly dry the tile before installing it. If you don't, the water on the tile can dilute the mortar, weakening its bond to the wall. Keep a terrycloth towel near the wet saw and wipe dry every tile after each cut.

4 **CUT THE LONG LINE.** Pull back the saw's sliding table and rotate the tile 90°. Cut along the second line up to, but not beyond, the first line to notch out the corner of the tile.

5 **SPREAD MORTAR.** Trowel thinset mortar onto the wall along the bottom and right side of the fireplace. Apply mortar to the back of the tile, as well.

6 **PRESS THE END TILE INTO THE MORTAR.** Check to make sure its notched corner fits easily around the bottom corner of the fireplace.

7 **CONTINUE TILING UP THE SIDE OF THE FIREPLACE.** Remember to insert two ⅛-in.-thick spacers between the tiles to maintain consistent grout joints.

Setting tiles above the fireplace

On our fireplace, there was a 7-in.-wide painted metal flange running horizontally along the top. Before tiling over the flange, we scuffed it up with a diamond pad to ensure the mortar bonded securely to the metal.

If necessary, mix up a fresh batch of latex-modified thinset mortar. Starting in the center of the fireplace, use the notched trowel to spread mortar across the metal surface and onto the wall above. Apply mortar to the back of a full tile, making sure to cover the entire surface. Set the tile onto the metal lip protruding from the bottom of the metal flange (if there is one), then firmly press the tile to the wall.

Check the tile for level by holding a level across the top edge of the tile. If necessary, slip a plastic wedge under the low end of the tile to level it. Now use a 4-ft. level to ensure that the end of the tile above the fireplace aligns perfectly with the end of the tile installed earlier below the fireplace. If the two tiles aren't in alignment, shift the tile above the fireplace to the left or right, as necessary, and then check again.

Mix and Match

The glazed-porcelain tile installed here resembles richly figured stone. The mottled surface has a subtle color range that varies from light gray to warm tan. And many tiles feature dramatic streaks of dark gray and brown. With such a wide difference between colors and patterns, it's important to mix and match tiles to avoid either repeating a pattern—dark tile, light tile, dark tile, light tile—or placing several darker tiles in one row, followed by several lighter tiles in the next.

Working from the center out in both directions, continue to install full-size tiles across the top of the fireplace. When applying thinset mortar to the metal flange, use the trowel to spread it at least 12 in. up the wall. Trowel mortar onto the back of the tile, then press it into place. After setting three or four tiles, use the 4-ft. level to check the tiles for level. If necessary, use wedges to raise any misaligned tiles. All remaining tile courses will follow this course, so it's important that it's perfectly level.

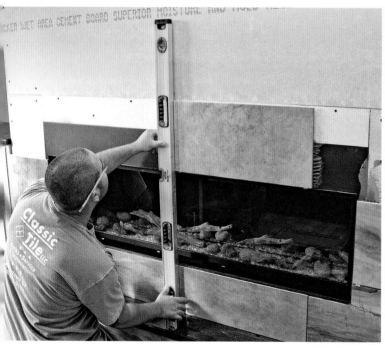

1 **CHECK THE LAYOUT.** Set the first tile above the fireplace. To maintain a precise tile pattern, use a 4-ft. level to confirm that the tile aligns with the tile below.

2 **CHECK FOR LEVEL.** Install three or four tiles above the fireplace, then check them for level with a 4-ft. level. Shim up any tiles that are out of alignment.

Installing the end tiles

In this particular installation, the tile courses below the fireplace butted into cabinets at each end. However, the tile courses above the fireplace wrap around the corner and return back to the room wall. If you have a similar situation with your installation, remember that the end tiles on the fireplace wall must extend past the corner to overlap and hide the edges of the tiles on the return wall.

Begin by standing a scrap piece of tile against the return wall. Hold a full-size tile in place at the end of the row so that its right end is ⅛ in. away from the adjacent tile and its left end extends past the return-wall corner. Mark the end tile where it intersects the face of the tile on the return wall. Now make a second mark ³⁄₁₆ in. beyond the first mark (this accounts for the thickness of the mortar). Use the wet saw to crosscut the tile on the second mark. The result will be a tile that extends approximately ½ in. past the wall corner.

1 **MARK FOR THE END TILE CUT. Stand a scrap piece of tile against the return wall. Mark where the end tile on the fireplace wall intersects the face of the scrap piece.**

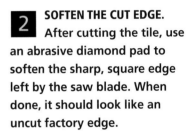

2 **SOFTEN THE CUT EDGE. After cutting the tile, use an abrasive diamond pad to soften the sharp, square edge left by the saw blade. When done, it should look like an uncut factory edge.**

Use the notched trowel to apply thinset mortar to the wall at the end of the row. Be sure to fully cover the metal flange at the top of the fireplace. Then back-butter the end tile in the usual way. Set the tile into place at the end of the row and press it firmly to the wall. Insert a ⅛-in. spacer to maintain a consistent grout joint. Then check the top edge of the tile to ensure it's even with the adjacent tile. If it isn't, slip wedges underneath to raise it flush. Use a 4-ft. level to make sure the tile wall is plumb (perfectly vertical). If the end tile is protruding out too far, tap it closer to the wall. If it's sunken in too far, carefully pry the tile off the wall with the trowel or a stiff-blade putty knife, apply more mortar to the rear of the tile, and press it back into place.

> **TIP** Before buying or even renting a wet saw, call a local tile contractor to see if he or she has a used saw for sale. Contractors often retire old but perfectly serviceable wet saws and then sell them at drastically reduced prices.

3 **SET THE TILE INTO PLACE AT THE END OF THE ROW.** Insert spacers, tip the tile forward, and press it into the mortar and tightly against the wall.

Why You Need Wedges

For this project, we used ⅛-in.-thick rubber spacers to maintain consistent grout joints between all the tiles. So then why, you might wonder, did we also have to install wedges? Good question.

In a perfect world, all tiles would be exactly the same size and wedges wouldn't be necessary. Unfortunately, that's simply not the case. In fact, tiles are seldom, if ever, the same size, making it impossible to align them perfectly. So, a wedge must be installed here and there to raise a tile flush with the adjacent tile.

There's no way to totally eliminate the need for wedges, but it helps to buy high-quality tiles, which are more likely to be manufactured under strict quality-control standards. These tiles will cost more—sometimes a lot more—but they'll be much more consistent in size and shape than inexpensive, bargain-bin tiles.

After installing an end tile, hold a full-size tile against the return wall. Mark the back of the tile where it meets the rear edge of the previously installed end tile. Then mark where the top edge of the end tile intersects the back of the return-wall tile. Set the tile on the wet saw, align the first mark with the blade, and crosscut the tile to length. Rotate the tile 90° and cut it lengthwise along the second mark.

Dry-fit (no mortar) the tile against the return wall, making sure it slips behind the end tile and lies flat against the wall. Apply mortar to the wall and press the tile into place. If necessary, slip a wedge beneath the tile to raise it flush with the end tile on the fireplace wall. Repeat the previous steps to mark and cut a tile to fit against the return wall at the opposite end of the tile course.

4 **MARK FOR THE RETURN TILE CUT. Hold a full tile against the return wall, allowing it to extend past the corner. Mark where it intersects the rear of the end tile.**

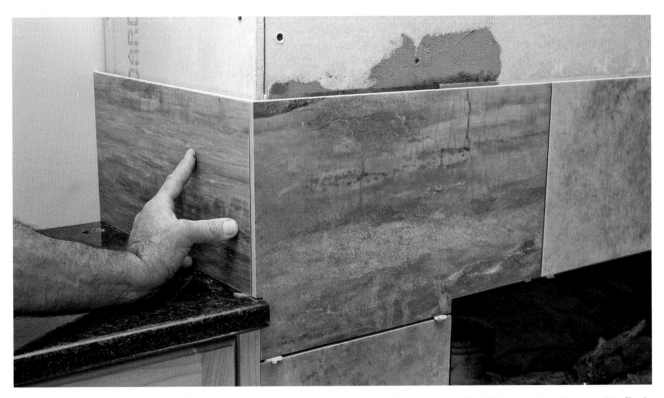

5 **SET THE RETURN TILE.** Trowel thinset mortar onto the return wall, then press the tile into place. Be sure it's flush with the end of the tile on the fireplace wall. If necessary, slip a plastic wedge beneath the return-wall tile.

Notching tiles around an outlet

There are two basic ways to tile around an electrical outlet. The method chosen will depend on how the outlet falls within the tile pattern. If the outlet spans the joint between two tiles, you'll need to notch each tile to fit around the outlet, as described below. However, if the outlet is located in the middle of a tile, then you'll have to cut a rectangular hole in a single tile, as shown on p. 164.

> **TIP** Before tiling around electrical outlets, be sure to first turn off the power to the circuit at the main electrical panel.

1 **MARK THE TOP EDGE.** To notch a tile around an electrical outlet, start by unscrewing the electrical outlet from its box and slip the tile underneath. Mark the top of the tile where it meets the right and left side of the box.

2 **MARK THE SIDE.** Reposition the tile and hold its right end against the side of the electrical box. Mark where the tile intersects the bottom of the box. Use a framing square or layout square to extend the three lines, outlining the notch.

3 **CUT THE LONG LINES.** Use the wet saw to cut down the center of the two vertical pencil lines. Be careful not to saw beyond the line at the bottom of the notch.

4 **CUT THE SHORT LINE.** Turn the tile over and align the saw blade with the bottom of the previous two cuts. Slowly raise the tile into the blade to cut out the notch.

5 **SET THE BOTTOM EDGE.** Pull the electrical outlet away from the wall, spread mortar onto the back of the tile, and then set the bottom edge of the tile into place, making sure the notch is aligned with the outlet.

6 **PRESS INTO PLACE.** Tilt the tile against the wall and check to make sure the notch fits around the electrical box. Then firmly press the tile into the mortar.

Tiling the Rest of the Fireplace Wall

Continue your way up the wall with the remaining tile courses. As with the previous courses, start tiling in the center of the wall and work out to the left and right. Mix up a fresh bucket of latex-modified thinset mortar as needed and apply it to the fireplace wall and to the back of the tile. Apply just enough mortar to set one 12-in. x 24-in. tile at a time. Insert ⅛-in. spacers between and beneath the tiles to maintain consistent, even grout joints.

At each end of the course, mark a tile to extend ½ in. past the wall corner just as you did before. Crosscut the tile on the wet saw and round over the fresh-cut end with a diamond pad. Install the tile to the wall, and then cut a tile to fit along the return wall.

INSTALL THE REMAINING COURSES. As you continue to work your way up the fireplace wall, one course at a time, always start in the center and work out to the left and right.

> **TIP** Mixing and spreading mortar all day can get a little messy, so it's inevitable that you'll get some on your tools, shoes, and clothing. Keep a scouring sponge and small bucket of water nearby and use the scouring pad to scrub off any mortar before it hardens.

The Suction Cup Cure

To create a professional-looking tile job, it's imperative that all the tiles are installed on the same plane to produce a perfectly flat wall. If the edge or corner of a tile is protruding past an adjacent tile, or is sunken in too far, the discrepancy will be blatantly obvious.

If a tile is protruding out too far, use a rubber mallet or the heel of your hand to tap it flush with the neighboring tiles. However, if you accidentally push a tile in too deeply, which is inevitable, you'll need to pull the tile off the wall, add more mortar, and then reinstall it.

Removing a tile, even a freshly set tile, takes some strength and a little finesse. If you're very careful, you can pry the tile off the wall with a putty knife or trowel, but an easier, safer method is to use a tile suction cup, as shown here. Simply press the suction cup onto the tile and pull with slow, steady pressure until the mortar bond releases; if you yank on the cup, it'll pop off the tile. And if the cup won't stick, wipe it—and the tile—clean with a slightly dampened cloth.

Drilling holes through tile

Since we were planning to install a flat-screen television above the fireplace, we had to customize the tiles to allow attachment of the TV-mounting bracket and to provide access to the electrical outlet and coaxial cable. If you're not mounting a TV above the fireplace, skip ahead to installing the last tile course.

For our project, the contractor who built the fireplace wall had located and marked the screw holes for the TV-mounting bracket. If you'll be installing the bracket, use the template provided by the manufacturer to locate the screw holes.

Hold a tile in position against the wall and directly below the screw holes. Transfer the position of each hole onto the top edge of the tile. Shift the tile to the side and mark the hole locations onto the end of the tile. While holding the tile in place, be sure to maintain the ⅛-in. grout joint. Now use a framing square or layout square to extend each line across the face of the tile. Where the lines intersect represents the center of a screw hole.

To drill the screw holes in the tile, use a cordless drill and 1⅛-in.-dia. diamond-grit hole saw. This type of abrasive hole saw cuts cleanly and quickly through the rock-hard porcelain tile, but it takes a little practice to use properly. Unlike a standard woodcutting hole saw, a diamond hole saw doesn't have a pilot bit to help guide the hole saw into and through the material.

Start by placing the tile on a flat, stable surface. Then set a sopping wet sponge on the tile close to the screw-hole location. Water from the sponge will cool down the hole saw, allowing it to cut easier and faster. Next, hold the drill at a slight angle—about 20°—to the surface of the tile. Squeeze the drill's trigger and lightly press the hole saw against the tile until its rim cuts through the glaze on the surface of the tile. Keep a firm grip on the drill to prevent the hole saw from skipping across the surface.

Once the rim of the diamond hole saw has cut a semicircular groove into the glazing, tip the drill upright and drill straight down into the tile. Stop occasionally and squeeze the sponge to flood the hole saw with water. Continue drilling until you've cut completely through the tile. Repeat to drill out the remaining screw holes.

1 **HOLD THE DRILL AT A SLIGHT ANGLE. Since a diamond-grit hole saw doesn't have a center pilot bit to guide it, start drilling with the drill held at about 20° to the surface of the tile.**

2 **DRILL STRAIGHT DOWN. Once the rim of the hole saw has cut through the hard, glazed surface, straighten up the drill and continue drilling down through the tile.**

Use the notched trowel to spread thinset mortar onto the wall and across the back of the tile. Press the tile to the wall and slip ⅛-in. spacers underneath. Check to confirm that the screw-hole locations marked on the wall are visible through the holes in the tile.

Cutting rectangular holes in tile

If you need to cut rectangular holes into the tile (as we did here to fit around the electrical-outlet box and coaxial-cable box), you can use a wet saw or a grinder (see the sidebar on p. 166). If the hole spans the joint between two tiles, notch each tile using the technique shown on pp. 160–161.

If the rectangular hole falls within the border of a single tile, hold the tile in place directly below the electrical box. Mark the top edge of the tile where it crosses the left and right sides of the box. Slide the tile to the left and mark where its end intersects the top and bottom edges of the box. Use a framing square or layout square to extend the lines across the face of the tile, outlining the rectangular hole. Cut the hole in the tile on the wet saw as shown in the photos below and then set the tile.

3 **SET THE DRILLED TILE. Press the tile into the mortar and tight to the wall. Be sure the screw-hole locations marked on the wall are clearly visible through the holes.**

Cutting a rectangular hole within the body of a tile

1 **MARK THE HOLE LOCATION. Hold the tile in position, aligned with the tile below, and mark where the top of the tile meets the right and left end of the electrical box. Then slide the tile to the left and mark where its end intersects with the top and bottom of the box.**

2 **CUT ALONG THE TWO LONG HORIZONTAL PENCIL LINES. Be careful not to cut beyond the shorter vertical lines.**

3 **CUT ALONG THE TWO SHORTER VERTICAL LINES.** Again, don't saw past the ends of the two longer horizontal cuts.

4 **TURN THE TILE OVER.** Align the saw blade with one of the short cuts made previously and lengthen the cut. Rotate the tile 90° and saw along each of the two long horizontal cuts. Cut just deep enough to free the rectangular waste piece from the tile.

5 **APPLY MORTAR.** Trowel thinset mortar onto the wall and across the back of the tile. Keep the mortar away from the edges of the rectangular cutout.

6 **SET THE TILE.** Press the tile tightly to the wall and then check to be sure the rectangular hole fits comfortably around the electrical box and doesn't overlap it.

Cutting Holes with a Grinder

A wet saw provides a quick, clean way to cut square and rectangular holes in tile, but you can also use a portable angle grinder. When fitted with an abrasive tile wheel (blade) or, better yet, a diamond-impregnated wheel, the grinder slices through tile with surprising speed. And it provides a bit more control and maneuverability than a wet saw because you're holding the tool in your hands.

The one drawback is that grinders use dry-cut wheels, which spew out thick clouds of dust. Never use a grinder indoors and always wear eye, hearing, and lung protection.

Cutting tapered tiles

In a typical room with a flat ceiling, the tiles in the last course are all cut to the same height. But the room shown here has a cathedral ceiling, so each tile in the last course had to be cut at an angle to match the slope of the ceiling.

The easiest, most accurate way to cut the tiles to the correct taper is simply to measure the wall space for each tile in two places: at the narrowest end and widest end. Then transfer those dimensions to the tile and cut the taper on the wet saw. When marking the cut line, don't forget to take into account the 1/8-in. space needed for the grout joint.

After transferring the measurements to the tile, use a level as a straightedge guide to draw the angled cut line across the face of the tile. Then cut the tile on the motorized wet saw. Use the notched trowel to apply mortar to the back of the tile and then gently press the tile to the wall, being careful not to snap off the narrow, pointed end.

Repeat to install the remaining tapered tiles to complete the top course. Allow the mortar to cure 8 to 16 hours before grouting.

1 **MARK THE CUT LINE. Measure the tapered space along the cathedral ceiling. Transfer those dimensions to a full-size tile, and use a level to draw the angled cut line.**

TIP Before applying any mortar to the tapered tile, hold the tile in place to check that it fits the angular space at the top of the wall. If necessary, return to the wet saw and trim the tile to fit.

2 **CUT THE TILE.** Align the tapered cut line with the saw blade. Turn on the saw and slowly feed the tile into the spinning blade. As you cut across the tile, guide the blade along the angled pencil line.

3 **SET THE TAPERED TILE.** Confirm that the tile fits evenly along the angled ceiling, press the tile into place, and then insert rubber spacers to maintain the ⅛-in. grout joints.

Grouting the Tiles

For this fireplace wall, we used unsanded masonry grout to fill the ⅛-in. spaces between the tiles. (If the grout joints were wider than ⅛ in., we would have used sanded grout.) And even though this is a pretty big wall, very little grout was used because the grout joints were small and the tiles were large.

There are three main phases of grouting: mixing the grout, applying the grout to the joints, and cleaning the

excess grout off the tile. However, before proceeding, take time now to mask off the area, which will make cleanup much easier later (see the sidebar on p. 168). Next, use a utility knife or slotted screwdriver to pry out all the rubber spacers from between the tiles. If you notice a grout joint that's completely filled with mortar, scratch out the mortar with a utility knife. Then vacuum the joints clean of all dust and debris.

Masking Off the Work Area

1. MASK OFF CABINETS AND WOOD TRIM.

2. MASK OFF THE ROOM WALL AND CEILING.

3. COVER THE FLOOR.

Start by using 1½-in.-wide painter's tape to mask off the area between the fireplace wall and any nearby cabinetry or trim work. As you apply the tape, be careful that you don't partially cover the grout joints.

Also, apply tape to where the room wall intersects the tiled fireplace, but don't bother taping the entire length of the wall. Instead, just put small strips of tape at the end of each grout joint. (Grout is only applied between the tiles, not between the wall and the tile.) Use this same short-strip taping technique to mask off the grout joints along the ceiling. Cover the floor in front of the hearth with 12-in.-wide masking paper. Roll out the paper across the room and tape it down to the floor.

TIP When masking off around the tiled fireplace, use painter's tape, not regular manila-colored masking tape. Painter's tape has a quick-release adhesive that peels off without harming painted surfaces. Regular masking tape can peel paint right off the wall or ceiling.

Mixing the grout

Add about 1 pt. of water to a small bucket, then slowly sprinkle in approximately 3 lb. of grout. Mix vigorously with a margin trowel until the grout is the consistency of thick yogurt. If it's too thin, add more grout and mix again. If the grout is too thick and dry, mix in a little water. Allow the grout to slake for five minutes, then mix again for a few seconds immediately before grouting. When the grout is ready, scoop some out with the margin trowel and scrape it onto a rubber grout float.

Applying the grout

Start grouting at the top of the wall and work your way down to the hearth. With both hands on the rubber float, force grout deep into the joints between the tiles. As you swipe the float across the surface, lift the leading edge at an angle so that the trailing edge of the float presses the grout into the joint.

Use the float to scrape any excess grout from the face of the tile and smear it into the next open joint. Apply grout to both the horizontal and vertical joints in one area. Then move down a few feet and repeat the process, filling all the joints in one area before moving on to the next.

After grouting the entire fireplace wall and hearth, rinse the bucket, rubber float, and margin trowel clean of all grout. Then wait 20 to 30 minutes before proceeding.

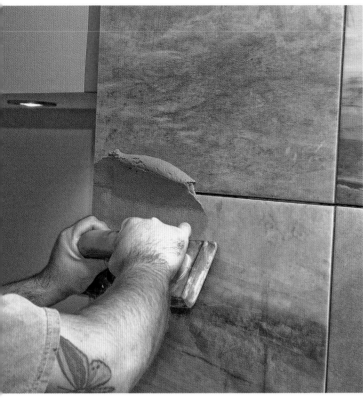

FORCE THE GROUT DEEP INTO THE JOINTS. Tip the rubber float up at an angle and then smear the grout across the surface of the tile.

USE A MARGIN TROWEL TO GROUT THE END JOINTS. The trowel's stiff, square-end blade is ideal for grouting narrow spaces (like the joint between the wall and rows of tile) and hard-to-reach areas.

WORK ONE AREA AT A TIME. Hold the rubber float with two hands and smear grout horizontally across the wall, packing the vertical joints with grout.

USE THE TOE OF THE FLOAT ON SHORT JOINTS. The front end of the float works best to pack grout into short vertical joints (here, the joints immediately below the fireplace).

Clean off the grout

The next step is to wash the excess grout from the surface of the tiles, using a grout sponge and bucket of clean water. Dunk the sponge into the bucket and wring out the excess water. Then, starting at the top of the wall, wipe the sponge at an angle across the grout joints, using light pressure. During this preliminary wipe-down step, don't try to wash off all the grout, just remove the heaviest buildups.

> **TIP** After grouting the joints, clean the tiles with a grout sponge, not a regular household sponge. Grout sponges are large, thick, and soft with rounded edges and corners. A regular sponge is more rigid with square edges and sharp corners that can carve the grout from the joints.

Wring out the sponge after every swipe across the wall. As you work your way across the face of the wall, don't forget to wipe down the tiles on the return wall. After cleaning grout from three or four tiles, go back over the same area with a clean, damp sponge to remove the remaining grout. Then carefully peel off the masking tape so as not to disturb the grout joints, which are still a bit soft.

Continue washing down the tile on the wall and around the fireplace. Then wait an hour or two for the grout to "set up" or partially harden. At that point, a light, cloudy haze of grout will be visible on the surface of the tiles. Use a dry cotton cloth to buff the grout haze off of the tiles. Let the grout harden for two to three days, then apply a clear silicone-based grout sealer to make the grout water- and stain-resistant.

> **TIP** Ordinarily it only takes about an hour or two for grout to become hard enough to allow you to buff the tile surface clean. However, if it's a very rainy or particularly humid day, the grout will take longer to dry. In such conditions, wait at least another hour or two.

1 **CLEAN OFF THE GROUT.** Wipe the excess grout from the tiles with a wet grout sponge. Rinse the sponge clean in a bucket of water after each swipe across the wall.

2 **BUFF OFF ANY HAZE.** Use a dry cloth to buff off any residual grout haze from the surface of the tiles. Don't upset the grout joints, which are still relatively soft.

BRICK FIREPLACE FACELIFT

Here's how to transform an ordinary bare-brick fireplace into a beautiful focal point
by installing Vermont slate tiles and a prefabricated mantelpiece.

1. TILE THE EDGES OF THE FIREPLACE OPENING.

Start by cutting slate to cover the ends of the bricks at the vertical edges of the firebox. You can cut slate with a motorized wet saw or a circular saw fitted with a masonry blade. Apply thinset mortar to the bricks with a ⅛-in. notched trowel, then press the slate tiles into place. Separate the tiles with ³⁄₃₂-in. spacers. (Here, we used strips of ³⁄₃₂-in.-thick cardboard.)

Next, apply mortar to the front of the brick fireplace, covering an area not larger than about 2 sq. ft. Use a rubber mallet to tap the slate tiles into the mortar. Again, insert ³⁄₃₂-in. spacers between the tiles and stagger all vertical joints by at least 3 in. from one course to the next.

Continue installing slate tiles up both sides of the fireplace opening. Next, apply thinset mortar across the top of the fireplace opening. Set slate tiles into the mortar above the fireplace. Note that the tiles rest on a wood cleat that's wedged against the top of the fireplace opening. The cleat holds the tiles in position and prevents them from sliding down the bricks. After installing all the slate tiles, allow the mortar to cure overnight.

2. SET TILES ON THE FRONT OF THE FIREPLACE.

3. BE SURE TO COMPLETELY FILL THE MORTAR JOINTS.

4. SET THE TILES ABOVE THE OPENING.

5. GROUT THE JOINTS BETWEEN THE TILES.

6. WIPE OFF EXCESS GROUT.

7. SCREW CLEATS TO THE WALL TO SUPPORT THE MANTELPIECE.

8. PUT STRIPS OF TAPE ON THE WALL TO LOCATE THE CLEATS.

9. SECURE THE MANTELPIECE.

Next, mix up a small batch of unsanded grout and put some into a plastic food-storage bag. Use scissors to snip off the corner of the bag, creating a ¼-in.-dia. opening. Remove all the spacers, then squeeze grout from the bag directly into the joints between the slate tiles. Press the grout into the joints with a plastic putty knife.

Wait about 30 minutes for the grout to stiffen up, then use a wet sponge to wipe off the excess grout. If there's any grout stuck in crevices, scrub it out with an old toothbrush. Wait another 30 minutes or so, then buff off any grout haze with a dry cloth.

Now temporarily install the prefabricated mantelpiece, centering it on the fireplace. Draw short pencil lines onto the wall along the top and sides of the mantel. Move the mantel out of the way. Measure down from the horizontal line above the fireplace the thickness of the mantel top, plus ⅛ in. Repeat for the two vertical lines along each vertical leg of the mantel.

Cut a 2x3 or 2x4 to about 40 in. long and screw it to the horizontal line above the fireplace. Position the cleat so that the prefabricated mantelpiece just slips over it. Then cut two 1x1 cleats about 12 in. long and screw them on the vertical lines marked on either side of the fireplace. Put tape strips on the wall, aligned with the top and bottom ends of the cleats. Repeat to mark the ends of the horizontal cleat above the fireplace. The tape strips are necessary because you won't be able to see the cleats once the mantelpiece is installed.

Stand the mantelpiece in place, centered on the fireplace opening. Secure the mantel by screwing down through the top and sides and into the cleats.

TILING A BACKSPLASH

MOST KITCHEN-REMODELING projects require a significant investment of time, money, and effort, but here's an exception: applying tile to the back-splash wall. This dead space, which spans between the countertop and upper cabinets, is the most visible wall surface in the kitchen. However, a majority of kitchen backsplashes are simply painted and left to blend into the background. That's too bad because tiling a backsplash is well within the capability of most do-it-yourselfers, and it's one of the simplest, most affordable ways to create an attractive, eye-catching focal point. And as a bonus, you get a durable, totally scrubbable wall surface.

You can put virtually any wall tile on a backsplash wall, including glazed ceramic, stone, porcelain, or glass. Here, we chose an Italian crema marfil marble subway tile, which provided a nice complement to both the beige-speckled granite countertop and the cherry-stained cabinets.

The 3-in. x 6-in. natural stone tiles were laid horizontally to accentuate and balance the long, horizontal shape of the backsplash wall. And to add a little extra style and visual interest, we cut the marble subway tiles to accept decorative 2⅛-in.-sq. glass-tile insets. We also designed a centerpiece feature behind the range, using 4-in. x 4-in. marble tiles and glass-tile insets framed by 2-in.-wide marble ogee chair rail.

Wall Prep and Tile Layout

Start by clearing the countertop of all small appliances, spice racks, drain boards, and other items. Then, turn off the power to the electrical outlets, switches, and other devices on the backsplash wall. Use a screwdriver to remove the cover plates and switch plates.

Before you lay out and set any tile, it's important to prep the wall surface to ensure the tiles adhere properly. Begin by scrubbing the wall with a nylon scouring sponge and hot, soapy water. Pay particular attention to the wall behind the range. Dry the wall with a terrycloth towel or clean cotton rags.

Next, cut a sheet of 100-grit sandpaper into four equal pieces. Wrap one piece around a 3-in.-wide x 4½-in.-long wood block and hand-sand the backsplash wall. The abrasive action will roughen the painted surface and remove any slick, glossy sheen. After sanding, vacuum the countertop and wipe down the wall with a tack rag or dampened cotton rag to remove any residual sanding dust.

Laying out the centerpiece

With the wall surface prepped, you can lay out the tile pattern, starting with the centerpiece over the range. Establishing the centerpiece first makes it easier to cut the tiles to fit within the confines of the limited space behind the range.

Begin by pulling the range out from the wall about 6 in. Measure the horizontal distance behind the range from

PREP THE WALL SURFACE. After scrubbing clean the back-splash wall, roughen up its surface by sanding with 100-grit sandpaper wrapped around a wood block.

TIP To avoid receiving an electric shock, go to the main electrical panel and turn off the breakers that power the receptacles and switches on the backsplash wall. Only then is it safe to unscrew and remove the cover plates and switch plates.

countertop to countertop. Cut a 1x2 or 1x3 about ⅛ in. shorter than that dimension, creating a ledger board. Set the ledger flat against the wall behind the range. Hold it flush with the top edge of the countertops, and then screw it to the wall. The ledger will support the centerpiece tiles and prevent them from sliding down the wall.

To find the exact center of the centerpiece, measure the horizontal distance between the two wall cabinets directly

ESTABLISH THE CENTERPOINT. Mark the center of the wall behind the range, then use a level and draw a vertical centerline to represent the middle of the tiled centerpiece.

CUT THE INSET PIECES. To create the 2⅛-in.-sq. decorative glass-tile insets, take a utility knife and cut a square block of nine tiles from a glass-tile mosaic sheet.

above the range. Divide the dimension by two and mark the centerpoint onto the wall. Then use a level to draw a perfectly vertical plumb centerline onto the wall.

Measure the overall height and width of the backsplash wall behind the range, as measured from the ledger to the underside of the range hood, and between the two upper wall cabinets. With those dimensions in hand, you can now cut and dry-assemble the tiles for the centerpiece.

A Good Level

When tiling walls, you'll need a level to mark precise level (horizontal) and plumb (vertical) layout lines. However, to ensure accuracy, you must use a high-quality level. Cheap levels are inaccurate and unreliable. When shopping for a level, remember that price is typically a good indication of quality. Plan to spend at least $20 for a 24-in. level and $30 to $50 for a 48-in. model.

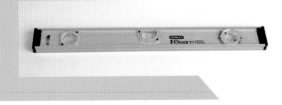

In general, it's best to size the centerpiece to fit comfortably—not precisely—within the overall height and width of the wall space. In this case, the centerpiece fit perfectly: about 1 in. narrower and 1 in. shorter than the overall height. The remaining space around the centerpiece is filled in with cut subway tiles, which eases the transition from the 4-in. x 4-in. centerpiece tiles to the 3-in. x 6-in. subway wall tiles.

Cutting the centerpiece tiles

Begin by cutting five glass-tile inset pieces from a mosaic-tile sheet. Each mosaic sheet is composed of ⅝-in.-sq. glass tiles adhered to a fiberglass-mesh backing. Place the mosaic-tile sheet face down on a piece of cardboard and then slice through the mesh backing with a utility knife, freeing a square of nine glass tiles. If you're following our design, repeat to cut out the remaining four glass-tile insets for the centerpiece.

Most of the centerpiece is made up of 4-in. x 4-in. marble tiles set diagonally at 45° to create a diamond pattern. However, to form the perimeter border around the diamond pattern, you must use an electric wet saw to cut tiles to fit. For the left and right vertical sides of the centerpiece, cut two 4-in. x 4-in. marble tiles in half on the diagonal to form four triangular half-pieces of tile; two for each side.

LAY OUT THE CENTERPIECE. Dry-assemble the tile centerpiece for the wall behind the range. Place ³⁄₁₆-in. spacers between the tiles and set the five glass-tile insets on top.

For the top and bottom horizontal edges of the centerpiece, cut three 4-in. x 4-in. marble tiles in half on the diagonal, creating six triangular half-pieces of tile: three for the top edge and three for the bottom edge. And finally, use the wet saw to slice a 4-in. x 4-in. tile into quarters on the diagonals, forming four quarter-tile pieces; one for each corner of the diamond-pattern centerpiece.

With all the border tile pieces cut to size, dry-assemble the centerpiece. Place ³⁄₁₆-in. rubber spacers between the tile pieces to create uniform grout joints. Then set 12-in.-long marble chair-rail pieces around the perimeter of the centerpiece, separated by ³⁄₁₆-in. rubber spacers. Here, we used 2-in.-wide chair rail, which produced the perfect size centerpiece. If necessary, choose a wider or narrower chair rail to achieve the desired overall height and width to match your wall space.

Set the five glass-tile insets on top of the centerpiece, positioning them as shown in the photo above. Note that the insets are aligned square to the diamond pattern, not parallel with it. In other words, the glass-tile insets are not set at 45°.

Check to be sure each glass-tile inset is precisely centered over the intersection of four marble tiles. Then, use a sharpened pencil to draw cut lines onto each of the four tiles beneath the insets. Position the cut lines ⅛ in. beyond the insets to create the proper-width grout joints.

MARK FOR CUTTING. Mark cut lines onto the four marble tiles below each glass-tile inset. Position the cut lines precisely ⅛ in. beyond the edges of the insets.

Existing Backsplash: Leave It or Lose It

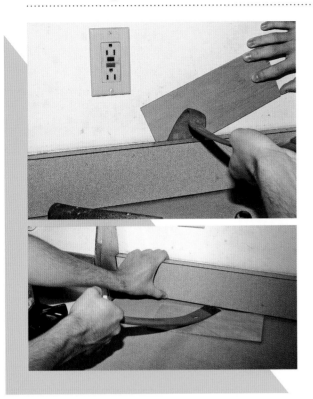

If your kitchen counter has an existing 4-in.- to 6-in.-tall backsplash, you have two options: Remove it and tile the entire backsplash wall down to the countertop, or leave the existing backsplash in place and tile above it.

The right decision is often based on the type of existing backsplash. For example, if there's a granite or solid-surface (i.e., Corian®) backsplash, it's best to leave it in place and simply tile above it. However, if the backsplash is made of plastic laminate or wood, you're better off removing it and tiling the entire wall.

The age and condition of the existing counter and backsplash also play a role. For instance, the owners of the kitchen where we installed the marble tile backsplash had recently replaced an old, worn-out plastic-laminate counter and backsplash with brand-new granite counters. But, the homeowners did not get a new granite backsplash, opting, instead, for us to install marble tiles down to the new countertop.

When removing an existing backsplash, pry it off the wall first, using a wood block to protect the wall surface. Then, slip the pry bar beneath the backsplash and pry up to release it from the countertop.

If you're wondering why 1/8-in. joints instead of 3/16 in. were used between the marble tiles, here's why: The spaces between the individual mosaic glass tiles are only 1/8 in. wide, and the centerpiece will look more balanced if the grout joint around each inset matches the joints between each 5/8-in.-sq. glass tile.

Disassemble the centerpiece and take all 20 marked marble tiles over to the wet saw. If your wet saw doesn't have a fence that adjusts to 45°, clamp a layout square to the saw's sliding table. Hold each 4-in. x 4-in. tile against the square and then trim off the corners of the marble tiles to accept the glass-tile insets.

Once all the marble tiles are cut to size, reassemble the centerpiece on the kitchen counter or nearby tabletop. Now you're ready to start tiling.

TRIM THE MARKED TILES. Use a wet saw to trim off the corners of the marble tiles at 45°. If necessary, clamp a layout square to the saw to support the 4-in. x 4-in. tile.

Tiling the Centerpiece

First, mix a batch of thinset mortar in a clean 5-gal. plastic bucket using an electric drill fitted with a mixing paddle. For this job, we used white polymer-modified mortar that's specifically formulated for setting stone and glass tiles, and features what the manufacturer calls "maximum non-sag performance." In other words, it tenaciously grips the tile, which prevents it from sliding down the wall. And because the mortar is modified with polymers, all you need to do is add water and mix for 5 minutes to reach a creamy-smooth consistency. Let the mortar slake for 10 minutes before proceeding.

Start by measuring and marking the center onto a 12-in.-long piece of marble chair rail. Then use a 3/16-in.-wide V-notch trowel to apply mortar to the back of the chair rail, a technique known as back buttering. Set the chair rail on top of the ledger board screwed to the wall behind the range. Align its center mark with the vertical centerline drawn on the wall, and tightly press the chair rail to the wall.

Next, back-butter two more pieces of marble chair rail. Only this time, apply very little mortar to the 12-in.-long tiles, just enough to stick them to the wall. These pieces will need to be removed shortly for cutting. Press one chair rail to either side of the center-positioned chair rail

MIX THE MORTAR. Mix a small amount of white thinset mortar in a 5-gal. plastic bucket using a ½-in. electric drill and mixing paddle. Blend for five minutes.

installed previously. Leave a 3/16-in. space between the chair-rail pieces.

Next, begin building the centerpiece, starting with the bottom course of tiles and working your way up the backsplash wall, as shown in the photos on the facing page.

The Benefits of Back Buttering

Most tiling jobs require you to trowel mortar onto the wall or floor and then press the tiles into place. Simple enough. But when tiling a backsplash, it's often easier—especially for DIYers—to back-butter the tiles. That is, to spread mortar onto the back of the tiles, not onto the wall.

The advantage of back buttering is that it allows you to work at a much more relaxed and comfortable pace. When you spread mortar onto a wall, the clock immediately starts ticking and you must install the tile before the mortar starts to dry. Work too slowly and you'll have to scrape the mortar off the wall and reapply a fresh coat.

And when back buttering, you're mortaring and setting tiles one at a time, so you can take a break or stop working at any point. You don't have to finish tiling a wall section simply because it's smeared with mortar.

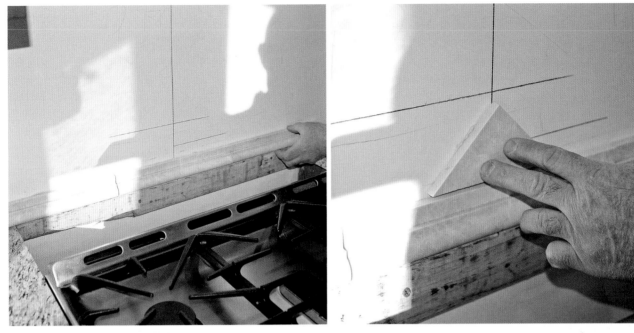

1 START WITH THE CHAIR RAIL. Install three 12-in.-long marble chair rails along the ledger board screwed to the wall behind the range. Space the chair rails ³⁄₁₆ in. apart.

2 SET THE FIRST TRIANGLE. Trowel mortar onto the back of a half-tile and press it to the wall, making sure its pointed tip aligns with the vertical centerline drawn on the wall.

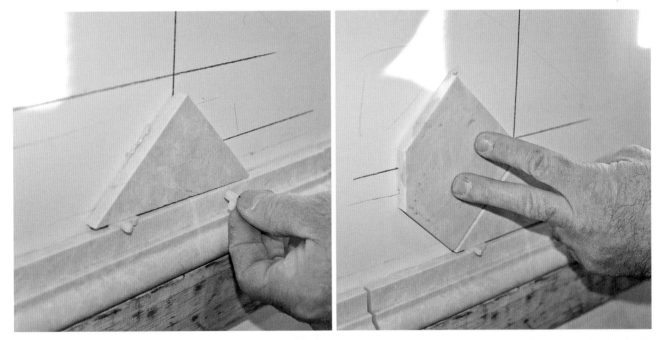

3 INSTALL THE TILE. To maintain a uniform grout joint, slip two ³⁄₁₆-in.-thick rubber spacers beneath the half-tile (left). Back-butter the tile with the clipped corner and press it into place next to the half-tile at the center of the pattern (right). If any mortar squeezes from under the tile, scrape it off the wall.

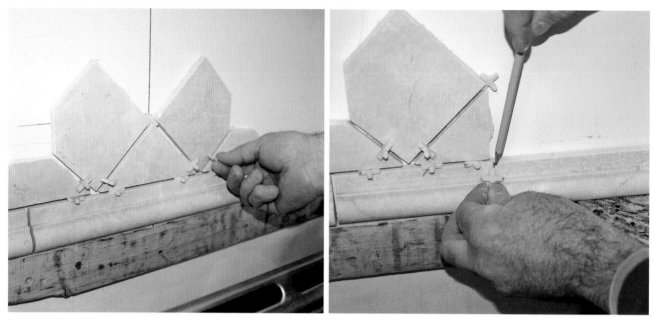

4 CONTINUE SETTING AND SPACING. Set a few marble tiles to the left and right of the centerline of the pattern, then stop and install ³⁄₁₆-in. rubber spacers between the tiles.

5 MARK FOR THE CHAIR-RAIL CUT. After completing the first course, hold a ³⁄₁₆-in. spacer against the quarter tile at the end of the row. Draw a cut line along the outer edge of the spacer and onto the chair rail below.

6 MITER-CUT THE CHAIR RAIL. Gently pry the chair rail from the wall, being careful not to disturb the tiles above. To miter-cut the chair rail to 45°, hold it against a layout square on the wet saw's table. Slide the table into the spinning blade to make the cut.

7 BUFF WITH A DIAMOND HAND PAD. To produce a precise, professional-looking miter joint, use an abrasive diamond hand pad to lightly sand smooth the mitered end of the chair rail.

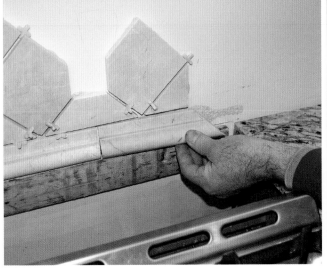

8 REINSTALL THE CHAIR RAIL. After trimming the chair rail to length, apply mortar and press it into place on the backsplash wall. Repeat to install the opposite chair rail.

9 INSTALL THE TILES FOR THE SECOND COURSE. Press the tiles into place, starting and ending the row with a half-tile and separating the tiles with 3/16-in. spacers.

10 LEAVE HOLES FOR THE GLASS INSERTS. As you work your way up the wall creating the 45° diamond pattern, arrange the clipped-corner tiles to accept the five square glass-tile insets.

Wet-Saw Setup

The spinning blade of a wet saw spews out a fine slurry of water and stone dust, so it's best to set up the saw outdoors. However, if you must cut inside a garage, porch, or other enclosed space, drape a small plastic tarp over the rear of the saw to catch some of the overspray. If you don't have a tarp handy, use an empty plastic mortar or grout bag. Slit the bag down one side and across the bottom to create a makeshift tarp.

11 SET THE CHAIR-RAIL SIDES. After setting all the centerpiece tiles, miter-cut and install one piece of chair rail along the left and right vertical sides of the centerpiece. Butt the miter joints together tightly. You'll install the remaining chair-rail pieces after setting the glass-tile insets.

Installing the Square Insets

Now it's time to install the five 2⅛-in.-sq. glass-tile insets in the centerpiece. Begin by using a 1½-in.-wide putty knife to apply thinset mortar to one of the square openings in the tile pattern. Because glass tiles are a bit thinner than marble tile, you must apply slightly more mortar—about ⅛ in. more—than when you set the marble. It's also important to smooth the mortar perfectly flat. Any deep ridges or grooves will be visible through the glass tile.

> **TIP** Don't back-butter mosaic tiles because the mortar will squeeze out from between the individual glass tiles.

Gently set the glass-tile inset into place, but don't press too hard or it'll sink below the marble and mortar will squeeze out between the glass tiles. If that happens, you'll have to pry out the glass-tile inset, clean the wall and glass tiles of all mortar, and try again, so be careful. Just barely press the inset into the mortar, then use a marble subway tile or small wood block to press the glass-tile inset flush with the marble. Again, don't press too hard or you'll disturb the marble tiles. If a little mortar squeezes out from between the glass tiles, scrape it off with the tip of a utility knife. And next time, apply a little less mortar.

To hold the inset perfectly centered within the square opening, slip one or two plastic tile wedges underneath the inset. Check to confirm that there's an even space around the glass-tile inset and that the inset sits square in the opening and isn't tilted to one side or the other. Repeat the previous four steps to install the remaining glass-tile insets.

Once all five insets are in place, cut and install the final few pieces of marble chair rail up the sides and across the top of the centerpiece.

> **TIP** To avoid dirtying or damaging the countertops, set hand tools down onto pieces of cardboard or thin plywood.

Installing glass-tile insets

1 **MORTAR THE OPENING.** Use a putty knife to apply thinset mortar to one of the square openings in the tile pattern. Spread the mortar perfectly smooth.

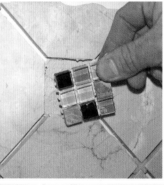

2 **SET THE INSET INTO PLACE.** Carefully press the glass-tile inset into the thinset mortar, making sure it doesn't drop below the surface of the surrounding marble tiles.

3 **FLUSH IT UP.** Use a 3-in. x 6-in. marble subway tile or flat wood block to gently press the glass-tile inset flush with the diamond-pattern marble tiles.

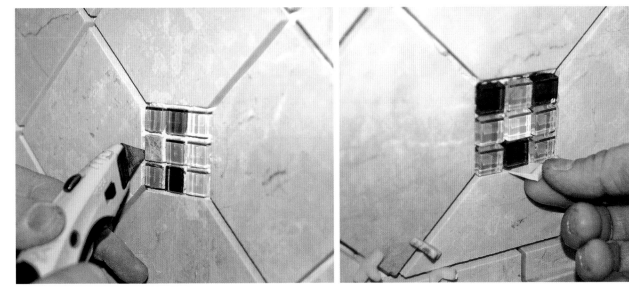

4 **CLEAN UP MORTAR SQUEEZE-OUT.** If any mortar squeezes out from between the glass tiles, use the tip of a utility knife, pocketknife, or similar tool to carefully scrape away the mortar.

5 **WEDGE IT.** Insert one or two wedges under the inset to hold it centered within the square opening. The plastic wedges are available at most tile stores.

7 **FINISH THE CHAIR-RAIL INSTALLATION.** Use the wet saw to miter-cut the final pieces of marble chair rail. Then install them up each side and across the top of the centerpiece.

6 **INSTALL THE REST OF THE INSETS.** Make sure each glass-tile inset sits squarely in its opening and perfectly flush with the surrounding marble tiles.

Tiling the Walls

The remaining kitchen backsplash walls are covered with 3-in. x 6-in. marble subway tiles set in an attractive running-bond pattern: The tiles in one row are centered over the vertical joints of the row above and below. The result is a repeating, staggered tile pattern that's similar to a traditional brick wall.

Establishing the layout

Begin by dry-fitting tiles along the length of the wall to determine if you must cut any tiles. Start laying out full 6-in.-long subway tiles, leaving a 3/16-in. space between each tile.

Chances are good that you'll have to cut the first tile or the last tile (or perhaps both) to create a balanced layout. If the space for the last tile in the row is 3 in. (half the tile length) or wider, then simply start with a full tile and cut the last tile to fit. However, if the space for the last tile is

less than 3 in., cut the first tile so that it and the last tile are approximately the same length. For example, if the space for the last tile is only 1½ in. wide, trim 2¼ in. from the first 6-in. tile, making it 3¾ in. long.

That calculated adjustment enlarges the space for the last tile by 2¼ in., making the first and last tiles the same size: 3¾ in. long. The goal of all these fussy mathematical calisthenics is to ensure you don't end a row with a thin sliver of tile.

In the kitchen shown here, the space for the last tile was just about 3 in. wide, so we started with a full tile and cut the last tile in half. The next row began with a half tile and ended with a full tile. Alternating this full-tile/half-tile starting sequence from row to row creates the desired running-bond pattern.

You also need to measure the height of the backsplash wall, even though balancing the tile pattern here is less of an issue because the top row is hidden beneath the upper

> **TIP** The running-bond pattern is ideal for setting subway tiles because it's easy to follow and attractive. And, its repetitive, repeating pattern does an excellent job of hiding slight imperfections in the wall, tiles, or installation.

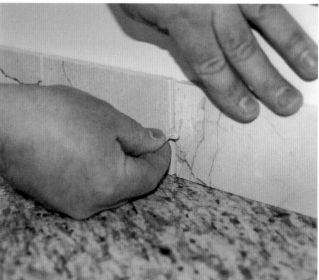

1 **START THE FIRST COURSE. Start tiling at the countertop and work up the wall. Set the tile on the** counter, tilt it flat against the wall, and then press firmly to ensure a good bond.

2 **INSERT SPACERS. Install several subway tiles, then go back and slip 3/16-in. rubber spacers** between the tiles. Set the remaining full-size tiles along the first course.

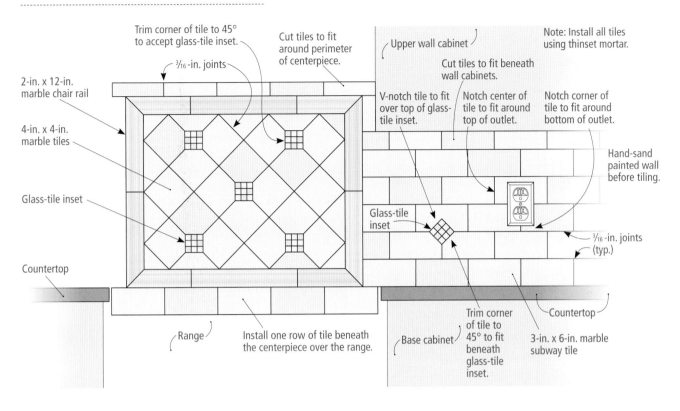

Trim corner of tile to 45° to accept glass-tile inset.

3/16-in. joints

Cut tiles to fit around perimeter of centerpiece.

Upper wall cabinet

Note: Install all tiles using thinset mortar.

Cut tiles to fit beneath wall cabinets.

2-in. x 12-in. marble chair rail

4-in. x 4-in. marble tiles

V-notch tile to fit over top of glass-tile inset.

Notch center of tile to fit around top of outlet.

Notch corner of tile to fit around bottom of outlet.

Glass-tile inset

Hand-sand painted wall before tiling.

Countertop

Glass-tile inset

3/16-in. joints (typ.)

Range

Install one row of tile beneath the centerpiece over the range.

Base cabinet

Trim corner of tile to 45° to fit beneath glass-tile inset.

Countertop

3-in. x 6-in. marble subway tile

cabinets. That's why we chose to simply run full 3-in.-tall tiles up the wall and then trim the last course to fit. Once you've determined the tile layout, you can begin setting the subway tiles.

Surface Sheen Options

Marble and other natural stone tiles are typically available in two different sheens or finishes: polished or honed. Polished marble provides the traditional look of a highly reflective, shiny surface. Honed marble has a more subtle finish. Its matte surface appears softer and is much less shiny.

For this backsplash project, we chose marble tile designated as "honed and filled," meaning it has a matte finish and all surface cracks and crevices are filled with an epoxy resin and sanded smooth.

Setting the subway tiles

Start by mixing up a fresh batch of white thinset mortar. Apply mortar to the back of a marble tile with a 3/16-in. V-notch trowel. Push down firmly with the trowel to produce sharply formed ridges of mortar.

Set the bottom edge of the tile down on the countertop and press it flat against the wall. Install five or six tiles in this manner, then stop and insert 3/16-in. spacers between the tiles. Repeat this process until you reach the last tile in the row. Measure the tile space at the end of the row, making sure you take into account the 3/16-in. grout joint. Use the wet saw to cut a tile to fit.

TIP Keep a bucket of water and small sponge nearby while tiling. If any mortar gets onto the face of the tile, immediately wipe it off with a damp sponge. Mortar left in place too long can etch the surface of the marble tile.

To begin the second row, measure and mark the center of a 3-in. x 6-in. subway tile. Back-butter the tile with mortar and press it to the wall, aligning the center mark with the joint between two tiles in the row below. Slip two ³⁄₁₆-in. spacers under the tile to create a uniform grout joint between the first two courses. Note that we set the first tile in the second row in the middle of the wall and then worked out in both directions, but you could just as easily start at the end of the row.

Notching for the insets

Continue installing subway tiles across the second course until you reach the location of the first glass-tile inset. Then, just as you did earlier, use a utility knife to cut nine-tile insets from a mosaic sheet of glass tiles. However, unlike the glass-tile insets in the centerpiece over the

Design Considerations

The second and third rows of subway tiles are punctuated by glass-tile insets, positioned every 18 in. across the wall. When using accent tiles, such as glass-tile insets, it's important to use them sparingly. They're meant to complement the field tile—in this case, the marble subways—not to overpower them. Plus, too many accents will make the wall look too busy.

Be sure to keep the accent tiles closer to the countertop. If you place them too high on the backsplash wall, the upper cabinets will block them from view while you stand at the counter.

START THE SECOND COURSE. Back-butter the tile with mortar and press it to the wall, aligning its center mark with the tile joint below. Then slip two spacers beneath the tile, separating the two courses.

ESTABLISH THE RUNNING-BOND PATTERN. Measure a 6-in. tile and make a small pencil mark at the 3-in. centerpoint. Now use this tile in the second row to establish the running-bond pattern.

range, these insets are installed at 45° to form diamond-shaped highlights on the backsplash walls. Just as before, dry-assemble the tiles and insets to ensure they fit together perfectly.

Start by laying out three tiles: Place two tiles end-to-end and center a third tile above the first two. Slip ³⁄₁₆-in. spacers between the tiles to represent the grout joints. Next, set a glass-tile inset over the intersection between the three tiles. Use a combination square to position the inset at precisely 45°. Then draw pencil marks along each edge of the inset and onto the tiles below. Position the marks ⅛ in. from the glass-tile inset.

Now use a combination square to draw 45° lines across the tiles at each pencil mark. Note that the two lower tiles will each have one corner trimmed off at 45°, but the upper tile requires a trickier V-shaped cutout in order to accept the glass-tile inset. Fortunately, the wet saw provides an accurate and easy way to produce these cuts.

TIP When using a wet saw, be sure to wear safety glasses to protect your eyes from flying tile chips and spray of gritty slurry.

To trim off the tile corners, set a layout square onto the saw's sliding table. Hold the tile in position at 45° with the cut line aligned with the spinning blade. Slowly push the table forward to slice off the corner. Repeat for the second tile.

To make the V-notch in the third tile, set the layout square to the right side of the saw blade. Hold the tile in position and carefully advance the table forward. Cut just up to—but not beyond—the bottom of the V-shaped cut. Pull back the sliding table and turn off the saw.

Reposition the layout square to the opposite side of the saw blade and make the second angled cut into the tile. Again, be careful not to cut past the V-notch. Pull the table back to clear the blade, remove the tile, and turn off the saw.

Laying out for the insets

1 **MARK FOR THE INSETS. Lay out three 3-in. x 6-in. marble tiles and one glass-tile inset. Center the inset over the intersection below, then mark cut lines onto the three tiles.**

2 **NOTCH THE TILE. Use the wet saw to cut a V-shape notch into the tile at precisely 45°. Hold the tile against a layout square and be careful not to cut beyond the notch.**

3 **DRY-ASSEMBLE THE TILES.** After making all the cuts, reassemble the marble tiles and glass-tile inset. Slip spacers between the tiles and check to ensure all the pieces fit together.

Jewel of a Tool

There's a little-known tiling tool, called a diamond hand pad, that's indispensable when working with marble, limestone, granite, and other natural stone tiles. This innocuous-looking tool is essentially a sanding block, except that its abrasive surface is impregnated with supersharp diamond grits.

Whenever you cut a stone tile, you remove the factory edge and create a sharp, square corner along the tile's edge. To restore the factory edge, simply rub the tile with a diamond hand pad. Then, you can install the restored tile anywhere on the wall or floor, resulting in less waste and a more professional-looking job.

Diamond hand pads are also useful for buffing away small chips or nicks, rounding sharp corners, and smoothing rough, uneven cuts. They're available in varying levels of coarseness, ranging from 60 grit (very coarse) to 3,000 grit (superfine). A 60-grit hand pad is suitable for use with most types of stone tiles.

You'll find that the V-shaped waste piece will still be attached by a small bit of uncut tile. Do not snap it off by hand; you might chip or crack the tile. Instead, turn on the saw, rest your forearms on the table for stability, and lift the tile up to the spinning blade. Carefully guide the blade into the kerf, then raise the tile to cut through the last bit of tile, but again, not beyond the bottom of the V-notch. Repeat for the opposite side of the notch, cutting just deep enough to free the waste piece.

After making all the necessary cuts, reassemble the three tiles and the glass-tile inset. Place rubber spacers between the tiles and check to confirm that all the pieces fit neatly together.

Now you can install the notched tiles as shown at right. Continue tiling the second and third rows, but don't install any glass-tile insets until you've tiled all the walls.

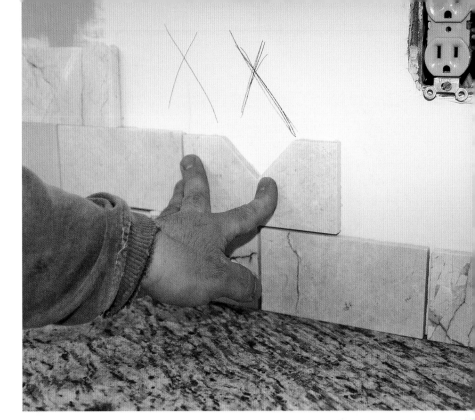

1 **SET THE V-NOTCHED TILE.** Trowel mortar onto the back of the notched tile and set it on top of the first course. Press the tile to the wall, centered directly over the tile joint below. Scrape off any mortar that squeezes out into the V-notch.

2 **SET THE TILES IN THE THIRD COURSE.** When you come to the V-notched tile, install one of the tiles with the corner trimmed off at 45°.

3 **MAINTAIN THE PROPER GROUT JOINTS.** Place 3/16-in. rubber spacers between the tiles, then check to confirm the V-notch lines up precisely with the angled cut in the tile above.

Tiling around Outlets

One of the most challenging and time-consuming aspects of tiling a backsplash is working around all the electrical outlets, switches, coaxial cable boxes, and other devices found on a kitchen backsplash wall. (To reduce the risk of electric shock, make sure the power is disconnected before tiling around electrical receptacles.)

To ensure a professional-looking installation, you must perfect two tile-cutting techniques: (a) notching the corners of two tiles to fit around each side of an electrical box, and (b) notching one tile to wrap around both sides of the box. Here's how to expertly perform each technique.

Tiling around an outlet: two-tile notch

1 **LOOSEN THE OUTLET.** After switching off the electrical circuit breaker to the backsplash wall, loosen the two retaining screws that hold the outlet to the electrical box. You don't have to remove the screws; just loosen them enough to allow a tile to slip behind the round metal ears of the outlet.

2 **MARK THE HORIZONTAL EDGE.** Hold a marble tile in place on top of a 3/16-in. spacer. Mark the end of the tile where it meets the horizontal bottom edge of the electrical box.

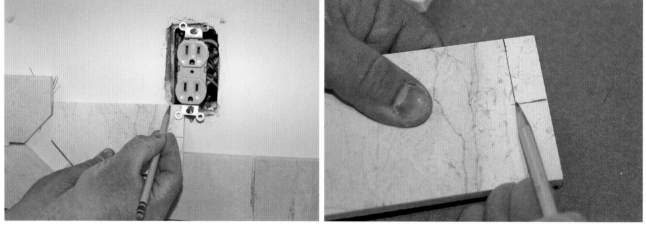

3 **MARK THE VERTICAL EDGE.** Slide the tile below the outlet with its left end spaced 3/16 in. from the adjacent tile. Mark the tile where it intersects the left side of the box.

4 **OUTLINE THE NOTCH.** Connect the two marks with pencil lines, outlining the corner notch that must be cut from the tile in order for it to fit around the outlet.

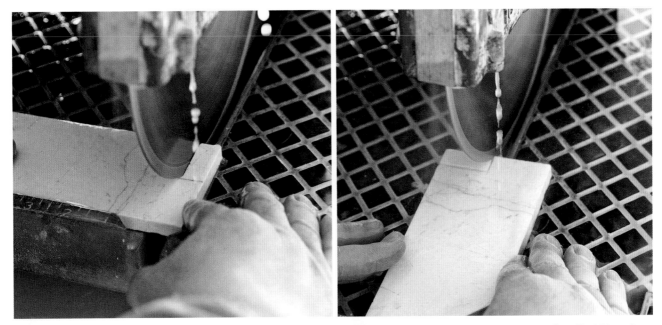

5 **MAKE THE FIRST CUT.** Use the wet saw to make the initial cut across the tile. Cut up to, but not beyond, the shorter perpendicular pencil line.

TIP After cutting a tile on the wet saw, thoroughly dry the tile with a terrycloth towel. Thinset mortar adheres best to bone-dry surfaces. Plus, excessive water can dilute and weaken the mortar and dramatically extend its drying time.

6 **MAKE THE SECOND CUT.** Rotate the tile 90° and set its end against the fence on the sliding table. Push the table forward and slowly saw up to the first cut. Flip the tile over and carefully cut along each kerf until the waste falls away, leaving a notched corner.

7 **BACK-BUTTER THE TILE.** Apply mortar to the back of the tile, then slip it into place behind the ears of the electrical outlet. Press the tile to the wall, then insert spacers. Repeat the process to create a mirror-image notched tile to fit around the lower right-hand corner of the outlet.

1 **MARK THE RIGHT SIDE.** To notch a single tile around an outlet, hold the tile in position and 3/16 in. from the neighboring tile. Mark the tile where it intersects the right side of the electrical box.

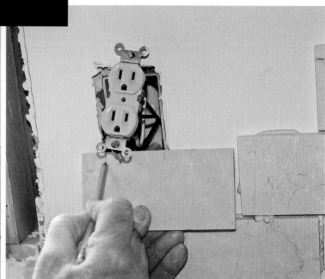

2 **MARK THE LEFT SIDE.** Without moving the tile, mark the tile where it crosses the left-hand side of the electrical box. Be sure to maintain a 3/16-in. grout joint between tiles before marking the lines.

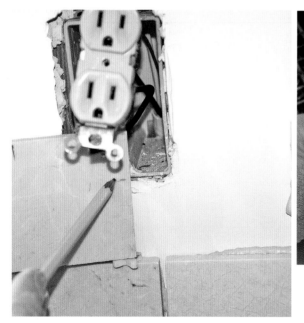

3 **MARK THE BOTTOM EDGE.** Reposition the tile, setting it on top of the course below. Slip a spacer beneath the tile and mark where it meets the horizontal bottom edge of the electrical box. Draw pencil lines connecting the three marks to outline the notch.

4 **CUT THE SHORT SIDES.** To form the notch, hold the tile against the saw fence and use the wet saw to cut along the two shorter, parallel lines. Don't saw past the horizontal pencil line.

TIP After breaking off the teeth, use the nippers to clean up the bottom of the notch by snipping off any remaining stubs. The notch will be hidden by the outlet's cover plate, so it doesn't have to be perfectly smooth and straight.

5 **CUT ACROSS THE BACK OF THE TILE.** Flip the tile face down and slice into the back of the tile, cutting a connecting kerf between the first two shorter cuts. Cut about halfway into the tile, not completely through it.

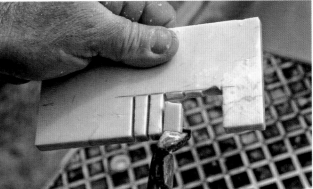

6 **MAKE A SERIES OF CLOSELY SPACED CUTS.** Set the tile on edge against the sliding table. Push forward to cut a series of closely spaced kerfs through the tile and up to the horizontal line.

7 **BREAK OFF THE TEETH.** Use a pair of tile nippers to snip off each "tooth" within the notch. To avoid cracking the tile, bite off the pieces of tile; don't grab and pry down to break them.

8 **SET THE TILE BELOW THE OUTLET.** Back-butter the notched tile and slide it into place around the bottom of the electrical box. Be sure to slip the tile behind the metal ears on the outlet.

9 **PRESS TIGHT TO THE WALL.** Firmly press the tile to the wall, but be careful not to put too much pressure on the upper corners of the notch or the tile may crack. Slip 3/16-in.-thick rubber spacers between the tiles to establish the proper-width grout joints.

Setting the remaining subway tiles

Continue tiling across the wall with full tiles. When you get to the next outlet or wall switch, mark and cut notches to fit around each electrical box.

Once you've tiled one wall, start tiling the adjacent perpendicular wall, if there is one. And remember, when tiling into a wall corner, it's imperative that the tile rows on one wall line up precisely with the rows on the adjacent wall. Even the slightest misalignment will be blatantly obvious in both the tile courses and grout joints. If necessary, use tile wedges to micro-adjust the first course on one wall to align perfectly with the first course of tiles on the opposite wall.

1 WORK YOUR WAY UP THE WALL. Continue setting 3-in. x 6-in. marble subway tiles up the wall, one course at a time. Whenever you encounter an outlet or switch, notch the tile to fit.

2 TILE THE ADJACENT WALL (IF THERE IS ONE). After completing one wall, tile the adjacent wall with the same running-bond pattern. Note in the corner, a cut tile always butts against a full tile.

Installing the Diamond Insets

Installing glass-tile insets to the backsplash walls is similar to the process used earlier when tiling the centerpiece over the range. However, in this case, the glass-tile insets are arranged in a diamond pattern to complement the horizontally laid subway tiles.

Begin by using a utility knife to cut the glass-tile insets from a mosaic-tile sheet. Each inset is composed of nine $\frac{5}{8}$-in.-sq. glass tiles, same as before.

Use a putty knife to apply thinset mortar to one of the diamond-shaped openings in the tiled wall. Spread the mortar perfectly smooth and then set the glass tile. Repeat for the remaining glass tile insets.

 TIP Replace your utility knife blade at the first sign of dulling. A new blade will cut quicker and cleaner but also more safely because you won't need to force it through the cut. And to reduce blade changes, consider upgrading to carbide-tipped utility knife blades. They cost a bit more, but they stay sharper and last many times longer than standard blades.

1 **SET THE INSET TILE PROUD.** Spread mortar into the opening and then gently press the glass-tile inset into place. It's best if the inset is sticking out from the surface a little bit.

2 **PRESS THE INSET TILE FLUSH.** To ensure that the glass-tile inset is set to the proper depth, use a spare subway tile or wood block to press it flush with the surrounding marble tiles.

3 **REMOVE EXCESS MORTAR.** Use the tip of a utility knife to scrape away any thinset mortar that oozes from between the glass tiles. (And next time, apply a little less mortar.)

4 **WEDGE TO CENTER THE TILE.** After pressing the glass-tile inset into place, slip two tile wedges beneath it to hold it perfectly centered within the diamond-shaped opening.

1. COVER THE ADJOINING COUNTERTOP.

2. SNUG UP THE SCREWS.

3. PROTECT WITH PAINTER'S TAPE.

4. PRY OUT THE SPACERS.

Prepping for Grouting

Grouting vertical surfaces can be a bit messy, so it's a good idea to cover the adjoining countertop. You can buy a 12-in.-wide roll of masking paper at any paint store. Unroll the paper onto the countertop and secure it with painter's tape. You don't need to cover the entire counter, just the area closest to the back-splash wall.

Next, tighten the retaining screws on the electrical outlets. Snug up the screws just until the round metal ears on the outlet press against the tile. Check to be sure the outlet is perfectly vertical. Then, to prevent any grout from getting inside the outlets, cover each one with a strip of painter's tape.

Finally, use a putty knife, awl, pocketknife, or similar tool to pry out all the rubber spacers from between the tiles. The spacers can be reused, so save them for your next tiling project.

Finishing Up

Once you've tiled the backsplash walls and installed all the decorative glass-tile insets, it's time to move on to the final tiling sequence.

Unscrew the ledger board from the wall behind the range and then install a single row of marble subway tiles below the tiled centerpiece. Use 3/16-in. spacers to maintain grout joints between each tile and between the tile row and the chair rail above. Now screw the ledger board back in place, directly below the row of tiles, to prevent the tiles from sliding down the wall; leave the ledger in place overnight. This row of tiles is installed so that when the range is pushed back into place you'll see a newly tiled surface, not a bare strip of painted wall.

After tiling below the centerpiece, turn your attention to the wall space above the centerpiece. Although this narrow strip of wall is hidden from view, tiling makes the job look complete. Cut 3-in. x 6-in. subway tiles to the proper height on the wet saw and set them into the space between the upper chair rail and range hood. Again, insert spacers to produce the correct-width grout joints.

The last tiling step is to install a decorative molding, called pencil rounds, to the perimeter edges of the wall tile. This step is optional, but it does add a nice finishing touch to the room. Pencil rounds, or just "pencils," are narrow strips of marble that have a bull-nose profile. They come in a few different sizes; the ones we installed were ¾ in. thick x 1 in. wide x 12 in. long. Cut the pencil rounds to length on the wet saw, then back-butter them with thinset mortar.

Install the pencils horizontally along the top edge of the backsplash wall. Also set them vertically along the outer ends of the tiled surfaces. Separate the pencils from the tile with spacers. Allow the mortar to set overnight before grouting the joints.

1 **UNSCREW THE LEDGER BOARD. Use a cordless screwdriver to remove the wooden ledger board screwed to the wall behind the range. Set the ledger and screws aside for reattachment.**

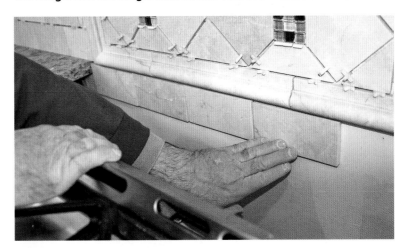

2 **INSTALL A SINGLE ROW OF TILES. Set a row of 3-in. x 6-in. marble tiles to the wall behind the range and below the chair rail running along the bottom edge of the tiled centerpiece.**

3 **REINSTALL THE LEDGER BOARD. After installing the bottommost row of tiles, screw the ledger board back in place; it'll help prevent the 3-in. x 6-in. tiles from sliding down the wall.**

TIP   After tiling the wall, you may find that the retaining screws holding the electrical outlets in place are now too short to reach the electrical box. If necessary, replace the original 1-in. screws with 1½-in.-long 6-32 machine screws, which you can buy at hardware stores and electrical suppliers.

4   **SET THE TOP ROW.** Use the wet saw to cut pieces of marble tile to fit into the narrow space running between the top of the tiled centerpiece and the range hood.

5   **TRIM THE TOP EDGE.** Install a decorative molding, called pencil rounds, to the top edge of the tiled backsplash wall. Secure each molding piece with thinset mortar.

6   **TRIM THE ENDS.** Trim the vertical ends of the tiled wall with marble pencil rounds. Here, the top end of the pencil had to be notched to fit around the cabinet.

TIP   After choosing a grout color, check with the grout manufacturer to see if it also carries colored caulk to match its line of grout. Depending on the manufacturer, you may just find a perfect color-match caulk for your tile grout.

Grouting the Joints

The next step is to fill the joints between the tiles with grout. Since these joints are wider than ⅛ in., you must use sanded grout (see p. 35). Grout is available in a wide array of colors. We chose one in the color Mushroom to reflect the darker earth tones in the crema marfil marble tiles.

Use a margin trowel to mix grout and water in a 1- or 2-gal. plastic bucket. Scoop some grout from the bucket with the margin trowel, deposit it onto a rubber grout float, and then spread the grout as shown in the photo sequence below.

1 MIX THE GROUT. Mix tile grout by hand in a small bucket using a margin trowel. Add just a little water, and mix until the grout is well blended and silky smooth.

TIP A little grout goes a long way, so don't mix up too much; start with about two or three cups of grout, and then mix more if you need to.

2 SMEAR ON THE GROUT. Apply grout to the backsplash wall with the rubber grout float held virtually flat against the tile. Don't worry if the grout is thicker in some areas; just get it onto the wall. Before proceeding, use the margin trowel to scrape the rubber float clean of grout.

3 LONG EDGE FOR THE FIELD. Hold the rubber float against the wall with its edge tipped up at about 45°. Then swipe the float across the wall, forcing the grout into the joints.

4 SHORT END FOR THE PERIMETER. Use the toe, or front end, of the float to grout the joints along the very bottom of the backsplash wall. Be careful not to tear the masking paper.

TIP Smear the grout at an angle across the joints. If you work parallel to the joints, the float will tend to pull grout from the joints.

5 **GROUT THE CENTERPIECE.** Use the same techniques on the tiled centerpiece, swiping the float at an angle to force grout between the marble subway tiles and the glass-tile insets.

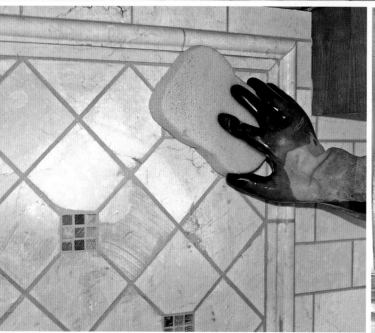

6 **SPONGE OFF THE EXCESS.** Use a damp grout sponge to clean off any excess grout. Wipe at an angle across the joints so you don't pull any grout out from between the tiles.

TIP When sponging off the excess, it's important to wring out the sponge after each swipe across the tile and to refill the bucket with clean, cold water every 10 to 15 minutes.

7 **REMOVE THE HAZE.** Let the grout firm up for 20 to 30 minutes, and then clean the tile of any remaining grout residue by gently wiping with a damp sponge. Be careful not to disturb the grout joints.

8 **BUFF WITH A DRY, SOFT COTTON CLOTH.** Let the grout cure overnight, and then apply just enough pressure to remove any grout haze or dirty-water streaks.

9 **CAULK THE EDGE JOINTS.** Use acrylic latex caulk to seal joints between the tile and cabinets. Overfill the joints slightly, and then smooth away excess caulk with a wet finger.

> **TIP** When cleaning grout from tiled surfaces, be sure to use a grout sponge, not a standard household sponge. Grout sponges are thick with large rounded edges and corners that glide over the tile without disturbing the grout joints. Standard sponges have square edges and corners that can dig in and carve grout from the joints.

Sealing the grout joints

The final step in any tile job is to seal the grout joints with a penetrating masonry sealer, which greatly increases stain and water resistance. However, in this case, you must seal not only the grout joints but also the marble tiles because natural stone is porous and susceptible to staining.

Before applying the sealer, you must wait for the grout to cure completely, a process that takes anywhere from 48 hours to a week or longer, depending on the grout manufacturer's recommendation, and the size and depth of the joints. In this case, we needed to wait 72 hours.

Once the grout has cured, use a small sponge to apply penetrating sealer to the backsplash wall. Start at the top of the wall and work your way down. The grout will absorb more sealer than the marble, but it also requires more protection, so be vigilant about sealing every inch of all the grout joints.

After sealing the tiled surfaces, slide the range back into position, screw on all the cover plates to the electrical devices, and turn the power back on.

10 **APPLY SEALER.** After the grout has fully cured, apply a clear penetrating sealer to the entire backsplash wall, including the grout joints and marble tiles.

CHAPTER TEN

A TILE-TOP TABLE

THE CHARACTERISTICS THAT MAKE

glazed tile an excellent choice for surfacing floors and walls—durability, stain and heat resistance, and ease of cleaning—also make it a great tabletop material. Here, I'll show how to build a versatile tile-top console table that's perfect for placement against a wall, behind a sofa, or in a kitchen or dining room. The table is constructed of stock pine lumber that's commonly available at home centers and lumberyards.

For the tabletop, we wanted to add a splash of color, so we tiled it with 4-in. x 4-in. handmade, hand-painted Mexican tiles purchased from Mexican Decorative Accessories. Each handcrafted tile has its own unique colorful design. The tabletop is sized to accept a whole number of tiles—40 in all—so there's no need to cut any tiles. And to further simplify the project, the tiles are set in premixed mortar and the joints between the tiles are filled with premixed grout.

You can, of course, tile the top with a different type or size of tile, if you'd prefer. Just keep in mind that to avoid having to cut any tiles, you must size the tabletop to fit the tiles. So, be sure to lay out the tiles and measure carefully before cutting any lumber. And you can easily alter the construction techniques shown here to make the table wider or longer.

Making the Table Legs

The legs of this table are made of pine 2x2s, which measure 1½ in. sq. We used a table saw to taper the legs down to 1 in. sq. at the bottom, which makes them look more delicate. If you prefer, you can leave the legs straight or buy ready-made legs that are available in various shapes, including tapered, turned, and fluted.

Crosscutting the legs

If you're following our design, the first step is to use a miter saw to crosscut the 2x2 legs to 28½ in. long. And to make sure each leg is exactly the same length, cut all four of them at the same time, a technique known as gang-cutting.

Start by cutting two 6-ft.-long pine 2x2s in half, making four 36-in.-long pieces. Next, place the four 2x2s on the miter saw table, arranged in two stacks of two 2x2s each. Trim an inch or so off the ends of the four 2x2s. Clamp the stack together to hold the just-cut ends perfectly flush and even. Now rotate the stack, set it back on the saw table, and cut all four legs to 28½ in. If you want to taper the legs, see the sidebar on the facing page.

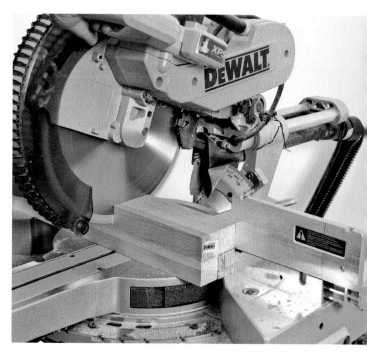

CUT THE LEGS TO LENGTH. Use a power miter saw to crosscut all four 2x2 legs to length at the same time. To produce a 30-in.-tall table, trim the legs to 28½ in. long.

Cutting the Tabletop Parts

After cutting the legs, the next step is to cut the three main tabletop components: plywood base, apron, and tabletop frame. The ¾-in. plywood base supports a layer of cement backerboard and the tiles. The 1x4 apron runs around the underside of the plywood base, providing rigidity and depth. And the 1x6 frame encircles the tabletop, creating a picture-frame border around the tiles.

Sawing the plywood base

Rip a 24-in. x 48-in. piece of ¾-in.-thick birch plywood down to 22¾ in. wide with a portable circular saw. Be sure to clamp a straightedge guide in place to produce a perfectly straight cut.

When cut to these dimensions, the plywood base will accept four rows of 4-in. x 4-in. tiles with 10 tiles in each row. If you're using different-size tiles or a larger or smaller number of tiles, you'll need to alter the dimensions of the plywood: First, lay out the tiles onto the uncut plywood. Don't forget to leave grout joints between the tiles. Then

CUT THE PLYWOOD BASE. Saw a 2-ft. x 4-ft. piece of ¾-in. birch plywood down to 22¾ in. wide. Clamp a 1x8 board in place to serve as a straightedge guide.

measure the length and width of the tile layout. Add 5¾ in. to each dimension and cut the plywood to size. That extra width and length allows the plywood to extend 2⅞ in. beyond the tile, creating a surface for mounting the 1x6 picture-frame border.

After cutting the plywood base to size, set a combination square to 2⅞ in., and use it to mark lines around the perimeter of the plywood base. Those layout lines represent the inner edge of the 1x6 frame.

Cutting Tapered Legs

1. FASTEN THE LEG TO THE JIG.

2. ADVANCE THE JIG TO CUT THE TAPER. (BLADE GUARD REMOVED FOR PHOTO CLARITY.)

In our design, each table leg is tapered on two sides, starting 7 in. down from the upper end. The two tapering cuts remove ½ in. of wood from each side, reducing the foot of the leg to 1 in. sq. Here, I'll show how to taper the legs using a tablesaw and tapering jig. You could also cut the tapers with a jointer, circular saw, or even a handplane. However, a table saw provides the quickest and most accurate way to taper the legs.

You can buy commercial tapering jigs, but we made our own simple jig from a piece of ¾-in. plywood; the jig tapers from 6⅞ in. wide on one end to 6⅛ in. on the other. A ¾-in.-sq. x 4-in.-long plywood stop block screwed to the 6⅞-in. end extends 1 in. past the edge of the jig, providing a safe way to push the leg past the saw blade (see the photos at left). Attach an auxiliary fence (made from a 1x6) to the table saw's rip fence to provide extra support for the tapering jig.

Place a table leg against the angled edge of the tapering jig and slide the leg down until it contacts the stop block. Secure the leg to the jig by driving a 1¼-in. drywall screw through the stop block and into the end of the leg.

Adjust the saw's rip fence so that the auxiliary fence is exactly 7⅞ in. from the saw blade. Lock the fence in place. Turn on the tablesaw, set the tapering jig against the auxiliary fence, and slowly push the jig toward the saw blade. Be sure to keep your hand well away from the line of cut.

The blade will begin cutting the taper 7 in. down from the top end of the 2x2 leg. As you continue to push the jig forward, the blade will cut deeper into the leg. As the blade exits the cut, it'll trim ½ in. off the end of the leg.

Turn off the saw and wait for the blade to stop spinning before sliding back the jig. Loosen the screw holding the leg to the stop block. Rotate the leg one-quarter turn and tighten the stop-block screw. Turn on the saw and cut a second taper into the leg. Repeat to make two tapering cuts on each of the three remaining table legs.

Cutting the table apron

Cut the four aprons from pine 1x4s. We cut the ends of the aprons to 45°, forming miter joints at each corner of the tabletop. You could square-cut the aprons and simply butt them together at the corners, but miter joints are much cleaner and neater looking.

Set two 6-ft.-long 1x4s on edge against the miter-saw fence. Adjust the saw blade to 45°, and trim about an inch off the ends of both 1x4s. Now from those two boards, miter-cut two 22¾-in.-long aprons and two 48-in.-long aprons.

> **TIP** We used clear pine to build this table, but virtually any wood species could be used, including hardwood, such as oak, maple, or mahogany. If you plan to paint the table, build it out of poplar, which accepts primer and paint beautifully.

Ripping the tabletop frame

The wood frame that borders the tiled top is made of pine 1x6s. The outer edge of the frame extends past the plywood base and is trimmed below by cove molding. However, to ensure that the frame extends only ⅞ in. beyond the cove molding, you must trim ½ in. off the width of the 1x6s.

To make the tabletop frame, you'll need three 6-ft.-long pine 1x6s. Crosscut one 1x6 in half on the miter saw to produce two 36-in.-long boards. Next, set the table saw's rip fence 5 in. from the saw blade. Then rip all four 1x6 parts down to 5 in. wide.

Routing the tabletop frame

Use a router fitted with a ⅜-in.-rad. cove bit to cut a cove profile into one edge of each tabletop frame part. This step is optional, but it does add a little visual interest and architectural detailing to the tabletop.

We used a router table to cut the coves, but a handheld router would work just as well. Note that the router bit shown has a ball-bearing pilot, which controls the depth of the cut. If your bit doesn't have a pilot, you'll have to clamp a wood fence in place. Bury half of the bit into the fence, leaving the other half exposed to rout the ⅜-in.-rad. cove profile.

Sanding the parts

Next, sand smooth all the pine table parts, including the legs. It's much easier to sand the parts now before assem-

CUT THE TABLE APRON. Adjust the miter-saw blade to 45° and trim the ends of two 6-ft.-long pine 1x4s. Then miter-cut the four table aprons from these two boards.

Cutter guard removed for clarity.

ROUT THE FRAME. Rout a ⅜-in.-rad. cove into each of the four tabletop-frame parts. Here, we used a router table, but a handheld router would work as well.

bling the table. It's not necessary to sand the birch-plywood base.

The best tool for smoothing the pine parts is a random-orbit sander, which has a round abrasive disk that spins in circles and vibrates in tiny orbits at the same time. Start by sanding each part with a 100-grit disk, then switch to a finer 120-grit disk.

If you don't own a random-orbit sander, use an orbital finishing sander, often called a palm sander. Or, hand-sand the parts with a simple sanding block made from a short piece of 1x3. However, don't use a belt sander, it's far too aggressive.

> **TIP** When using a router table, feed the board into the bit from right to left. However, if using a handheld router, advance the router in the opposite direction: left to right. Routing in the wrong direction will cause the bit to skip along the board's edge, instead of cutting into it.

TABLETOP (TOP VIEW)

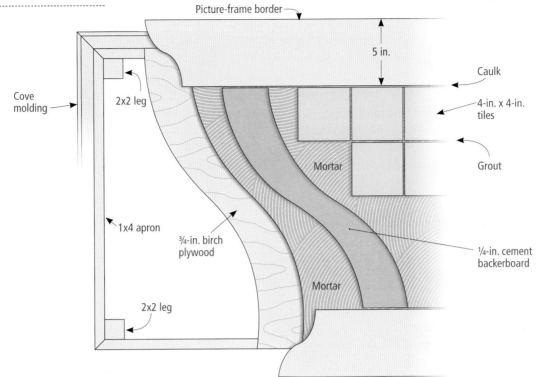

Picture-frame border

5 in.

Caulk

4-in. x 4-in. tiles

Grout

Cove molding

2x2 leg

Mortar

1x4 apron

¾-in. birch plywood

Mortar

¼-in. cement backerboard

2x2 leg

TABLETOP (SIDE VIEW)

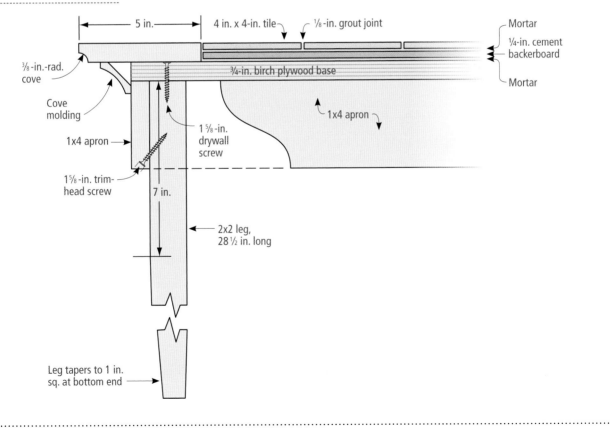

5 in.

4 in. x 4-in. tile

⅛-in. grout joint

Mortar

¼-in. cement backerboard

Mortar

¾-in. birch plywood base

⅜-in.-rad. cove

Cove molding

1x4 apron

1x4 apron

1⅝-in. drywall screw

1⅝-in. trim-head screw

7 in.

2x2 leg, 28½ in. long

Leg tapers to 1 in. sq. at bottom end

Assembling the Table

We used a pneumatic nailer to join together the parts, but you can hand-nail them with finishing nails. Just be sure to bore pilot holes first. Otherwise, the nails might split the wood.

Attaching the aprons

Apply a thin bead of yellow carpenter's glue to the top edge of one of the 48-in.-long aprons. Set the plywood base on top of the apron. Hold the face of the apron flush with the edge of the base, then secure it with 1½-in. nails. Space the nails 6 in. to 8 in. apart. Use a damp cloth to wipe away any excess glue.

Now apply glue to the edge of one of the 22¾-in.-long aprons. Also spread a little glue onto the mitered end of the previously installed apron. Slip the 22¾-in.-long apron into place beneath the plywood base. Align it flush with the edge of the base, then push the corner joint closed to form a tight-fitting miter. Secure the apron with 1½-in. nails by nailing down through the plywood base. Repeat to install the two remaining 1x4 aprons.

Fastening the legs

Turn the tabletop upside down on a workbench to prepare to install the legs. Apply glue to the top 3 in. of the table leg on two sides (if your legs have tapers, make sure that the tapered sides face out). Set the leg down into the corner of the tabletop and press it against the apron corner.

Now you could simply nail through the aprons to secure the leg, but then you'd have nail holes to fill. To fasten the leg without any visible fasteners, first drill a ⅛-in.-dia. pilot hole at an angle through the bottom edge of the apron. Then, use a cordless drill or impact driver to drive a 1⅝-in.-long trim-head screw through the apron and into the leg. Drive one screw into each side of the leg and tighten them just deep enough to conceal their tiny heads.

Repeat to install the other three legs, and then flip the table over and set it on the floor. Now secure each leg with one more screw: Drive a single 1⅝-in.-long drywall screw down through the plywood base and into the top end of each leg. To ensure that the screw hits the center of the 2x2 leg, place it 1½ in. from the edge of the plywood.

ATTACH THE APRONS. Glue and nail the plywood base to the 1x4 table apron. Be sure the pine apron is perfectly flush with the edge of the plywood.

TIP Trim-head screws have square-recess heads, so you must have a square-drive bit to drive in the screws. Most trim-head screws include a free bit in the box, but check to make sure before leaving the store. If necessary, buy the appropriate-size square-drive bit.

1 **GLUE THE OUTSIDE FACES.** Set the tabletop upside down on a workbench, then install the table leg in the apron corner. (If installing tapered legs, be sure to apply glue to the two tapered sides of the leg.)

2 **ATTACH WITH HIDDEN FASTENERS.** Drill pilot holes in the bottom edge of the apron, then secure the leg with two trim-head screws.

3 **SECURE FROM THE TOP.** Stand the table upright and secure each leg with a 1⅝-in. drywall screw driven through the plywood base and into the top of the leg.

Laying out the tile pattern

Before installing the tabletop picture frame, check one last time to confirm that the tiles will fit within the 2⅞-in. layout lines marked onto the plywood base. Set two rows of tiles onto the plywood: 10 tiles across and 4 tiles down.

Place ⅛-in.-wide spacers between the tiles, then confirm that the tiles fit within the 2⅞-in. lines. It's okay if the tiles fall a little short of the line; you can widen the gaps between the tiles to fill the space. If the tiles overlap the line by ⅛ in. or so, that's okay, too. Just set the tiles a little closer together. However, if the tile pattern overlaps the lines by ¼ in. or more, you'll have to rip down the width of the 1x6 tabletop frame.

LAY OUT THE TILE PATTERN. Confirm that the tiles fit within the layout lines on the plywood base. Dry-assemble two rows of tiles: 10 across and four down.

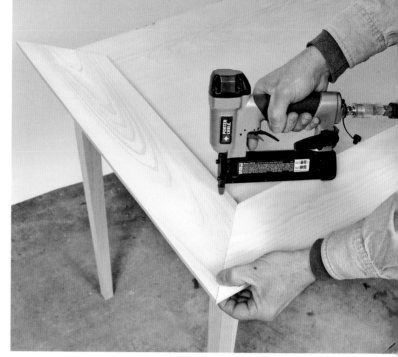

Attaching the tabletop frame

Clamp the two 6-ft.-long tabletop frames on the miter saw with the coved edges facing out. Adjust the saw blade to 45°, then make a miter-cut at the end of the boards. Measure 52$\frac{7}{16}$ in. from the point of the mitered ends, and miter-cut the parts to length.

Apply a continuous bead of glue to the plywood base, centered between the 2$\frac{7}{8}$-in. layout line and the plywood edge. Set one of the 52$\frac{7}{16}$-in.-long frames down into the glue. Align its inner edge with the layout line, then fasten the frame to the plywood base with a 23-gauge pin nailer and 1-in. pins. Space the nails 6 in. to 8 in. apart along the inner and outer edge of the frame.

Next, miter-cut one of the 36-in.-long frame parts to 27 in. long. Again, be sure its coved edge is facing out when making the miter cuts. Set the part into place along the end of the tabletop. Check to be sure it forms a tight miter joint with the previously installed frame. Secure the frame with the pin nailer.

Install the remaining 52$\frac{7}{16}$-in.-long frame to the opposite side of the tabletop. Fasten it with glue and 1-in. pins. Now, miter-cut one end of the remaining 36-in.-long frame. Hold it in place at the end of the tabletop. Mark where it overlaps the frame at the inside corner. Miter-cut the frame to length and then glue and nail it in place to complete the picture-frame border.

> **TIP** A pin nailer shoots superthin headless nails that are so small it's not necessary to putty the holes. If you don't own a pin nailer, use an 18-gauge pneumatic brad nailer or hammer and 1¼-in. (3d) finishing nails. If hand-nailing, be sure to bore pilot holes first to avoid splitting the pine frame.

Installing the cove molding

Turn the table over and set it back on top of the workbench. Miter-cut four pieces of ⁹⁄₁₆-in. x 1¾-in. cove molding to fit around the underside of the tabletop frame. Cut two 50⁹⁄₁₆-in.-long pieces of cove to fit along the front and rear of the tabletop, and two 25³⁄₁₆-in.-long pieces for the tabletop ends.

ATTACH THE FRAME. Glue and nail the four sides of the mitered frame to the plywood base. Here, we used a pin nailer, but you could also hand-nail the frame to the base.

> **TIP** Make a couple of test cuts in scrap lumber with your miter saw to ensure it's cutting precisely at 90° and 45°. Check the cuts with a combination square, and readjust the saw, if necessary.

INSTALL THE COVE MOLDING. Trim the underside of the tabletop frame with 1¾-in. cove molding. Fasten the cove to the apron and tabletop frame with the pin nailer.

Apply a little glue to the back of the cove and then fasten it with the pin nailer and 1-in. pins. Space the pins 6 in. to 8 in. apart and drive them into the apron and down into the tabletop frame.

Spread glue onto the mitered end of the cove molding you just nailed in place. Set the next piece of cove into position along the end of the tabletop. Press it against the end of the first piece of cove to form a tight miter joint at the corner. Fasten the cove to the end of the tabletop with the pin nailer. Install the final two pieces of cove, then stand the table upright.

Tiling the Tabletop

With the table built, it's time to tile the tabletop, starting with installing cement backerboard. The ¼-in.-thick backerboard serves two purposes: First and foremost, it provides an ideal surface for setting the tiles in mortar. And second, it raises the tiles so they'll be just about even with the tabletop's picture-frame border.

Installing the backerboard

Purchase a 2-ft. x 4-ft. sheet of ¼-in.-thick cement backerboard. Then cut it down to 17 in. wide x 42⅜ in. long with a carbide-tipped scoring tool (see the sidebar on p. 66).

Next, use a ¼-in. square-notch trowel to spread mortar across the surface of the plywood base. We used premixed mortar, which comes ready-to-use in a plastic pail, but if you prefer, buy a bag of modified thinset mortar and mix it with water.

Immediately after spreading the mortar, set the cement backerboard into place. Then, to ensure a good bond with the mortar, tap down the backerboard with a rubber mallet and wooden tapping block. Fasten the backerboard with 1-in. screws placed 2 in. from the perimeter edges and spaced 6 in. apart across the sheet.

1 **SET THE BACKERBOARD DOWN INTO THE MORTAR.** Check to be sure it's evenly spaced within the picture-frame border.

2 **FASTEN WITH 1-IN. DRYWALL SCREWS.** Keep the screws 2 in. from the perimeter edges or the sheet might crack.

Applying the wood finish

There's one more step to complete before tiling can commence: Apply a wood finish to the table. Applying the finish now, instead of waiting until the end, eliminates any chance of getting stain on the tiles or in the grout joints.

Since this table is made of pine, a porous softwood, it's necessary to first brush on a coat of wood conditioner. The prestain conditioner partially seals the wood and allows the stain to be absorbed more evenly without blotching or streaking. Let the conditioner soak in for about 10 minutes, then wipe off any excess with a clean, dry white cotton cloth.

It's important to stain the table within two hours of applying the wood conditioner. Put on a pair of rubber gloves and rub on the wood stain with a cotton cloth, starting with the picture-frame border. Next, set two 30-in. to 40-in.-long 2x4s on a workbench. Flip the table upside down and set it on the 2x4s, making sure it rests on the cement backerboard, not on the just-stained wood border. Now apply stain to the rest of the table. Allow the stain to dry for 10 to 15 minutes, then wipe off any excess stain with a clean, dry cotton cloth.

If you want to darken the color of the table, wait about four hours and apply a second coat of stain. Allow the stain to dry overnight and then brush on two coats of satin polyurethane varnish. Lightly hand-sand between coats with 220-grit sandpaper. Let the polyurethane dry overnight before proceeding.

Setting the tiles

The first step in setting tile is spreading mortar onto the cement backerboard with the ¼-in.-notch trowel. Next, start in one corner of the tabletop and press 4 or 5 tiles

APPLY WOOD FINISH. Rub the stain into the wood grain with a cloth. When staining the border, stain the inner edges, too.

down into the mortar. Leave a small gap between each tile, but don't insert any spacers just yet. Install 5 or 6 more tiles across three rows. After installing 10 or 12 tiles, stop and insert ⅛-in. spacers between the tiles.

Use the trowel to spread more mortar onto the cement backerboard. Only cover enough area to install 12 to 16 tiles. Continue setting tiles, using spacers, whenever possible, to maintain consistent grout joints.

After setting 20 or so tiles, embed each tile into the mortar by gently tapping it with a rubber mallet. The clay-body tiles are relatively soft, so tap lightly to avoid cracking a tile. Spread mortar across the last section of exposed cement backerboard and install the remaining tiles. Use the rubber mallet to tap the tiles down into the mortar.

> **TIP** Don't apply mortar to the entire surface; just cover enough area to set 12 to 16 tiles. That way, you can work at a leisurely pace and not feel rushed to set all the tiles before the mortar begins to harden.

Spacing Mexican Tiles

Handmade Mexican tiles, while beautiful, are imperfect. They vary in size and aren't always perfectly square or flat. Depending on the extent of these imperfections, the use of tile spacers might prove futile. In those instances, forget the spacers and simply space the tiles by eye while trying to maintain ⅛-in.-wide grout joints.

1 SET THE TILES. Start setting tiles in the tabletop corner and work out along the picture-frame border. Press down each tile with a slight twisting motion.

2 ADD SPACERS. After installing 10 or so tiles, insert ⅛-in. spacers in between the tiles. The circular spacers shown straddle the intersection of four tiles.

3 WORK IN SMALL SECTIONS. Trowel mortar onto the next section of cement backerboard. If any mortar gets smeared onto the wooden border, wipe it off immediately.

4 EMBED THE TILES. To make the tiles bond permanently to the mortar, lightly tap them down with a rubber mallet. Strike the center of the tiles, not the corners.

5 **CLEAN UP THE JOINTS.** Use the tip of a putty knife to scrape excess mortar out from between the tiles. It's much easier to do this now when the mortar is soft.

Now, inspect the grout joints between all the tiles. When you find one that's completely filled with mortar—and you will—scrape out the excess mortar with the tip of a narrow putty knife. It's important to clear out the joints to make room for the grout. Allow the mortar to cure overnight.

TIP Hand-painted Mexican tiles come in a riotous collection of bright colors and patterns. Mix and match the tiles to avoid having too many of one color pattern or design bunched together on the tabletop.

Grouting the tiles

Start by masking off the picture-frame border with 1½-in.-wide masking tape. Position the tape precisely along the edge of the tiles, covering the seam between the tiles and wood border. The seam will be caulked later and the tape prevents it from being filled with grout. The tape also helps protect the wood frame from the grout and makes cleanup much easier.

Next, apply grout to the tiled tabletop with a rubber grout float. Tilt the float up on edge and forcefully smear the grout diagonally across the joints. Work on about one-third of the tabletop at a time, stopping occasionally to confirm that each and every joint is filled with grout.

After grouting the entire tabletop, grab the float with both hands and scrape the surface clean of any excess grout. Then take a slightly dampened grout sponge and wipe off the remaining grout from the tiles. Lightly work the sponge in a circular motion. If you scrub back and forth in straight lines, you'll pull the soft grout out of the joints. Rinse the sponge frequently in water and continue wiping until the tiled surface is clean. Peel off the masking tape and allow the grout to cure overnight.

Next, prepare to caulk the seam that separates the tiles from the picture-frame border. The reason for using caulk, not grout, is that wood and ceramic tile expand and contract at different rates, depending on humidity and temperature. Caulk remains flexible and is able to accommodate a certain amount of movement. Grout dries hard and will crack under the same conditions.

Start by placing strips of masking tape along both sides of the seam. Then, apply a bead of white caulk in between the tape strips, filling the seam around the perimeter of the tiled tabletop. Put on a pair of rubber gloves and smooth the caulk with a wet fingertip. Then immediately peel off the masking tape.

Sealing the grout joints

Tile grout is porous and susceptible to staining. Therefore, it's important to protect the grout joints with silicone-based grout sealer. There are a wide variety of sealers available in a broad range of prices. Cheap sealers provide very little stain resistance, so it's best to pay a little more for maximum protection.

Some grout sealers have a built-in applicator. If you buy one that does not, apply the sealer with a narrow artist's brush. Allow the sealer to penetrate the grout for 10 to 15 minutes, then wipe off any excess sealer with a dry white cotton cloth or paper towels.

A second sealer coat can be applied for extra protection, but you must first wait until the initial coat has fully dried. Check the label on the sealer container for dry times.

1 **GROUT THE TILES.** Use a rubber grout float to smear grout diagonally across the tiles. Tilt the float on edge and force the grout down into the tile joints.

2 **SCRAPE OFF THE EXCESS.** Scrape grout from the surface of the tiles with the rubber float. Then scoop up the excess grout with a wide plastic putty knife and discard it.

4 **CAULK THE PERIMETER.** Squeeze a bead of caulk into the seam between the tiles and wood picture-frame border. Masking tape makes cleanup easy.

3 **CLEAN THE TILES.** Using a slightly dampened—not wet—grout sponge, lightly scrub the surface in a circular motion until all the grout is gone.

5 **SEAL THE GROUT JOINTS.** Protect the grout from staining by brushing on grout sealer. Use an artist's brush to apply the clear sealer to the grout joints between the tiles.

MAKING A MOSAIC-GLASS TILE MIRROR

HERE'S A FUN DO-IT-YOURSELF

tiling project that you can build, even if you've never before worked with tile. In fact, you can make this beautiful tiled mirror without cutting a single tile or mixing a drop of mortar or grout.

The mirror consists of a plywood frame covered with mosaic-glass tiles. The frame is trimmed with wood moldings, which conceal the plywood edges, and, more important, create a decorative picture frame around the mosaic tiles.

For this mirror, we selected a beautiful mosaic-glass tile from Daltile called South Beach, which features brilliant sea-kissed colors ranging from foamy white to iridescent blue. The individual tiles measure about ⅝ in. sq. and come adhered to sheets that are 11½ in. x 11½ in. Each sheet contains 324 tiles laid out in 18 rows with 18 tiles in each row.

The mirror, which measures about 25 in. wide x 29 in. tall, is sized to accept a whole number of tiles, thus eliminating the need to cut any tiles. And to avoid mixing any materials, we adhered the tiles to the plywood frame with premixed tile adhesive and used premixed grout to fill the spaces between the tiles. Note that you can easily alter the construction techniques described here if you'd like to make the mirror smaller or larger.

Making the Frame

The rectangular frame of the mirror is made from ¾-in.-thick birch plywood, which provides a flat, smooth surface for setting the glass-mosaic tiles. Most home centers and lumberyards sell partial plywood pieces cut to 2 ft. x 4 ft. or 4 ft. x 4 ft., so there's no need to buy a full sheet of plywood (unless you're planning to make several mirrors). We used a tablesaw to rip the plywood frame pieces, but you could also use a portable circular saw. Just be sure to guide the saw along a clamped-in-place straightedge guide to produce perfectly straight, accurate cuts.

To make the frame shown here, cut two 4-ft.-long pieces at 6³⁄₁₆ in. wide. Then stack the two plywood pieces on a miter saw. Hold the ends flush, and cut through the stack to create two pieces that are 11¹³⁄₁₆ in. long. Cut the stack again to make two 28¹⁄₁₆-in.-long pieces. These four pieces make up the mirror frame (see the drawing on the facing page).

> **TIP** When using a tablesaw to cut the plywood frame, place the "good" side of the plywood facing up. That way, any splintering will occur in the bottom surface of the plywood. However, the opposite is true when using a circular saw: Place the plywood with the good side facing down so any splintering will occur on the top surface.

Assembling the frame

We joined the four plywood pieces with pocket screws, but you could also use biscuit splines or wooden dowels. The advantage of using pocket screws is that you don't have to clamp the parts together and then wait for the glue to dry. Immediately after driving in the last pocket screw, you can move on to the next step.

Draw three parallel pencil lines onto each of the two short plywood pieces, positioned as shown in the drawing. Stand each piece on end in the pocket-hole jig and drill three pocket-screw holes into the face of each end. Lay out the four plywood pieces to form the mirror frame, with the pocket-screw holes facing up. Apply yellow glue to the four joints and then fasten the two short pieces to the two long pieces with 1¼-in.-long pocket screws.

2 **DRILL FOR POCKET SCREWS.** Clamp the frame part into a pocket-hole jig, then drill three pocket-screw holes into each end of both 11¹³⁄₁₆-in.-long plywood parts.

> **TIP** Wear hearing protection and a dust mask when using a table saw. And never operate the saw without its blade guard in place. (Here, the guard was removed for photo clarity.)

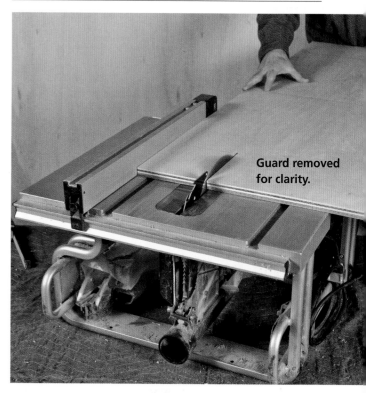

Guard removed for clarity.

1 **CUT THE MIRROR-FRAME PARTS.** To make the frame shown here, first set the tablesaw's rip fence 6³⁄₁₆ in. from the blade and rip the parts to width. Then use a miter saw to cut the four parts for the mirror frame to length.

STANLEY

MOSAIC-GLASS TILE MIRROR

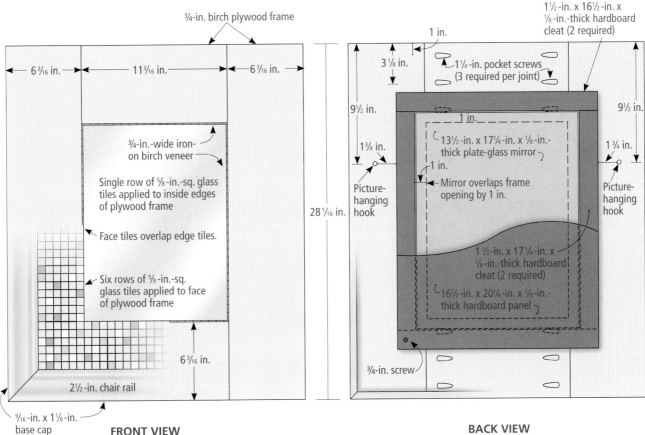

¾-in. birch plywood frame

6 ³⁄₁₆ in.

11 ³⁄₁₆ in.

6 ³⁄₁₆ in.

¾-in.-wide iron-on birch veneer

Single row of ⅝-in.-sq. glass tiles applied to inside edges of plywood frame

Face tiles overlap edge tiles.

Six rows of ⅝-in.-sq. glass tiles applied to face of plywood frame

6 ³⁄₁₆ in.

2½-in. chair rail

⁹⁄₁₆-in. x 1⅛-in. base cap

28 ¹⁄₁₆ in.

FRONT VIEW

1½-in. x 16½-in. x ⅛-in.-thick hardboard cleat (2 required)

1 in.

3 ⅛ in.

1¼-in. pocket screws (3 required per joint)

9½ in.

1 in.

9½ in.

1¾ in.

13½-in. x 17¼-in. x ⅛-in.-thick plate-glass mirror

1¾ in.

Picture-hanging hook

1 in.

Mirror overlaps frame opening by 1 in.

Picture-hanging hook

1 ½-in. x 17 ¼-in. x ⅛-in.-thick hardboard cleat (2 required)

16½-in. x 20¼-in. x ⅛-in.-thick hardboard panel

¾-in. screw

BACK VIEW

3 **ASSEMBLE THE FRAME. Fasten together the mirror frame using yellow glue and 1¼-in.-long pocket screws. Secure each of the four butt joints with three screws.**

Veneering the edges

The exposed plywood edges around the inside of the frame aren't suitable for tiling because tile adhesive can't form a lasting bond to the multilayered plywood edge. Therefore, it's necessary to cover the inside edges of the frame with wood veneer. To make that job easier, we used iron-on birch veneer.

The ¾-in.-wide veneer has heat-sensitive glue applied to its back surface. When warmed with a clothes iron, the glue melts and adheres the veneer in place. Turn on the iron and adjust to the cotton setting with no steam. It's important to use dry heat, so be sure the steam is turned off. Wait about five minutes for the iron to heat up.

Cut four strips of veneer to fit around the inside of the mirror frame. Hold the veneer on the plywood edge and press it down with the iron. Apply heat for about 10 seconds, then slide the iron down a few inches and repeat until you've ironed down the entire strip. Immediately after ironing on the veneer, use a small wood block to forcefully rub down the veneer. The pressure applied by the wood block increases the bond strength of the heat-sensitive glue.

Now lay the mirror frame flat on a workbench. Wrap a piece of 100-grit sandpaper around a wood block and sand the edges of the veneer flush with the plywood.

Tiling the Inside Edges

The first tiling step is to apply tile to the inside edge of the frame, which comprises the four edges you just veneered. Each edge receives only a single strip of ⅝-in.-sq. tiles, but the visual effect of tiling all four edges is quite powerful: Once the plate-glass mirror is installed, the single row of edge tiles is reflected in the mirror, creating what appears to be a 1¼-in.-thick tiled edge that's two rows wide.

TIP Be sure to adhere the tiles with white tile adhesive. Gray—or any other color—adhesive will show through and change the color of the glass tiles.

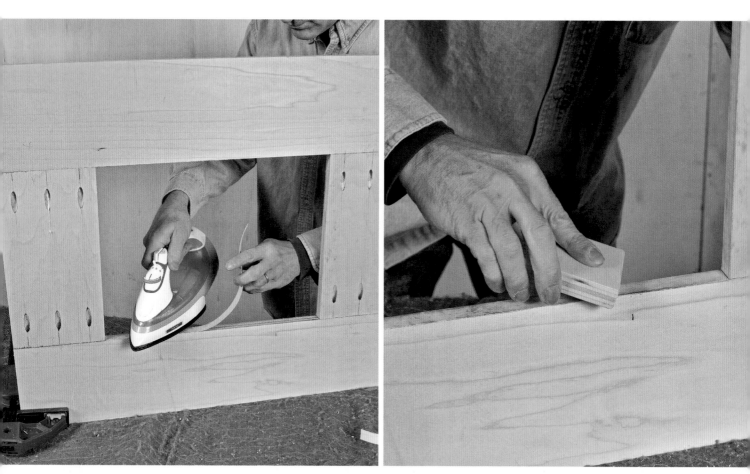

1 **VENEER THE EDGES.** Cover the inside edges of the plywood frame with iron-on birch veneer. Press down the adhesive-backed veneer with a hot clothes iron.

2 **RUB DOWN THE VENEER.** While the adhesive is still warm, use a wood block to rub down the veneer. This will help ensure a good bond with the plywood edge.

Cutting the tile strips

One side of each sheet of mosaic-glass tiles is covered with paper. The paper protects the face of the tiles, and is removed after installation. Lay a tile sheet upside down on a workbench; that is, with the papered surface facing down. Use a sharp utility knife to cut enough single rows of tiles to cover the four inside edges. Also cut six wider strips (6 tiles wide and 18 tiles long), which will be used later to cover the face of the mirror frame.

Applying the edge tiles

Start tiling along one of the short inside edges, then work your way around the frame. Use a ³/₁₆-in. V-notch putty knife to apply white tile adhesive to the inside veneered edge. Flatten the ridges in the adhesive with a smooth (unnotched) putty knife. If you don't smooth the adhesive, the V-notch ridges will show through the glass tiles. Also, when smoothing the surface, be careful not to wipe off any adhesive. Apply only enough pressure to flatten the ridges.

Set a single strip of tile into the adhesive along the edge of the frame. Be sure the papered surface is facing up. Gently press the strip down into the adhesive, then check to make sure the tiles are perfectly centered on the plywood edge. Continue applying the strips around the inside edges. To ensure a lasting bond with the edge, use a short wood block to gently tap the tiles down into the adhesive. Once done, allow the tile adhesive to cure for 24 hours.

1 **CUT THE TILE STRIPS. Cut one-tile-wide strips from a sheet of mosaic-glass tiles. These will cover the inside edge of the mirror frame.**

TIP Tile adhesive can be irritating to bare skin, so be sure to wear rubber gloves when applying the adhesive and cleaning up the tools.

2 **APPLY THE ADHESIVE. Use a V-notch putty knife to spread the premixed tile adhesive along the inside edge of the mirror frame and then flatten the ridges with a plastic putty knife.**

3 **SET THE STRIP. Gently press the tiles into the adhesive with the papered surface facing up.**

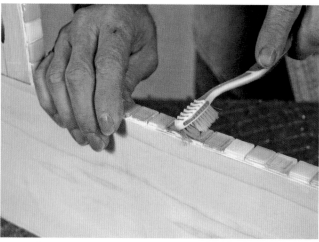

4 **REMOVE THE PAPER FACE.** After using a warm, damp sponge to soften the glue, peel the paper strip off the tiles. If the glue doesn't release, set the sponge back in place.

Removing the paper face

Set a warm, damp sponge on top of the paper-covered edge tiles and hold it in place for a minute or two to dissolve the glue that's holding the paper in place. Once the glue has released its grip, carefully peel the paper from the tiles. Now use a dry cotton cloth to buff the tiles clean of any residual glue. If you encounter any particularly stubborn patches of glue, dampen the cloth with warm water and then wipe the tiles clean.

Inspect the grout joints between the ⅝-in.-sq. glass tiles. If you find a joint that's completely filled with tile adhesive, slice through the excess adhesive with the tip of the utility knife. Then use an old toothbrush to scrub the space between the tiles free of any leftover bits of dried adhesive.

Tiling the Mirror Frame

With the inside edge of the mirror frame tiled, you can now begin tiling around the face of the frame. And since you'll be setting the tiles in six large strips, this process goes pretty quickly. You should be able to spread the adhesive and set the six tile strips in about 20 minutes.

5 **CLEAN UP THE JOINTS.** Remove any adhesive from between the tiles with the tip of a utility knife and then use an old toothbrush to scrub each joint free of any bits of dried adhesive.

TIP When using a utility knife to clean adhesive from between tiles, be careful not to twist the knife or you'll dislodge a tile. If you do accidentally pop loose a tile, simply stick it back into place with a dab of premixed tile adhesive.

1 **SPREAD THE ADHESIVE.** Use a 3-in.-wide V-notch putty knife to spread tile adhesive around two sides of the plywood mirror frame; save the other two sides for later.

2 SET THE FIRST FACE STRIP. Lay a strip of mosaic tiles into the adhesive with its papered surface facing up. Align the six-tile-wide strip flush with the edge tiles.

3 INSTALL THE NEXT STRIP. Butt it end-to-end against the first strip, leaving a ¹⁄₁₆-in. gap.

Spreading the adhesive

Start by drawing layout lines onto the mirror frame to represent the edge of the mosaic-tile strips. If you're following the dimensions of the frame shown here, measure 2 ⁷⁄₁₆ in. in from the outer perimeter.

Use the ³⁄₁₆-in. V-notch putty knife to apply tile adhesive around two sides of the mirror frame. Spreading adhesive on just two sides, instead of all four, allows you to work at a more leisurely pace. Otherwise, you'd have to rush to set the tiles before the adhesive started to dry. Spread the adhesive from the inside tiled edge out to the layout lines, but don't obscure the lines. Then, just as you did before, use an unnotched putty knife to smooth the surface of the adhesive.

Setting the mosaic-tile strips

Lay the first tile strip into place with its papered surface facing up. Set the end of the strip on the layout line and overlap the tiles previously installed along the inner edge of the frame. Shift the tile strip, as necessary, so that its grout joints align with the joints between the tiles on the inner edge.

Install the next tile strip in a similar manner, butting it end-to-end against the first strip. Separate the two strips by ¹⁄₁₆ in. to form a grout joint. Once satisfied with the position of the two strips, use a small wood block to gently tap the tiles down into the adhesive.

Now install a six-tile-wide strip of tiles along the second side of the mirror frame in the same way. Repeat to tile the remaining two sides of the mirror frame.

4 TILE THE SECOND FACE. Slide the strip flush with the edge tiles, then tap it down into the adhesive.

5 TILE THE OTHER TWO FACES. Space the tile strips ¹⁄₁₆ in. apart to create the proper grout joints.

Allow the tile adhesive to cure for 24 hours before removing the paper from the surface of the strips; use the same warm, damp sponge technique as used to remove paper from the edge tiles. Buff the tile surface clean of any sticky glue residue, and then clean out any grout joints that are filled with adhesive to make room for the grout.

> **TIP** Before installing a mosaic-tile strip, carefully inspect each glass tile. If you find one that's cracked or chipped, use a utility knife to cut it from the strip. Then, install the strip and set a single glass tile into the space that was originally occupied by the damaged tile.

Grouting the Tile

The grout joints between the mosaic-glass tiles are only about 1/16 in. wide, so you need to use unsanded grout to fill the joints. (Sanded grout is used for joints wider than 1/8 in.) You can mix up a batch of standard unsanded masonry grout, but again, to simplify this project, we used premixed white grout. Ordinarily, you'd use a rubber grout float to apply the grout, but since there's very little area to grout, we used a 3-in.-wide plastic putty knife.

6 **REMOVE THE PAPER FACE.** Use a warm, damp sponge to release the paper from the surface of the tile. Then buff off any sticky glue residue with a soft cotton cloth.

Grouting the tile frame

1 **APPLY THE GROUT.** Use a 3-in.-wide plastic putty knife to apply white unsanded tile grout. Smear the grout across the surface, forcing it deep into each joint.

2 **SCRAPE OFF THE EXCESS.** After filling all the tile joints, including those around the inner edge of the frame, use the putty knife to scrape away all the excess grout.

TIP Apply the grout with a plastic—not metal—putty knife. A plastic knife is more flexible and it won't scratch the glass tile, as a metal putty knife might.

4 **BUFF OFF THE HAZE.** Let the grout cure for about four hours, then use a cotton cloth and buff off the grout haze. Scrub off any stubborn spots with warm water.

3 **CLEAN OFF THE GROUT.** Wipe the tiles clean of any remaining grout using a damp sponge. Work the sponge in a circular motion, and rinse it often in clean water.

TIP If you accidentally wait too long before buffing off the grout haze, the tiles will appear cloudy. Try removing the dried grout haze with a scouring sponge and hot water. If that doesn't work, use a liquid grout and tile cleaner.

Trimming the Mirror

The mirror featured here is trimmed with two types of decorative wood moldings, which are commonly available at home centers and lumberyards. The outer perimeter edges of the plywood mirror frame are trimmed with 9/16-in. x 1 1/8-in. base-cap molding. This L-shaped molding wraps around the edge of the frame, concealing the exposed plywood edges.

The picture-frame detail that surrounds the mosaic-glass tiles is created with 2 1/2-in.-wide Colonial chair-rail molding. Both moldings are cut to 45° on a miter saw to create mitered corners joints. We attached the moldings with a 23-ga. pneumatic pin nailer. If you don't own a pin nailer, you can use a hammer and 3/4-in. brads.

Priming and painting the wood moldings before you install them is much easier and neater than trying to apply the finish after nailing the moldings to the mirror frame. Brush on a coat of primer, allow it to dry, hand-sand lightly with 220-grit sandpaper, and then apply two coats of high-gloss acrylic-latex paint.

1 **CUT THE BASE-CAP MOLDING AT 45°.** Hold the molding with its rabbet facing out and its flat surface down against the miter-saw table. Be sure to keep your hand well away from the path of the saw blade.

2 **FASTEN WITH GLUE AND PINS OR BRADS.** Hold the edge of the molding flush with the top of the frame.

TIP If you're hand-nailing the molding, be sure to first bore 1/16-in.-dia. pilot holes to avoid splitting the molding. This is particularly important when nailing close to the end of the molding.

Installing the trim

Start by installing the base-cap molding around the perimeter edges of the mirror frame. Adjust the power miter saw for a 45° miter cut. If you don't own a power miter saw, you can get satisfactory results with a traditional miter box and backsaw.

Trim one end of a length of base-cap molding to 45°. Hold the molding in place against the corner of the frame and allow its other end to run long. Now mark the opposite end of the molding where it meets the frame corner. Trim the molding on the mark to 45°.

Next, apply a thin bead of yellow glue to the back of the base-cap molding, and nail it to the edge of the mirror frame. Be sure to keep the top edge of the molding flush with the plywood surface. Cut and install the next piece of base cap, making sure it forms a tight miter joint at the corner. Repeat to install the remaining two pieces of base cap.

The chair-rail molding is installed similar to the base cap: Miter-cut each piece to length and then glue and nail the molding to the mirror frame using ¾-in.-long pins or brads. Cut the fourth and final piece of chair rail a bit too long, and then test to see how it fits. If necessary, trim off a bit more until it forms a tight miter joint at each end.

 TIP A pneumatic pin nailer is ideal for attaching thin, narrow wood moldings. Unlike other types of finishing nailers, a pin nailer shoots superthin headless pins, which produce holes so small they're virtually undetectable. However, since the pins are headless, be sure to apply glue to the wood moldings.

3 **MITER-CUT AND INSTALL THE REST OF THE BASE CAP.** Check to confirm that each piece fits tightly at the corner, then apply glue along its back surface.

4 **GLUE AND NAIL THE CHAIR-RAIL MOLDING TO THE FACE OF THE FRAME.** Hold the inner edge of the molding about ¹⁄₁₆ in. away from the tile.

5 **CHECK THE FIT.** Test-fit for tight-fitting mitered corner joints, trim as necessary, and then install the final piece of chair-rail molding to complete the decorative picture frame that surrounds the glass tiles.

Attaching the Mirror

Order the plate-glass mirror from a local glass shop. For the design shown here, we used a piece of ⅛-in.-thick mirror cut to 13½ in. x 17¼ in. At that size, the mirror will be 2 in. wider and longer than the tiled opening in the frame. When the mirror is installed, it'll overlap the opening by 1 in. on each side.

To make the mirror easy to install and to remove should it ever break, we secured it to the frame without mastic, glazing compound, silicone sealant, or clips. Instead, it's held in place by a hardboard panel screwed to the back of the frame. The hardboard also protects the reflective coating on the back of the mirror from scratches. (Hardboard is more commonly known by the trade name Masonite.)

> **TIP** When you order the mirror from a glass shop, ask the glazier to polish the edges. It costs a few dollars more, but polishing removes the sharp edges that can cut you.

Fastening the cleats and back

Place the tiled frame upside down on a cushioned work surface. Set the plate-glass mirror face down over the opening in the frame. Use a tape measure to center the mirror on the frame.

Cut four 1½-in.-wide cleats from a piece of ⅛-in.-thick hardboard to fit around the perimeter of the mirror (see the drawing on p. 221). Apply two beads of yellow glue to the back of each cleat, and then secure the cleats alongside the mirror with ½-in. pins or brads. The mirror is now trapped within the four cleats, but it's not yet secured to the frame.

To secure the mirror, cut a ⅛-in.-thick hardboard back. Fasten the hardboard panel with ¾-in. No. 6 pan-head screws. Drive the screws through the panel, through the cleats, and into the plywood frame.

2 FASTEN THE CLEATS. Glue and nail the hardboard cleats along the perimeter edges of the mirror. Wipe away any excess glue with a slightly dampened cloth.

3 ATTACH THE PROTECTIVE BACK. Lay the ⅛-in.-thick hardboard panel over the mirror, align it flush with the four cleats, and attach with ¾-in.-long screws.

1 CENTER THE MIRROR. Set the plate-glass mirror face down on the back of the tiled frame. Use a tape measure to make sure that the mirror is centered on the frame.

Mounting the hanging wire

The completed tiled mirror weighs only about 18 lb., but don't take any chances when hanging it on a wall: Use metal swivel hangers and braided-steel wire that's rated to support 100 lb. And note that we attached the wire to hang the mirror vertically, but the same technique can be used to hang it horizontally.

Begin by screwing a metal swivel hanger to each side of the mirror. Mount the hangers one-third of the way down from the top edge of the mirror, securing each hanger with a single ⅝-in.-long screw. Feed the braided wire through the eye of the swivel hanger, then twist it around itself several times. Tie off the wire with a couple of half hitches, then secure it with duct tape.

Feed the opposite end of the wire through the other swivel hanger. Pull up on the wire near the center of the frame. When taut, the wire should be about 3 in. down from the top edge of the frame. Tie off the wire to the second swivel hanger.

The mirror is now ready for hanging. For maximum strength, it's best to fasten the hanging screw or hook to a wall stud. When that's not possible, use a hollow-wall anchor that's rated for at least 50 lb.

Sealing the grout

The final step is to seal the grout to prevent staining. The reason we saved this step for last is that grout must dry for two or three days before it can be sealed.

The grout sealer we used had an attached brush, which made application easy: Turn the bottle upside down and give it a slight squeeze to dispense some sealer. Don't squeeze too hard or sealer will squirt out everywhere. Glide the tip of the brush along every grout joint. The porous grout will immediately soak up the sealer.

Allow the sealer to penetrate for about five minutes, then buff the surface clean with a dry white cotton cloth. Wait 30 minutes, then apply a second coat of sealer.

> **TIP** It's much easier to screw on the hardboard panel if you first bore ⅛-in.-dia. screw-pilot holes. Drill the pilot holes ¼ in. deep, which is deep enough to pass through the hardboard panel and cleat but not penetrate the plywood frame.

4 **MOUNT THE HANGERS.** Screw a metal swivel hanger to each side of the plywood frame. Position the hangers one-third of the way down from the top of the frame.

5 **THREAD THE HANGING WIRE.** Twist braided-steel wire around the eye of the hanger. Tie off the end of the wire to prevent it from unraveling or slipping.

SEAL THE GROUT. Apply a liberal coat of sealer to all the grout joints. The clear sealer helps prevent staining and makes the grout much easier to clean.

CHAPTER TWELVE

TILE MAINTENANCE AND REPAIR

OF ALL THE FINISHED SURFACES in your home, tile is arguably the most durable and easiest to maintain. In fact, being low-maintenance is one of the main reasons why so many people choose tile. However, low-maintenance doesn't mean no-maintenance; even tile requires a little attention every now and then to stay in like-new condition. Besides, you've invested a considerable amount of time and expense to buy and install tile, so it only makes sense to protect that investment with some occasional maintenance.

In this chapter, I'll focus on the two most common tile issues: cleaning and replacing grout, and replacing cracked tiles. And while there are valid cosmetic reasons to repair missing grout and cracked tiles, the most important reason runs much deeper: Once damaged, the entire tiled surface is compromised. If the problem isn't fixed in a timely manner, water will seep in and eventually create a much bigger and more expensive repair.

Over time, moisture penetration can lead to mold and mildew growth, wood rot, bug infestation, and structural damage to walls and floors. The good news is that you don't need any specialized skills or expensive tools to repair tile. Most problems can be fixed in a couple of hours using a few simple hand tools.

Grout Repairs

Masonry grout is the weak link in any tiled surface. While glazed tiles are impervious to water penetration and staining, grout is susceptible to both.

Tile grout is typically stained by dirt, dropped food, spilled drinks, soap scum, mold, and mildew. Most people deal with stained, grungy grout joints by simply scratching out the old grout and regrouting the surface. And that'll certainly solve the problem, but it's a pretty aggressive first step and seldom necessary. It's best to try to clean the grout first. If that fails, then you can regrout the joints. But cleaning is very effective and can be done in a fraction of the time.

Cleaning grout stains

There are specially formulated grout cleaners available at hardware stores and home centers, and they work pretty well on most stains. But you can make a less expensive homemade cleaner that's just as effective.

Pour a few ounces of water into a plant mister and add an equal amount of chlorine bleach; gently shake the bottle to mix. Spray the bleach solution liberally over the entire tiled surface, not just the stained grout joints.

Wait five minutes or so for the solution to dissolve the stains and then aggressively scrub the grout joints with a stiff-bristle plastic scrub brush. Rinse the tiled surface with lots of clean, cool water and inspect the grout joints. If any stains remain, dry the surface and repeat the previous steps.

1 **MIX UP THE BLEACH SOLUTION. Pour some clean water into a spray bottle, then add an equal amount of liquid chlorine bleach. Screw on the spray top and gently shake to mix.**

2 **SPRAY ON THE TILED WALL. Saturate all the stained grout joints and allow the solution to soak in for at least five minutes. Grout is rather porous, so it'll absorb quite a bit of the solution.**

3 **SCRUB THE GROUT JOINTS CLEAN. Use a stiff-bristle plastic scrub brush rather than a brush with metal bristles, which could damage the grout.**

TIP Wear rubber gloves and tight-fitting eye goggles when handling and spraying the bleach solution. Also, open a nearby window when working, and leave it open for an hour or so afterwards to clear the air of any remaining bleach odor.

STANLEY

Removing old grout

It's necessary to regrout tile joints when the existing grout is too badly stained to be cleaned or when the grout is cracked and crumbling out of the joints. As grout ages, it shrinks, pulls away from the tile, and eventually starts to fracture. At that point, the tiled surface becomes susceptible to water penetration. So, be sure to regrout at the first sign of grout failure.

Start by using a carbide-grit grout saw to scratch out the grout from between the tiles. Work on the vertical joints first. Apply pressure directly behind the blade with one hand, and use your other hand to pull down on the handle. Repeat as many times as necessary to clean out the old grout. Then use the same technique to remove the grout from the horizontal joints. Stop occasionally to vacuum up the area of all grout dust and grit.

It's important to note that it's not always necessary to remove every last bit of grout from each joint. In some cases, removing just the top 1/8 in. or so will reveal sound, stable grout. However, if the grout is cracked straight through to the substrate, or is crumbly or soggy, then remove it all.

Once you've scratched out the grout, use a plastic-bristle grout brush to clean the joints of any dust or dirt. You could use a household scrub brush, but a grout brush has a narrow scrubbing head and stiff bristles, which are perfectly suited for cleaning grout joints. After brushing, vacuum the joints to remove any remaining dust and grit.

> **TIP** When shopping for a grout saw, look for one with a long offset handle. It provides better leverage and extra clearance for your knuckles.

1 **SCRATCH OUT THE GROUT JOINTS.** Use a carbide-grit grout saw to remove the grout. Depending on the condition of the grout, you may have to rake each joint several times.

2 **CLEAN OUT THE JOINTS.** Before regrouting the tile, use a plastic-bristle grout brush to scrub the joints. The new grout won't stick if the joint is filled with dust or grit.

Regrouting the tile

Buy grout in the same color as the original grout. You can use latex-modified masonry grout or premixed tile grout; just remember to use unsanded grout for joints ⅛ in. wide and narrower, and sanded grout for joints wider than ⅛ in.

Smear the grout diagonally across the tiled surface with a rubber grout float. Tip the float up on edge and force the grout deep into the joint. Don't worry about applying too much grout; it's better to overfill the joints than to underfill them.

After regrouting the tile, use the rubber float to scrape any excess grout from the surface. Then, clean off any remaining grout with a damp grout sponge. Wait 10 to 20 minutes, then buff the tiles with a dry cotton cloth to remove any grout haze.

1 **SMEAR THE GROUT DIAGONALLY. Apply the grout to the tiled surface with a rubber grout float. Swipe the float diagonally across the tile to force the grout into the joints.**

2 **REMOVE EXCESS GROUT. Clean the grout off the tiles with a damp grout sponge. Use the rounded edges of the thick sponge to smooth and tool the grout joints, too.**

Two More Grout-Removal Tools

The carbide-grit grout saw is a terrific all-purpose grout-removal tool, but there are two other options to consider. For very small repairs, you can often get by with an ordinary can opener. Use the pointed tip of the opener to scratch grout out from between the tiles, as shown below left. This works best for narrower joints up to about ⅛ in. wide.

For large regrouting jobs or tiles with wide grout joints, you can save a considerable amount of time and trouble by using an oscillating multi-tool. When

fitted with a carbide-grit grout blade, this versatile power tool will grind through the hardest grout in just seconds.

Simply hold the pointed edge of the blade against the grout joint and turn on the tool, as shown below right. The blade will vibrate—or oscillate—back and forth and grind through the grout. If the tool has a variable-speed motor, choose a lower speed for greater control; as you gain more experience and confidence, you can increase the speed.

USE A CAN OPENER ON NARROW JOINTS.

AN OSCILLATING MULTI-TOOL WORKS WELL ON WIDER JOINTS.

Cracked Wall Tile Repair

In this section, we'll show how to replace a cracked 4-in. x 4-in. tile in a shower stall, but the process is basically the same for any size wall tile. This technique is also useful when you need to remove a perfectly good tile to install a soap dish or accent tile.

Note that there's no subtle way to remove a wall tile; it requires quite a bit of hammering, drilling, chiseling, and prying. The key is to work carefully and deliberately so you don't damage any neighboring tiles. One small slip of the chisel, one errant hammer blow, and you'll have to replace two tiles instead of one. Also, be sure to protect your eyes with wraparound safety goggles.

Scratching out the grout

Start by taping a paper bag to the wall directly below the cracked tile. This step is optional but worth the trouble: The bag will catch the dust and debris, making cleanup a whole lot easier. Next, use a carbide-grit grout saw or other grout-removal tool to scratch the grout from the joints around all four sides of the cracked tile.

Use a grout brush to clean the grout joints of any dust or grit. Inspect the four joints to ensure that all the grout has been removed. If any grout remains, rake the joints again with the grout saw. The cracked tile will be much easier to remove once all the grout joints are cleared out.

Removing a cracked wall tile

1 **REMOVE THE GROUT.** Scratch out the grout from around the damaged tile. Here, we used a compact grout saw, but you can use any grout-removal tool.

Removing the cracked tile

The next step is to drill several ¼-in.-dia. holes into the tile. However, to keep the drill bit from skipping across the hardened glazed surface, you must first punch a series of shallow divots with a hammer and nail set. Arrange the divots in a diagonal line across the tile, spaced no more than ½ in. apart. When punching the divots, tap the nail set very lightly. You just want to chip the glazing, not shatter the tile.

Next, make a depth-stop drilling guide from a 1-in.-sq. block of wood about 2¾ in. long. Drill a ¼-in.-dia. hole lengthwise down the center of the block. Now use the block as a depth stop for drilling through the tile but not into the substrate behind it.

Remove the ¼-in. twist drill bit from the drill and insert a ¼-in.-dia. carbide-tipped masonry bit. Slip the depth-stop block over the masonry bit, and then adjust the bit in the chuck so that it protrudes from the block a distance equal to the thickness of the tile. In our case, that was ⁵⁄₁₆ in. Tighten the drill chuck to securely lock the bit in place.

Drill a ¼-in.-dia. hole through the tile at each of the divots punched into the tile's surface. Drill all the way in until the depth-stop block contacts the tile and prevents the bit from drilling any deeper.

Next, use a hammer and ¼-in.- or ⅜-in.-wide cold chisel to crack the tile along the line of ¼-in.-dia. holes. The tile will crack across to the next hole. If it doesn't, strike it again. Repeat to crack the tile between the remaining holes. At this point, the tile should be split into four large pieces. Lightly tap the tile with a hammer until it cracks into several smaller pieces. The tile will be much easier to remove once it's fractured. However, be careful not to pound on the tile too hard or you'll damage the substrate.

Use a stiff-blade putty knife to pry the broken tile pieces from the wall. If necessary, tap the handle of the putty knife with a hammer to loosen the tile. Once all the tile pieces have been removed, use a narrow cold chisel to scrape off any old grout that remains stuck to the edges of the surrounding tiles.

> **TIP** Drilling the center hole in the depth-stop block is much easier if you first clamp the block into a vise. You can make the depth stop from a 1-in.-sq. wood block, but a short piece of 1-in.-dia. wood dowel works just as well.

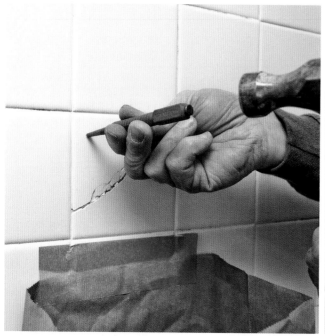

2 **PUNCH DIVOTS INTO THE TILE.** Before drilling holes into the tile, use a hammer and nail set to punch a series of closely spaced divots into the glazed surface of the tile. Be sure to wear eye goggles as protection from flying chips of glazing.

3 **DRILL THROUGH THE DIVOTS.** Bore through the tile at each divot mark with a ¼-in.-dia. masonry drill bit. The depth-stop block will prevent the bit from drilling too deep.

4 **CRACK THE TILE.** Use a hammer and cold chisel to crack the tile along the line of ¼-in.-dia. holes. Set the beveled tip of the chisel against the edge of the hole, then strike the chisel with the hammer.

5 **FRACTURE THE TILE.** Lightly tap on the tile with a hammer to fracture it into several smaller pieces. Be sure to protect your eyes with tight-fitting goggles.

6 **REMOVE THE PIECES.** Pry the pieces of shattered tile from the wall with a stiff-blade putty knife. Be careful not to scratch or damage any of the surrounding tiles.

7 **CLEAN UP THE EDGES.** Use a ¼-in.-wide cold chisel to carefully scrape away any remaining grout that's stuck along the edges of the neighboring tiles.

Installing a new tile

Use a ³⁄₁₆-in. V-notch putty knife or trowel to apply tile adhesive or thinset mortar to the back of a clean, new tile. Firmly press the tile into place against the wall.

Slip a spacer beneath the tile to create the proper width grout joint along the top and bottom of the tile. If you don't have a rubber tile spacer, use a couple of strips of thin card stock, as we did here. Now, shift the tile to the left or right to create an even joint along each vertical edge of the tile. Secure the tile to the wall with 1½-in.-wide masking tape.

Wait 24 hours for the tile adhesive or mortar to cure. Then, use a 3-in.-wide plastic putty knife to fill the joints around the tile with grout. Wipe off the excess grout with a sponge, then wait 20 minutes or so before buffing the tile clean with a dry cloth.

1 **BACK-BUTTER THE NEW TILE.** Spread an even coating of tile adhesive or thinset mortar to the back of a clean, new wall tile. Be sure to coat the entire surface.

2 **SET THE TILE.** Vacuum the substrate, then firmly press the tile into place. Wipe away any adhesive or mortar that squeezes out from behind the tile.

3 **SPACE AND TAPE.** Slip a spacer beneath the tile to maintain the proper grout joint, then hold the tile to the wall with a long strip of painter's masking tape.

4 **APPLY THE GROUT.** After the tile adhesive or thinset mortar hardens, fill the gaps around the tile with grout. Here, we applied ready-to-use premixed grout.

Cracked Floor Tile Repair

The steps for replacing a cracked floor tile aren't much different than replacing a damaged wall tile, except that floor tiles are typically larger, thicker, and much harder. That's because ceramic tiles are often used on walls, but most floor tiles are made of porcelain, which is much denser than ceramic.

Floor tiles are also normally set in a thicker bed of mortar, which makes them more difficult to pry up. With that said, any competent do-it-yourselfer should be able to repair a cracked floor tile with nothing more than a few simple hand tools and the following step-by-step instructions. (Note that we had to replace several cracked floor tiles, but the tools and techniques are the same to repair a single tile.)

Removing the grout

As with any tile repair, the first step is to remove the grout from around the cracked tile. If you don't, it's nearly impossible to pry up the tile without damaging the adjacent tiles.

> **TIP** Wear a dust mask or dual-cartridge respirator as protection from the fine grout dust.

Start by using a carbide-grit grout saw to lightly scratch a groove into the grout joints around the damaged tile. Once the initial grooves are formed, apply greater pressure to the saw and rake out all of the grout. The saw is less likely to jump out of the joint once the initial groove is formed.

> **TIP** When scratching out grout with a grout saw, stop occasionally and vacuum up the grout dust. Otherwise, you risk stepping into the dust and tracking it throughout the house.

Busting out the old tile

Use a hammer and nail set or center punch to break the cracked tile into smaller pieces. However, don't make the mistake of starting at the edge of the tile. That increases the chance of damaging the adjacent tile. Instead, start at the crack in the tile. Hold the nail set against the tile and about ½ in. away from the crack. Tilt the nail set at a slight angle, then strike it with the hammer to break off a small piece of tile. Move down the line of the crack about an inch or so and repeat. Once you've busted out a few pieces of tile, the remaining pieces will come out much easier.

1 **REMOVE THE GROUT.** Scratch out the old grout from around the damaged tile with a carbide-grit grout saw. Save time by using a grout saw with a thick blade.

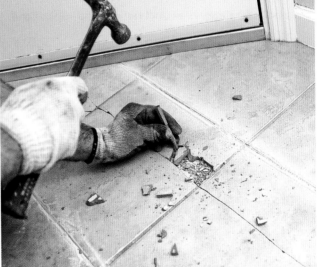

2 **BUST OUT THE OLD TILE.** Break the damaged floor tile into pieces with a hammer and nail set. Start along the line of the crack and bust the tile into small chunks. Be sure to protect your eyes with tight-fitting goggles.

3 **SWITCH TO A PUTTY KNIFE. As you near the tile edge, use a stiff-blade putty knife and hammer to break the tile into pieces. Be careful not to strike the adjacent tile.**

4 **WORK FROM THE CENTER TOWARD THE EDGE. Remove half of the tile, then set the putty knife against the cracked edge in the middle of the tile. Hammer on the knife to break the tile.**

> **TIP** Shattered tile pieces have incredibly sharp, jagged edges that can easily slice your hands and fingers. Always wear thick work gloves when handling broken tile.

As you get within 2 in. of the tile's edge, switch to a stiff-blade putty knife. Hold the tip of the putty knife against the subfloor with its beveled edge facing up. Tap the handle of the knife with the hammer to break the tile into two or three larger pieces. Be careful not to hit the putty knife too forcefully or it might strike and damage the edge of the neighboring tile. Repeat until you've removed half of the tile.

Now slip the putty knife under the cracked edge near the center of the tile. Strike the knife handle with the hammer to break off a piece of tile. Continue to work from the center of the tile toward the opposite edge. Again, use caution as you approach the edge of the tile; you don't want to chip the adjacent tile.

If you must remove the next tile, there's no need to start with the nail set. Just continue to use the hammer and putty knife to fracture the tile into pieces. And if you run into a particularly stubborn tile, resist the temptation to pound on the putty knife with more force. Instead, hold the putty knife at a shallow angle and tap it as far as it'll go under the tile. Then strike the top of the tile with the hammer directly over the tip of the putty knife. The tile will crack into slightly larger pieces.

The most difficult pieces of tile to remove are the smaller triangular pieces that remain stuck in the corners. If you try to use the putty knife to pry the corner piece free,

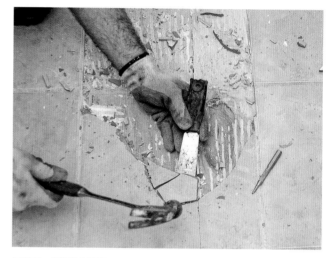

5 **ANGLE THE PUTTY KNIFE. Tap the tip of the putty knife beneath the tile, then use the hammer to strike the top of the tile. The tile will shatter into several large pieces.**

there's a good chance that it'll break off a piece of the adjacent tile. So, switch back to the nail set. Hold the nail set in the raked-out grout joint beside the corner piece, and very lightly tap it with a hammer. Move down along the grout joint ½ in. and repeat. Keep tapping the nail set into the grout joint, along each side of the corner, until the tile piece breaks free.

Once you've removed all the cracked tiles, inspect the edges of the surrounding tiles. If there's any old grout stuck to the edges, chip it off with the hammer and putty knife. Again, be careful not to damage the adjacent tiles.

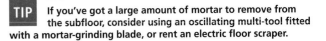

TIP If you've got a large amount of mortar to remove from the subfloor, consider using an oscillating multi-tool fitted with a mortar-grinding blade, or rent an electric floor scraper.

6 **REMOVE STUBBORN CORNERS.** Use the nail set to bust loose any tile pieces that are stuck in the corners. Hold the nail set in the grout joint and tap it with the hammer.

7 **CLEAN UP THE OLD GROUT.** Remove the old grout from the edges of the neighboring tiles with the putty knife. Hold the knife vertically and strike it with a hammer.

Mosaic-Tile Demolition

1. POUND WITH A HAMMER

2. SCOOP WITH A DUSTPAN

Most homeowners shudder at the thought of having to clear a room of mosaic floor tiles. After all, even a small room would contain thousands of tiny tiles. But, as is the case with many other challenges, perception is often worse than reality.

Mosaic tiles actually come up pretty easily. Not neatly, cleanly, or quietly but relatively easily. And the tile-removal technique used, while effective, isn't very subtle. In fact, it could be referred to as blunt-force trauma.

Start by donning work gloves, kneepads, dust mask, hearing protection, and tight-fitting eye goggles. Next, use a hammer to repeatedly pound on the tile floor, as shown at top left. A nail hammer works well, but a 3-lb. sledge works even better.

Continue to pound on the floor until tiles start popping loose. Stop occasionally and scoop up the tiles with a dustpan, as shown at bottom left. Empty the dustpan into a trashcan and repeat the previous steps until all the tiles are removed.

Prepping the subfloor

Before setting the new tiles into place, you must first prep the subfloor. If the surface of the subfloor isn't completely smooth and clean, the new tiles won't fit properly.

Start by chipping off the old mortar with the stiff-blade putty knife and framing hammer. Don't worry about removing every last bit of mortar; just chip off the high spots and thick deposits. Loosen any stubborn bits of thinset mortar by repeatedly striking the subfloor with the claw end of the hammer. Then vacuum the entire subfloor of any debris.

Grind off the remaining mortar with a masonry rubbing stone, which is simply a coarse stone fitted with a handle. Rub the stone back and forth across the surface to smooth and clean the subfloor.

Tiles will often crack when the subfloor flexes as people walk across the room. Take this opportunity to reinforce and stiffen the subfloor: Use a cordless drill to drive 1⅝-in.-long screws through the subfloor and into the joists below. It's particularly important to drive in screws along any exposed seams in the subfloor. Space the screws 6 in. to 8 in. apart along both sides of the seam. Vacuum the subfloor clean before proceeding.

Installing the new tile

Mix up a fresh batch of latex-modified thinset mortar. Spread the mortar across the subfloor with a square-notch trowel. Don't worry if mortar gets onto the neighboring tiles; you can wipe it off later. Just be sure to cover the entire surface of the subfloor.

Next, set the new tile down into the fresh mortar bed. Shift the tile, as necessary, to create equally spaced grout joints along each edge. Allow the mortar to cure overnight.

Mix up a small batch of latex-modified grout in the same color as the existing grout and apply in the usual manner.

1 **CHIP OFF THE OLD MORTAR. Hold a stiff-blade putty knife at a slight angle and try not to gouge the surface.**

2 **SMOOTH THE SUBFLOOR SURFACE. Scrub the subfloor with a masonry rubbing stone to quickly grind away any remaining mortar.**

3 **REINFORCE THE SUBFLOOR. Use a cordless drill and 1⅝-in. screws to fasten the subfloor to the floor joists. Be sure to screw along any exposed seams.**

1 **SPREAD THINSET MORTAR ACROSS THE SUBFLOOR.** Firmly press down on the square-notch trowel to produce crisp rows of mortar.

2 **SET THE NEW TILE.** Be careful not to push too hard or it will sink below the height of the surrounding tiles. If that happens, pry up the tile, apply more mortar, and reinstall it.

4 **CLEAN THE TILES.** Use the rubber float to scrape off excess grout, and then clean up with a thick, damp grout sponge. After 10 to 20 minutes, remove any grout haze by buffing the tiles with a dry cotton cloth.

TIP Lay a level or other straightedge across a newly installed tile to ensure it's flush with the surrounding tiles. If the ends of the level aren't touching the surrounding tiles, press down on the level to lower the new tile. If the level is resting on the surrounding tiles but not touching the new tile, then the tile is too low. Pry it up, add more mortar, and reinstall it.

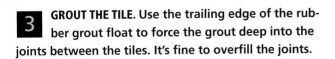

3 **GROUT THE TILE.** Use the trailing edge of the rubber grout float to force the grout deep into the joints between the tiles. It's fine to overfill the joints.

RESOURCES

General information about tiles and tiling

American Society for Testing and Materials
www.astm.org
(877) 909-2786

Tile Council of North America
www.tcnatile.com

Tile manufacturers

American Olean
www.americanolean.com

Arizona Tile
www.arizonatile.com

Classic Terra Cotta Company
www.terracottapavers.com
(888) 837-7286

Crossville Incorporated
www.crossvilleinc.com
(931) 484-2110

Daltile
www.daltile.com

Eleganza Tile
www.eleganzatiles.com
(714) 224-1700

Florida Tile
www.floridatile.com
(800) 352-8453

Florim Tile
www.florimusa.com

Malibu Ceramic Works
www.malibuceramicworks.com
(310) 455-2485

Marazzi Tile
www.marazziusa.com
(972) 232-3801

Mexican Decorative Accessories
(956) 242-4417

Stonepeak
www.stonepeakceramics.com
(312) 506-2800

Tile substrate

CertainTeed Corporation (Diamondback Tile Backer)
www.certainteed.com
(800) 233-8990

Custom Building Products (WonderBoard® Backerboard)
www.custombuildingproducts.com
(800) 272-8786

Georgia-Pacific Corporation (DensShield® Tile Backer)
www.buildgp.com
(800) 225-6119

James Hardie (Hardiebacker® Cementboard)
www.jameshardie.com
(888) 542-7343

Schluter Systems (Kerdi-Board Polystyrene Panel)
www.schluter.com
(800) 472-4588

USG Corporation (Durock® Cementboard)
www.usg.com
(800) 874-4968

Diamond hand pad

Alpha Professional Tools®
www.alpha-tools.com
(800) 648-7229

Uncoupling membrane

Schluter Systems
www.schluter.com
(800) 472-4588

Thinset mortar and tile grout

Ardex Engineered Cements
www.ardex.com
(888) 512-7339

Laticrete International
www.laticrete.com
(800) 243-4788

Mapei Corporation
www.mapei.com
(800) 992-6273

Liquid waterproofing membrane

Mapelastic™ AquaDefense
Mapei Corporation
www.mapei.com
(800) 992-6273

Shower floor system

Quick-Pitch Float Stick System
www.goofproofshowers.com
(866) 771-9470

Shower system

American Standard
www.americanstandard-us.com
(800) 442-1902

Tile-able shower pans

KBRS Inc.
www.showerbase.com
(866) 912-3211

Tile-Redi
www.tileredi.com
(855) 750-7334

Pocket-hole joinery

Kreg Tool Company
www.kregtool.com
(800) 447-8638

Hand tools

Stanley Tools
www.stanleytools.com
(800) 262-2161

Power tools

Black & Decker
www.blackanddecker.com

DeWalt
www.dewalt.com
(800) 433-9258

Porter-Cable
www.portercable.com
(888) 848-5175

INDEX

STANLEY

STANLEY®

Publications

Exper
advic
fo
DIYer

MASTER
EVERY PROJECT

OPEN A TOOLBOX OF ~~...~~ **with th** *STANLEY Quick Guide* series.

Highly visual and easy to ~~...~~ uides are packed with how-to
photographs and no-nons ~~...~~ e home projects with confidence.

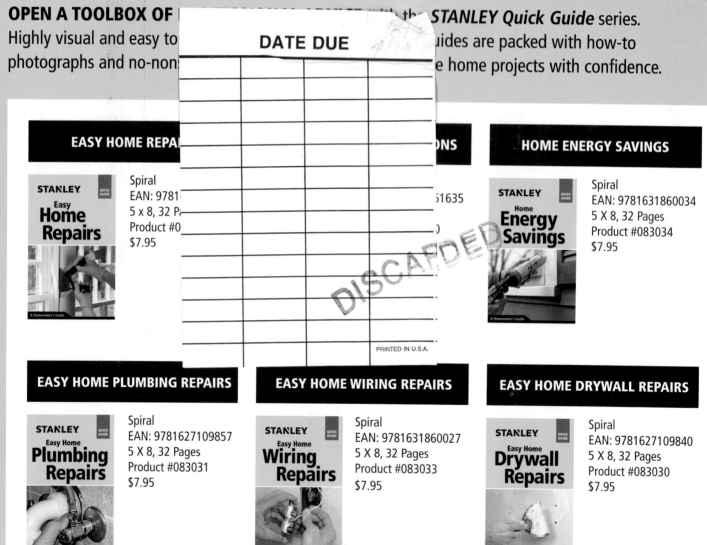

EASY HOME REPA

Spiral
EAN: 9781 ~~...~~
5 x 8, 32 Pa ~~...~~
Product #0 ~~...~~
$7.95

...ONS

...1635
...0

PRINTED IN U.S.A.

DATE DUE

DISCARDED

HOME ENERGY SAVINGS

Spiral
EAN: 9781631860034
5 X 8, 32 Pages
Product #083034
$7.95

EASY HOME PLUMBING REPAIRS

Spiral
EAN: 9781627109857
5 X 8, 32 Pages
Product #083031
$7.95

EASY HOME WIRING REPAIRS

Spiral
EAN: 9781631860027
5 X 8, 32 Pages
Product #083033
$7.95

EASY HOME DRYWALL REPAIRS

Spiral
EAN: 9781627109840
5 X 8, 32 Pages
Product #083030
$7.95

Available at TauntonStore.com or wherever books are sold.

Taunton